The Metaphorical Brain:

AN INTRODUCTION TO CYBERNETICS AS
ARTIFICIAL INTELLIGENCE AND BRAIN THEORY

The Metaphorical Brain

An Introduction to Cybernetics as Artificial Intelligence and Brain Theory

MICHAEL A. ARBIB

DEPARTMENT OF COMPUTER AND INFORMATION SCIENCE
UNIVERSITY OF MASSACHUSETTS AT AMHERST

ILLUSTRATED BY AURO LECCI

WILEY-INTERSCIENCE, a Division of John Wiley & Sons, Inc.
New York · London · Sydney · Toronto

Library of Congress Cataloging in Publication Data:

Arbib, Michael A
  The metaphorical brain.

  Bibliography: p.
    1. Cybernetics. 2. Artificial intelligence.
    3. Neuropsychology. I. Title.

Q310.A72   001.53'5   72-2490
ISBN 0-471-03249-2

Printed in the United States of America

10 9 8 7 6 5 4 3 2 1

FOR KEITH, DOROTHY, AND ADRIAN BURROWS

with love and gratitude
for their friendship and kindness

Preface

A tourist is accosted by a thief in a dark alley. A moment's indecision and his brain has committed him to a mode of action—to fight or to flee.

A frog sits on a lily pad. Two flies buzz into view and the pattern of electrical activity passing from retina to brain changes. The brain integrates this new pattern and selects one of the flies for a target. The frog turns and "zaps" and only one fly remains.

A robot is in a cluttered room. Its "eye"—a TV camera—feeds data to its "brain" —a computer. The computer resolves its input into a representation of objects and their locations. It then charts a path, and the robot moves to perform an assigned task, avoiding all obstacles as it does so.

We want to understand how people think and behave, and in particular we wish to understand the role of the brain in thought and behavior. In some ways the brain of a man is like the computer of a robot, in others it is more akin to the brain of a frog. Our aim here is to convey an understanding of the brain in terms of two main metaphors: The cybernetic metaphor, "Humans are machines", and the evolutionary metaphor, "Humans are animals". We shall not downgrade the differences, but we hope to learn much from the similarities.

Thus, when we call this book *The Metaphorical Brain* we do not imply that the understanding of the brain that it affords will be any less "real" than that afforded by other books—rather we are simply making explicit the aid that metaphor provides us, as well as lessening the risk of misunderstanding that results when an implicit metaphor is mistaken for reality.

Before giving a chapter by chapter account of the approach and contents of this book, let me briefly discuss the level of exposition. The book as a whole, although by no means light reading, should be accessible to anyone who reads *Scientific American*; but it is hoped that the material in Part III merits the attention not only of "the intelligent layman" but also of experts and serious students of cybernetics, artificial intelligence, or neuropsychology. Unlike my earlier *Brains, Machines and Mathematics*, which sought to introduce a reader with some knowledge of modern algebra to a number of mathematical models—unfortunately left somewhat unrelated to one another—relevant to a cybernetic approach to the brain, the present volume requires no mathematical background and is self-contained. It gives the reader all the background she needs in system theory, artificial intelligence, and neuropsychology to appreciate the novel and integrated view of brain function which this book seeks to provide. Occasionally, a few mathematical symbols are scattered around to reward the mathematically trained reader with a somewhat deeper understanding, but other readers will still be able to grasp the essential ideas from the surrounding text and so may read on without fearing that the book will become increasingly confusing.

A great deal of work has gone into the drawings. Auro Lecci transformed my rough sketches and twenty-six pages of typed suggestions into the beautiful graphics that grace this volume. I cannot thank him enough for the care and artistry with which he has produced these drawings, and the willingness with which he changed the pictures when new ideas presented themselves. The captions were then written in such a way that the pictures could be sampled without continual reference to the text, thus enabling the reader to orient herself by browsing through the illustrations before plunging into the more detailed written exposition.

The book is divided into four parts:

Part I, An Introduction, starts with a chapter on Brain, Behavior and Metaphor, which expands on the role of our two metaphors and notes that the cybernetic metaphor lends itself to two approaches: the *artificial intelligence* approach, which seeks to model intelligent behavior without regard for the structure of the model; and the *brain theory* approach, in which we require the internal structure of the model to be similar to that of some brain. The second chapter then serves to introduce a problem relevant to both approaches, the coding of information received by a system (be it animal or robot) in a form useful for guiding the action of the system. In particular, we study some of the coding of information that takes place in the visual systems of cats and frogs, introducing the reader along the way to some basic vocabulary from neurophysiology and neuroanatomy.

Part II, System Theory and Artificial Intelligence, pays little attention to the structure of the brain. Chapter 3 places within the context of the behavior of an active organism or robot such basic concepts from system theory as states (the residue of past experience), algorithms (programs for computers), feedback (which allows a system to compensate for unexpected disturbances), and adaptation (which allows a system to change with time to better interact with its environment). Chapter 4, Artificial Intelligence and Robotics, starts with a discussion of aspects of intelligence, stressing the need for an intelligent system to be able to use "internal models of its world" to perceive its environment and interact with it intelligently. The rest of the chapter then discusses how computers may be programed to plan courses of action, or analyze pictures to determine the objects located therein; and how such programs may be integrated into the overall design of the control system for a robot.

Part III, Brain Theory, is the heart of the book. Chapter 5 discusses the neural control of movement, working up from a discussion of feedback within the spinal cord through the neuroanatomy of the motor system to an overview of the multitude of tasks the brain must handle even in controlling so simple a behavior as taking a walk. The final section discusses various brainlike schemes for distributed control of movement, to provide the basis for the discussion of organizational principles which introduces Chapter 6, Memory and Perception in a Layered Computer. The discussion of output feature clusters complements the discussion of action-coding in Chapter 2. We then see how transformations may adjust the perception of an animal appropriately as its relationships with its environment changes, and we study the hologram metaphor in search of a distributed memory structure for our system. Chapter 7, Resolving Redundancy of Potential Command, then closes Part III by suggesting brain mechanisms for the two behaviors which introduced this preface, the tourist's commitment to a mode of action and the frog's "choice" of one of two flies.

Part IV, Prospects, asks "Where do we go from here?" Two types of answer are given. One suggests how the theory of Parts II and III might be built upon to understand more about such aspects of human thought and behavior as mental development and language; the other tries to identify some more general implications of our whole field of study.

The ideas of Warren McCulloch have especially influenced me in writing this book, but many of the researchers whose works I have cited are personal friends whose ideas and debate—as well as writings—have contributed much to this volume. They and other colleagues have provided invaluable, and valued, comments upon earlier drafts of this book. To all of them, my warm thanks. Students in my courses on Brains, Machines and Mathematics at Stanford University and the University of New South Wales and on Cybernetics and the Brain at the University of Massachusetts and Hampshire College have helped strip away much confusion. In particular, I am grateful to Richard Didday, Curt Boylls, and Parvati Dev, the first three students to venture a doctoral thesis on neurocybernetics with me. Finally, I wish to express my gratitude to the National Institute of Neurological Diseases and Stroke of the Public Health Service which, under grant no. NS 09755-01 COM, supported much of the preparation of this book.

MICHAEL A. ARBIB

Amherst, Massachusetts
December 1971

Contents

An Introduction

1 | Brain, Behavior and Metaphor

Rocks "survive" for billions of years without being alive, and a tree may live for hundreds of years though it has no brain. A tree can grow toward the sunlight, and a Venus fly trap can close to a touch. But a tree cannot escape a forest fire—it has neither the mobility to flee the fire nor the ability to perceive its approach. The burns upon its trunk may mark the passage of the fire, but the tree cannot use this "memory" to better react should it live to meet another fire. By contrast, an animal can perceive change in its environment and act to take advantage of, or reduce the harm from, such changes for it has the brain and the mobility to interact with, and adapt within, a constantly changing environment. Further, humans (at least) are able to base their current behavior on a rich pool of personal and cultural experiences to act within a long time-base of planned-for futures, and to make extensive use of artifacts and of language.

Our aim is to study the brain to enhance our understanding of human thought and behavior. Where some psychologists would study thought and behavior with little concern for the mechanisms which generate them, and where some biochemists would study chemical changes in neurons (the cells we consider most important in the brain) with little emphasis on their role in overall function, we—call us cyberneticians, model-builders, brain theorists—would seek to bridge the gap, searching for organizational principles which will help us understand how neurons can work together to yield complex patterns of behavior. Many psychologists and biochemists are model-builders, too, and the best cybernetics is built on a firm foundation of experimental knowledge. But too many psychologists and biochemists are *not* model-builders, and when such a psychologist speaks of the role of the brain, or such a biochemist speaks of memory, the "explanations" remain at a level of general vagueness which encourages neither detailed understanding nor careful evaluation.

It is useless to theorize if one lacks empirical data to shape and constrain one's thinking; and empirical data can form meaningless piles of garbage unless one has concepts and hypotheses to shape and constrain one's experimentation. We must develop theories of sufficient logical depth to do justice to the evolutionary and developmental histories of biological organisms, without losing the ability to test whether our theories are workable. Our strategy will then often be to construct the theory in the form of a machine (which we may build, simulate on a computer, or simply analyze through mathematical formulas) and show that the assumptions on its components and connections accord well with our experimental data at the biochemical or neurophysiological level, while its behavior agrees sufficiently well with behavioral or psychological data—"If you understand something, you can 'build' a machine to imitate it." In this book we shall present a number of cases in which such rigorous explanation has been achieved. This domain must be extended if we are to break out of constricting beliefs that behaviorism or biochemistry *alone* can yield a real understanding of human behavior.

In Section 1.1 we introduce two metaphors which structure our thinking. That "humans are machines" expresses our touchstone for explicit explanation. We shall see that it yields two approaches, which we shall label brain theory and artificial intelligence, depending on whether or not we insist that the units in our model correspond to units or regions in the brain. That "humans are animals" will remind us of the rich store of theoretical constructs and experimental data that evolutionary and comparative studies make available to us. In Section 1.2 we shall analyze what it might mean to understand the brain, so that we may place our methodology in perspective, suggesting the broad realm of questions it will help us answer.

1.1   THE EVOLUTIONARY AND CYBERNETIC METAPHORS

In seeking to understand brain and behavior, we shall be guided by two exploratory metaphors.

The first metaphor, "humans are animals," points us to evolutionary and comparative studies of animal behavior and brain function. Over a hundred years ago, Darwin convinced us that humans are biological organisms that have evolved from ancestors common to other biological organisms. Because of this commonality, we believe that there are similarities between our brains and those of other animals. We can gain only sketchy information about the functioning of the human brain from data gathered during brain operations upon human patients, but we are relatively unconstrained in our experimentation upon animals as long as proper care is taken to avoid pain. We thus hope to gain a great deal of information about human brain function by stimulating, recording from, or excising, portions of an animal's brain and seeing how the animal's behavior changes, and then comparing such results with, for example, the effect of excising a portion of a human patient's brain, when we know of no alternative way to cure epilepsy or remove a tumor. In this way, we hope to build up our understanding of how different parts of the brain contribute, alone and together, to such diverse aspects of mental function as the control of action, perception, and learning.

We do not claim that humans are no different from other animals. We expect to learn from the metaphor "humans are animals" by exploring both the *similarities* and the *differences* between humans and other animals. For instance, we know that humans can use tools far more ably than other animals, and we know that human language transcends the communication systems of virtually all other species. We also know that humans have certain brain developments which are lacking in other animals. By trying to correlate our behavioral uniqueness with our biological uniqueness, we may expect to gain insights into brain function, just as much as we can gain insights from seeing how mechanisms in other animals may carry over to mechanisms in the human brain.

Turning, then, to our second metaphor "humans are machines," it will again be the case that while trying to learn from the similarities between humans and machines—for example, trying to capture various aspects of human behavior in that of a robot—we must also stay alive to the fact that human action, memory, learning, and perception are far richer than those of any machine yet built or likely to be built in the near future. Thus, when we suggest that the brain can be thought of in some ways as a programmed computer, we are not trying to reduce humans to the level of extant machines, but rather to understand ways in which machines can give us insight into human attributes. We shall refer to this type of study as *cybernetics*, extending the usage of Norbert Wiener [1948] who defined the subject as "the study of control and communication in man and machine." For our present purpose, we may say that a worker in the field of cybernetics seeks to design, at least in principle, sophisticated information processing machines, which parallel human intellectual behavior or brain function.

Great care must be taken with our second metaphor, for we shall use it in two distinct ways. In the first, which we shall emphasize in Part II and refer to as the *artificial intelligence approach,* we simply see how existing computers may be programmed to yield "intelligent" behavior, without any attempt to provide a correlation between structures in the program and structures in the brain. Here we show that the idea of a stored program is more powerful than the old stimulus-response approach to behavior; and that some surprisingly complex behaviors can be broken down into conditional sequences of simple units. In the second use of this metaphor, which we shall emphasize in Part III and refer to as the *brain theory approach,* we shall emphasize the design of machines whose structure parallels that of brains. Our version of the latter approach will emphasize "distributed action-oriented computation in layered somatotopically organized machines" (this arcane terminology will be explained in Part III—for now the reader need simply note that this will prove to be an important catch-phrase in our brain theory), and will make heavy use of clues provided by comparative studies (the "humans are animals" metaphor) to suggest what structures should figure in our models. Whereas most of the artificial intelligence approach is based upon carrying out series of simple operations upon data passively stored, our brain theory will emphasize parallel activity of a multitude of operations within an array of interacting data and control schemes relevant to action.

In distinguishing the artificial intelligence and brain theory approaches, we must take care to avoid the error, all too common in the psychological literature, which has each mental process requiring a separate region of the brain, and vice versa. For the psychologist this may not matter, but for the student of brain evolution, or the neurosurgeon about to cut, the physical locus of a function may be crucial. Just because we may analyze a system S and find it to be equivalent in behavior to an interconnection of two systems S_1 and S_2 each with well-defined functions—and feel that we have learned much about S from such a decomposition—we may *not* infer that there is any way of carving S up *spatially* in such a way as to yield two systems equivalent to S_1 and S_2, respectively. The point is worth emphasizing by a detailed, although simple, example.

Consider the simple network of Figure 1a. We are to imagine each line as either "firing" or "not firing" at each time t on some fixed time scale, with the output of a cell bearing the inscribed number θ (called the "threshold" of the "formal neuron") firing at time $t + 1$ only if at least θ of its inputs fired at time t. Thus neurons 1 and 2 in a, both having threshold 1, just function as delay elements—their output pattern is precisely the input pattern one interval earlier. Neuron 3 fires at $t + 1$ if at least one

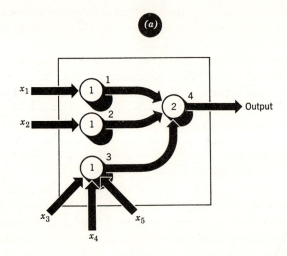

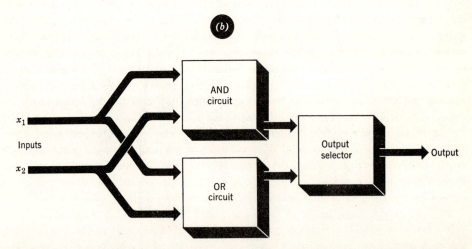

FIGURE 1   An illustration of the fact that two systems with the same function may possess quite distinct internal structures. In (a) we see a network of formal "neurons". "Neurons" 1 and 2 serve to feed the input variables to "neuron" 4 after a slight delay. "Neuron" 4 combines these variables in a way that depends on the "selector variables" x_3, x_4, and x_5 via its input from "neuron" 3. If any of the selector variables is active, "neuron" 4 behaves like an OR circuit; if none is active, it behaves like an AND circuit. Thus this "neural network" is equivalent in function to the circuit of (b) in which the AND circuit and the OR circuit reside in spatially separate subsystems.

of x_3, x_4, or x_5 fires at t. Neuron 4 fires if at least 2 of its inputs fire in the previous interval. Thus if all of x_3, x_4, and x_5 are quiet, the output of the whole net will fire at time $t + 2$ only if x_1 AND x_2 fire at time t, whereas if any of x_3, x_4, or x_5 fires at t, then the output will fire at time $t + 2$ only if x_1 OR x_2 or both fire at t. Thus we may regard x_3, x_4, and x_5 as control lines to determine whether or not the network acts on x_1 and x_2 as an "AND circuit" or an "OR circuit."

Let us imagine that x_1 and x_2 are input lines to the system, but that, as experimenters looking at the box from outside, we do not know about x_3, x_4, and x_5, which perhaps come from other subsystems which we are not studying. We might then deduce that our system can compute the AND-function and the OR-function, but it requires some output selector to determine which of these two results becomes the output of the system—and so draw up a block diagram like that of Figure 1*b* to summarize our observations upon the function of the system. However, in our *"actual" network,* Figure 1*a,* the AND and OR circuits *cannot* be separated.

Hence, even if we know completely the function or behavior of a device, we cannot deduce from this a unique structural description. Our brain theory must then use clues from anatomy and physiology about internal structure and states before it can yield details of the internal interactions which underlie observed behavior.

We should also add that we cannot deduce, just because a function is missing, that there exists a corresponding region of the brain which must thus be inactive. If one of the control lines x_3, x_4, or x_5 were to be severed, then the box would exhibit an apparently erratic behavior, failing to act as an OR-gate on many occasions when it should. Or suppose a "disease" were to cause x_3 to go into a mode of continual firing. Then neuron 4 would always function as an OR-gate, and the *function* AND would never be activated. Thus failure to activate a function does not imply failure to activate a neuron net, only failure to activate the net in a certain way. We may have a brain in which all neurons are activated, all gross neural tracts are connected appropriately, but errors of detailed connections or thresholds may lead to malfunction (cf. the example of "howl inhibition" on p. 8). The reader may also understand that we can describe neural networks where not only does each neuron take part in several functions, but also where functions are distributed over several anatomically distinct parts of the network. In fact, this seems to be a good strategy for obtaining reliable behavior from a brain composed of often unreliable neurons.

We cannot understand certain peculiarities of function unless we know of the constraints imposed by the underlying structure. We cannot make sense of a complex structure unless we have some hypotheses about its overall function. Thus in brain theory neither structure nor function is primary—rather the study of the two go hand in hand.

1.2   ON UNDERSTANDING THE BRAIN

Millions of *receptors* in our bodies continually monitor changes in our external and internal environment. Hundreds of thousands of cells called *motoneurons* control the movement of our muscles and the secretion of our glands. In between, an intricate network of billions of cells called *neurons* continually combine the signals from the receptors with signals encoding past experience to barrage the motoneurons with signals which will yield adaptive interactions with the environment. This network is called the *central nervous system* (CNS), and the *brain* constitutes the most headward part of this system—though we shall often speak of the brain when we really mean the CNS as a whole. Figure 2 gives us a rough picture of how the brain is situated in a *human* head, indicating the view we would get were we to slice down the middle of the head, and the side view we would get after removal of the skull. We shall discuss this figure in more detail in Section 2.3.

What would it mean to understand the brain? Would it mean that one day we could peer into a person's brain awhile, and then predict with perfect accuracy all his action? This seems unlikely. The human brain contains billions of neurons. (The estimate is rough—no one has the time to count all the neurons in a brain. At best one can estimate the number of cells in slices of brain, and then estimate what fraction these slices are of the whole brain.) Many neurons contact thousands of other cells. Thus if we regard the "coupling coefficients" of such places of neuronal interaction as being the adjustable parameters of the nervous system (and there may be many more, to do with fine chemical structure) we have say 10^4 parameters for each of say 10^{10} cells—a total of 10^{14} parameters to specify the interconnections of a single brain. (With less than 2×10^9 seconds in the average human lifetime, that gives us more than 5×10^4 parameters to record each second of our existence, although I would argue that human memory does not entail the second-by-second "tape-recording" that such a figure might suggest to be possible.) Such number games tend to be highly misleading, but they serve to remind us that if physics is still unable to solve the problem of the interactions of three particles, our goal cannot be detailed prediction of all the activity of an individual brain. In fact, if we tried to measure even a small fraction of these parameters in a brain, we would destroy it so completely that any prediction would be vacuous.

What we may hope to do, rather, is to gain reasonably accurate understanding at different levels. At the psychological level we might predict gross parameters of a person's emotional reactions from information about his personality, family relationships, and social milieu or, in more detail, we might seek to describe the strategies used by an individual in solving certain problems. In either case, we take the "black box" approach—we eschew all attempts to analyze the internal structure of the system and study only its external behavior—and characterize a human by a fairly small repertoire of actions and reactions.

The next level of study is that of the neuropsychologist, who tries to correlate the behavior analyzed by the psychologist with the function of various gross subdivisions of the brain. The neuropsychologist tries to relate aspects of behavior to a decomposition of the brain into a relatively small number of visually definable subsystems removing portions of an animal's brain to see how behavior is modified, hoping thus to learn the function of the ablated subsystem. This is a somewhat crude approach. As Richard Gregory remarked in his study, *The Brain as an Engineering Problem,* if we remove a resistor from a radio set which then emits a howl, this does not justify calling the resistor a "howl inhibition centre" (recall, too, our discussion of Figure 1). However, this approach should not be belittled. It is impractical to study subsystems of complex brains in isolation, not only because of the difficulties of keeping isolated chunks of brain alive and healthy, but also because of the fact that the neural messages reaching such chunks are already highly coded and transformed, making it difficult to stimulate such pieces of brain in a meaningful way.

Be that as it may, neuropsychologists are making progress in giving us a crude

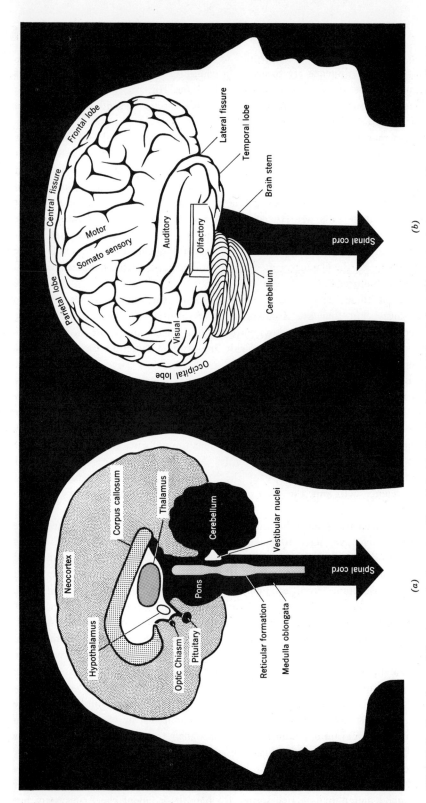

FIGURE 2 Two views of the human brain as positioned inside the head. The left-hand view diagrams what we would see were we to slice down the middle of the head, while the right-hand view suggests what would be seen from the side after removal of the skull. The *spinal cord*, the part of the CNS running up through the vertebrae of the spine, receives signals from the limbs and trunk, and contains the motoneurons that control the muscles of the limb and trunk. The spinal cord leads into the *brainstem* behind which is the outswelling of the *cerebellum*. Then, swelling out and overshadowing all, is the great outfolding of the *neocortex* of the cerebral hemispheres. In the "middle" view (a) we can see the *midbrain* and other structures which are obscured by the great outfolding of neocortex in the "side" view (b).

9

decomposition of the brain into structurally defined subsystems. At a similar level, students of artificial intelligence try to program computers to exhibit behavior such as playing a winning game of checkers, or proving theorems. But relating chunks of brain or subroutines of a program to various functions still cannot be said to constitute a complete understanding of the brain or the mind.

The next step may be to see how we might constitute arrays of cells to function in ways akin to that of the subsystems dissected out by the neuropsychologist. How might we design filtering networks, or networks for pattern recognition, or networks for combining auditory and visual information? Working at another level, one could spend a whole lifetime correlating the geometry of the membranes and subcellular systems which constitute cells with the way cells transform incoming patterns or the way in which they might subserve memory by changing function with repeated inter-actions. At another level, we may call on physics and biochemistry to explain the function of membranes, the chemistry of cellular interaction, and the detailed electrical conductivity of the neuron.

The presence of these "levels" makes it possible for the individual researcher to preserve her sanity, but they are ill-defined and a scientist who works on any one level needs occasional forays both downward to find mechanisms for the functions studied, and upward to understand what role the studied function can play in the overall scheme of things.

Of the many paths to understanding the ways in which people think and behave, we have selected that which seeks the principles of organization of the brain as a complex machine. But the path is not completed, and though a few portions of it are well-worn, we shall have to follow a number of trails unsure as to whether or not they really lead to greater understanding. There is an excitement in exploring little known regions which is lost when the superhighway is built. A similar excitement pervades our current attempts to construct a theory of the brain. Perhaps an amateur sketch of philosophy of science will put the status of our present approach into better per-spective.

There is more to science than accumulating more and more data on more and more objects. At some stage, we have to make an educated gamble that concepts which appear relevant to discussions of a few known examples are concepts that can be used to structure a whole range of phenomena of which the examples form a very small part. Concepts must come from somewhere, and biologists have often turned to technology for metaphors. Consider two versions of the "humans are machines" metaphor. "The human body is a steam engine" was a metaphor which finally shucked off its false importations and gave rise to a careful science of human metabolism. Similarly, we are somewhat creatures of current technological fashion when we try to transform the metaphor "the brain is a computer" into a serviceable basis for brain theory. Since a metaphor is a starting point for the evolution of a theory rather than a theory itself, a few words of caution may be appropriate here to remind us that the metaphors we use must not be taken too literally. A metaphor, by comparing a system to another which we may understand better, is designed to aid comprehension of the first system. But, besides properties which the two systems may share, there are many that they do not share. To say that "My love is like a red, red rose" does not imply that she will appreciate having the hose turned on her. Even for similes, so for metaphors. A good metaphor is a rich source for hypotheses about the first system but must not be regarded as a theory of the first system. If we bear such strictures in mind, then the metaphors "humans are animals" and "humans are machines" may well help us. Further, *when we have refined them and discarded many of their false importations,* they may well provide terms and concepts with which we shall perceive ourselves. In other words, during a period of concept formation, we must be well aware of the metaphorical nature of our concepts. However, during a period in which the concepts can accommodate most of our questions about a given subject matter, we can afford to ignore their metaphorical origins and confuse our description of reality with that reality. The title of this book reminds us that brain theory has not yet established its concepts to the point where we can afford to forget their metaphorical nature, but the brain we seek to explain is no less real for our self-conscious emphasis on the provisional nature of our theories.

We must also stress that there are so many different questions to be asked about a system as complex as the human brain that there are different approaches appropriate to investigating different clusters of such questions—it being a later task, once successful approaches are established to the various areas, to ascertain how best they may be reconciled on their "overlap."

For example, we do not claim to encompass all of psychology and the brain sciences within our scheme of "distributed action-oriented computation in layered somatotopically organized machines." This may be seen by contrasting it with the "molecular biology" approach. Having seen genetics transformed by an understanding of the role of DNA in "encoding" cellular materials, many biologists seriously believe that all biology can be reduced to the study of complex molecules. We would instead view this approach neither as irrelevant nor as all-encompassing—rather, we see it as addressing a class of questions complementary to those to which our methods are suited.

Where the molecular biologist goes "up" from the basic biochemistry and physics, we go "down" from overall functional questions. To point up this distinction we may look at computer science, where we see a corresponding division of labor. On the one hand, we have the electrical engineer using solid-state physics to reduce the size, and increase the speed of operation and flexibility of function, of the devices which are to be built into computers. On the other we have the computer system designer, not at all concerned with the actual physics involved, but rather—given a guarantee that the components have certain function—concerned to put those components together to get some overall sophisticated function. Thus, the component level—or the cellular level, to be more biological about it—is the meeting ground for two quite different approaches, and it is that of the "systems designer" that we are taking here.

The necessity for organizational principles to guide us in the analysis of any complex system, even if man-made, is well demonstrated by the following anecdote related by Jim Horning when a graduate student at Stanford University:

In December 1966 the Stanford Computer Science Department installed a 2116A computer for instructional use. I was one of a group of graduate students who attempted to use the computer before instructional manuals arrived. Our principal problem was deducing enough information about its structure to write meaningful programs.

We of course started with several advantages. The front panel was labelled; we knew it was an electronic digital computer of a certain general class; we knew quite a bit about the theory of digital computers, and had each programmed several. Nevertheless, we found it surprisingly hard to deduce non-trivial information about the 2116A.

We quickly located the power switch, the data entry switches, the register displays and the principal control push buttons. We did not have much trouble entering data into the registers, and were soon able to enter and execute instruction words. But that was about the limit.

In several hours of experimentation we completely failed to deduce such simple items as the format of the instruction word (or even the location of the op-code). We were unable to program the addition of two numbers or the simplest input-output.

When manuals arrived, we learned that our difficulties were not caused by any particular perversity on the part of the 2116A. It is a rather typical small-scale single-address computer of exactly the class we had expected. It seems unlikely that we would have done any better on any other comparable machine.

Perhaps this merely means that graduate students are not as clever as they think they are. But in pondering this experience I have concluded that it was illustrative of the problems that will be encountered in studying any complex information processing system. . . . The study of the brain [may be] very like the study of an *unknown* computer system.

Again some of the less subtle research on the chemistry of memory may serve as ample testimony to the dangers of relying on molecular biology to the exclusion of all organizational principles. We all agree that cells are living systems and that learning involves changes in the brain. Thus, in some sense, learning is a growth phenomenon, and so it is hardly surprising that substances which block RNA synthesis—and thus cell growth—interfere with an animal's learning. But to go from this to making such statements as "Therefore, RNA is the memory molecule" is as useful as noting that cutting off the electricity supply disrupts the storage of information in a computer and deducing that "Therefore, electrons are the building blocks of memory." We have a theory of complex computer memory structures based on the properties of switching and storage elements. It is irrelevant to this theory whether component properties are mediated by electrical, magnetic, hydraulic, or chemical mechanisms. Similarly a theory of the brain will not be so much in terms of biochemistry as in terms of organizational principles for neurons. Biochemistry is irrelevant to such a theory of organization per se—but it is vitally important in helping us understand the detailed properties of the components. In studying human perception, biochemistry may be of little relevance, while organizational principles predominate. In studying drug therapy, precisely the opposite balance may hold.

Thus although this volume is almost completely devoted to the search for organizational principles, we do *not* try to argue the superiority of this approach to that of the molecular biologist, but rather argue the complementarity of the two approaches. In fact, the organizational approach—"If cells can do such-and-such, then an array of them with certain properties will function in a way which is thus explained"—will always raise complementary questions—"Is it physically possible for a cell to do such-and-such, and if so what biochemical mechanisms are involved?" That we do not attempt to answer these latter questions does not diminish their importance—it is simply that they require volumes of their own for their proper elaboration.

Much of this book focuses upon the theme that "the brain is a complex information processor with distributed action-oriented computation taking place in a layered somatotopically organized network", but our contention that this is a useful approach does not imply that it exhausts all approaches to brain theory. It is only by dramatic reconfiguration and extension that such a scheme can come to encompass the insights of Freud or someone's experiences with drugs. Eventually, a unified theory (or a collection of interlocking complementary theories) will emerge that is not so limited. The cyberneticians may then claim that cybernetics is vindicated as they trace the evolution of their scheme by the incorporation of elements from psychoanalysis and chemistry; others will see molecular biology vindicated by the incorporation of computer science and verbal therapy into their own approach. Good science is a strange mixture of passionate conviction that one's own approach is correct—to get the sense of personal involvement that makes hard work a pleasure—and an openness to the virtue of other approaches. If the scientist can subscribe to the grand synthesis when it emerges, perhaps we can forgive her her human weakness in ascribing a somewhat exaggerated role to her own contribution to that synthesis.

At the present time, only a fragment of human thought and behavior can be explained from a cybernetic viewpoint, though there are many areas where this viewpoint can make some contribution to our present sketchy understanding. In this volume we shall see that certain aspects of intelligent problem-solving may be fitted into the artificial intelligence approach, while our brain theory approach provides insights into the interaction of an organism with the environmental space and structures around it. The book by no means exhausts the achievements in either of these areas, but is intended to convince the reader of the viability of a long-range investigation designed to yield a model of "distributed action-oriented computation in layered somatotopically organized machines" which will provide powerful insights into the brain mechanisms underlying perception, thought, language, and action.

2 | Action-Coding and Neural Networks

In answering the question "How does the organism extract relevant information from its environment?", we must realize that there is implicit here the further question "How does the organism avoid overloading its processors with irrelevant information from its environment?" In this chapter, we study some psychological data on this "discarding of the irrelevant" as well as some neurophysiological data on neuronal mechanisms which signal environmental features relevant to the action of the organism.

As we stressed in the introduction, what distinguishes an animal from a plant is that it has increased mobility coupled with a brain that allows it to perceive change in its environment and act to take advantage of, or reduce the harm from, such changes. It can also learn, so that subtle properties of past interactions can be incorporated to yield improved behavior. In Section 2.1 we wish to study how an initial component of perception—the "preprocessing" of visual stimuli in relatively peripheral stages of the nervous system—may be shaped by the range of likely interactions of the system.

In fact, our general discussion of "action-oriented perception" in Section 2.1 is also applicable to *robots*: For many applications a computer is a symbol-manipulator (see Section 3.2). It is provided with data encoded as a stream of symbols, and it processes these data to provide the required output as another stream of symbols. But in some applications, the computer must operate "on-line," as in monitoring an assembly line, where the computer receives its data from sensors and must process these data in time to order the rejection of faulty products by the time they reach an ejection mechanism on the line. Such a system of sensors and computer and effectors may be called a *robot*. Most robots, circa 1970, are—like the defect monitor just mentioned—limited in their activity, but in Chapter 4 we shall consider, by way of contrast, robots which are designed to use artificial intelligence techniques to guide their interactions with the environment, and for which the discussion in this chapter of preprocessing of visual information is highly relevant.

Section 2.2 introduces the basic neurophysiology we need for our discussion of visual preprocessing in cat and frog in Section 2.4, while Section 2.3 provides some basic neuroanatomy which places the gross structures to be introduced in Section 2.4 in some perspective. Learning will not come up *explicitly* in this chapter—we shall meet it in passing in our discussion of states and adaptation in Chapter 3, and then develop it in our discussion of internal models of the world in Section 4.1.

2.1   ACTION-ORIENTED PERCEPTION

Try out the following experiment upon a friend: Write down in front of her a list of six items, writing some of the items in script and some of them in hand printing. Ask your friend to memorize them. After they have been memorized and you have erased them, do not ask what the items on the list were, but rather ask which were printed and which were written. About nine people out of ten will have no idea of the answer to this question. This emphasizes that we do not perceive in a neutral way, but rather extract information which *may* be relevant to our interaction with the world. Since we cannot predict precisely what information will be useful to us in the future, it is not unreasonable that we perceive and remember far more than we may actually need. If we have sufficient time we "explore" our environment, noting novel features even though we have no reason at the time to think them significant. Later, we may be in a situation where the information does, surprisingly, prove to be useful— as for the one in ten who noticed the script-print distinction. Presumably, the longer the list is scanned, the more likely is "exploration" to disclose such features.

Nonetheless, a great deal of information that we might extract from current stimulation is "thrown away." It is worth noting in the preceding example that the subject presumably had to be able to call up different "routines" to recognize a word when it was printed and a word when it was written in script. Nonetheless, the choosing of these routines was subconscious, and it seems to be the *result* of their execution rather than the *execution itself* that was consciously remembered. Only some sort of abstract representation of the items to be remembered (some people seem to picture a "standard" typeface during recall)—the "output" of the recognition routine—was processed into memory. If you were to give your friend the test again, she would probably ask more questions and so would process more information into memory—and then you might trip her up by asking whether or not you dotted your i's.

We see then that the organism is not just a passive creature, being given a series of "photographs", which are to be classified one by one into one of some small number of categories. Nor does the organism have any use for storing unprocessed "photographs". Rather, it is constantly seeking information which is relevant to its actions. Again, if it has miscomputed what is relevant to it, it will ignore much relevant information— just as a student may curse herself for not taking notes at a certain portion of a lecture course, when she finds that that is the very portion that gets so many questions on the final exam. The problem of encoding information to make explicit the relevant kernel was brought home to me by considering a computer program which was designed to "recognize written words". The writer of the program felt that he had succeeded when the machine could take script, and type out in standard format the sequence of letters which comprised the written word, but I noted that the program was a complete failure if you were to ask it not, "What is the word written there?" but rather,

"Whose handwriting is it?" or, "Is that signature a forgery?" This is not to deny that—as in the script-versus-print test—some of the features previously used in processing may help in solving the new problem, but certain features which were previously lumped together must now be distinguished if subtle differences in writing style are to be distinguished.

Thus, as we shall see again and again, the question of the appropriate representation of information depends crucially upon the sort of questions we expect to be asked about that information now or in the future—noting that, in the case of an animal, and in much of our action as humans, the question is not asked verbally, to be responded to verbally, but is rather a problem posed by the environment, and is to be answered in terms of our action within that environment, contributing to our own well-being, or that of our fellow creatures.

This last point is worth emphasizing. In speaking of human perception, we often talk as if a purely passive process of classification were involved—of being able, when shown an object, to respond by naming it correctly. However, for most of the perception of most animals and much of human behavior, it is more appropriate to say that the animal perceives its environment to the extent that it is *prepared* to *interact* with that environment in some reasonably structured fashion. We can show that we have perceived a cat by naming it, true, but our perception of it often involves no conscious awareness of its being a cat per se, as when it jumps on our lap while we are reading and we simply classify it by the action we take as "something-to-be-stroked" or "something-to-be-pushed-off". In computer jargon (of which the reader may find some elementary exposition in Section 3.2) we might say that perception of an object generally involves the gaining of access to "programs" for controlling interaction with the object, rather than simply generating a "name" for the object, and this is precisely what distinguishes the control-computer of a robot from a computer programed, say, to read numbers from bank checks.

The reader may reasonably object that much of human behavior is verbal rather than involving activity of the body and limbs, and regret that our emphasis on "perception as preparation to interact" would seem to exclude most of people's more intelligent behavior from study! This is not so—for recalling our stress on the importance of comparative studies (Section 1.1), we note that human brains have evolved from the brains of animals which interacted complexly with their environments without the aid of language. Consequently, I believe that language can best be understood as a device which refines an already complex system—thus turning around the approach of many psychologists who take language as their starting-point. In Section 8.1, we shall briefly outline how naturally language might arise as an extension of our action-oriented approach to perception and memory. We would note that it is the evolutionary history of brains that gives brain theory its biological character, for whereas in brain theory, language is to be explained as a "recently" evolved refinement of an underlying ability to interact with the environment, in robotics we start from computers which are primarily linguistic (or at least symbol-manipulating) devices and try to evolve better programs to guide robot behavior.

An important disclaimer is necessary at this point. Our stress on *action-oriented perception* must not be confused with the radical behaviorism that confuses thought with action. We shall shortly comment upon the fact that gaining access to a number of programs does *not* entail a decision to act upon any of them; but here let us stress that in complex systems, perception is oriented toward the future as much as the present, "exploring" features of the current environment which may be incorporated into an "internal model of the world" (Section 4.1) to guide future action more and more adaptively. Thus—as we evolve toward the full flexibility of language—we may expect perception to be less bound to actions of the present and more involved with relational structures between the environment and the model with no *immediate* orientation to action. It should also be added (Section 8.1) that evolution has provided the brain with many genetically determined mechanisms which automatically relate sensed environmental features to an appropriate framework for action.

We should now note some implications of our contention that the primary purpose of recognizing objects is not to classify them, but to be prepared to interact with them. It is not enough to perceive the presence of a table on which to place our papers if we then release our grasp of the papers some two metres from the table. Perception is not so much of "what" an object in the environment is, as it is of relations between the object and the subject. Since spatial relationships are of particular importance in guiding action, we may say that perception involves not so much "what" as "how to relate" and (in particular) "where".

The observant reader may have noted that we have smuggled a rather large proposition into the argument, for we have implied that perception involves objects within the environment, rather than the environment *in toto,* even though we have stressed that this perception may simply raise the possibility of some simple interaction with such an object, rather than yield any awareness of its detailed shape, color, or texture. This is in fact so, if "object" is defined in a sufficiently loose way—as when I perceive a-row-of-trees as I walk by, without any awareness of the nature or even spacing of the individual trees. Thus our thesis must also be that all the more complex animals (and robots) will perceive their world in terms of "objects," even though the nature of that perception will vary greatly from animal to animal: Both people and dogs perceive telegraph poles in terms of communication systems, yet the perceived means of communication are very different. It is the ability of brains to mediate perception of the environment in terms of objects which will make the evolution of language seem so natural in Section 8.1. But now we must face up to the immediate implications of this ability, for if an animal or a robot can perceive that there are many "objects" in its environment, it is likely that the possibilities for interaction will exceed its capabilities for simultaneous interaction.

Related considerations led Warren McCulloch to stress the importance for brain theory of his *principle of redundancy of potential command* which states, essentially, that command should pass to the region with the most important information. He cited the example of a World War I naval fleet where the behavior of the whole fleet is controlled (at least temporarily) by the signals from whichever ship first sights the enemy, the point being that this ship need not be the flagship, in which command normally resides. In fact (cf. our discussion of structural versus functional decomposition in Section 1.1) it would be wrong to think that control of the brain in any conflict situation *must* devolve to any one region. We shall see an example where it does, and an example where it does not, in Chapter 7. However, while resisting this false implication we shall use McCulloch's terminology, and say that *it is an important property of any system interacting with a complex environment that it be able to resolve redundancy of potential command.*

To clarify the meaning of this statement, recall that in discussing its action-orientation we were careful to caricature perception as a gaining of access to a program

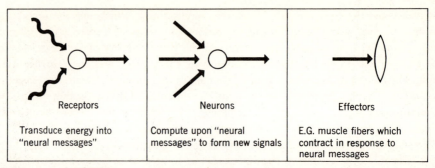

Receptors	Neurons	Effectors
Transduce energy into "neural messages"	Compute upon "neural messages" to form new signals	E.G. muscle fibers which contract in response to neural messages

FIGURE 1   Basic elements for the study of the nervous system: receptors, neurons, and effectors.

rather than the execution of a program—you perceive something and yet may still leave it alone. Thus in gaining access to the program, the system only gives it *potential* command, that is, capability to determine the course of action, further processing being required to determine whether or not to act. Further, as our stroke versus push example of the cat shows, there will be redundancy of potential command, with computation required to determine which of the accessed programs will actually control the ensuing actions of the organism. If we have been scratched frequently by cats, the "push program" may take command. In Chapter 7, we shall discuss two implementations of this resolution of redundancy of potential command—in modeling how a frog might come to snap at only one of several flies, and how a vertebrate might decide to fight or to flee. In both these cases, our discussion will make rich contacts with real data from neuroanatomy and neurophysiology.

We shall try to provide a better feel for some of the implications of the foregoing general considerations, by studying the coding of visual stimuli in cat and frog in Section 2.4. But first, we must introduce some basic properties of neurons in Section 2.2, and some of the overall "geography" of the brain in Section 2.3.

2.2   THE BRAIN AS A NETWORK OF NEURONS†

In Section 1.2, we introduced the basic "components" of receptors, neurons, and effectors schematized in Figure 1. The vast network of billions upon billions of neurons is interconnected in chains and loops and tangled skeinworks so that signals entering the net from the receptors interact there with the billions of signals already traversing the system, both to modify activity within the system and also to yield the signals which control the effectors. In this way, the CNS (central nervous system) enables the current actions of the organism (Figure 2) to depend both upon its current stimulation and upon the residue of past experience expressed in the activity (and changed structure) of its network.

We may abstract these architectural considerations to say that in our theory *we shall view the brain as a network of neurons*, which in some sense establishes the reference level for the explanations which constitute our brain theory. In other

---

† This section introduces such basic terms as axon, dendrites, synapse, and threshold, and may be omitted by any reader who has studied the bare elements of neurophysiology.

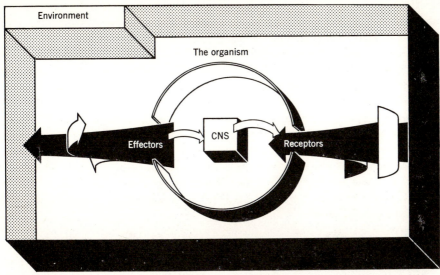

FIGURE 2   The organism in interaction with its environment: receptor responses to environmental energies and feedback signals from the effectors modify activity in the CNS
(central nervous system) which, among other things, controls the effectors that express
the activity of the organism.

words, the emphasis of our brain theory (though, of course, not of our study of
artificial intelligence) will be, as indicated in our discussion of levels of explanation
in Section 1.2, upon the properties of systems of interconnected neurons rather than
upon a purely psychological level or upon the analysis of biochemical systems. We
fix upon certain properties of neurons, or even larger regions of the brain, and
build up from there, rather than building up from—for example—biochemical
studies of the effects of drugs upon neural function. We are also ignoring other
cells in the brain, such as the glial cells which definitely play a role in metabolism
and which some have suggested may also play a role in memory.

We expect to solve many important problems despite these restrictions—and by
no means preclude later unification of our approach with others, such as that
emphasizing chemical systems.

We all know of the five classical senses of vision, hearing, touch, taste, and smell.
Specialized receptors in the eyes respond to light; receptors in the ears respond to
the pressure of air waves; some of the receptors in the skin respond to pressure;
while others in the tongue and the mouth respond to subtle traces of chemicals.
But—despite the popular belief that to have a sixth sense is somehow uncanny—
we all have a sixth and a seventh sense, and many more besides. In addition to the
"classical" touch receptors, there are others in the skin responsive to temperature,
or which signal painful stimuli such as tissue damage.

In addition to the external receptors, there are receptors located in the muscles
which monitor the activity of the muscles, tendons, and joints to provide a continual
source of "feedback" about the tensions and lengths of muscles and the angles of the
joints, and so on, for the appropriate activity of the effectors must depend not only
on where the system should be, but also on where it is now. The vestibular system
in the head monitors gravity and accelerations. Further, there are receptors located

within the body which monitor the chemical level of the bloodstream, and the state of the heart and the intestines, and so on. Since the brain is the most important sub-system of the body, and the most delicate, it is the appropriate place at which to monitor crucial levels of some metabolites in the bloodstream. Thus there are various receptors in the brain which signal inadequate water content, others which monitor sugar content, and so forth. If we stimulate these cells in its brain, an animal will drink copious quantities of water, or eat enormous quantities of food, even though it is properly supplied—for the brain has received a signal that water or food is lacking, and so instructs the animal accordingly irrespective of whatever contradic-tory signals may be coming from a distended stomach.

To understand the processes that intervene between receptors and effectors we must have a closer look at "the" neuron. In fact, *there is no such thing as a typical neuron* (Figure 3). What we shall do, then, is to schematize properties shared by

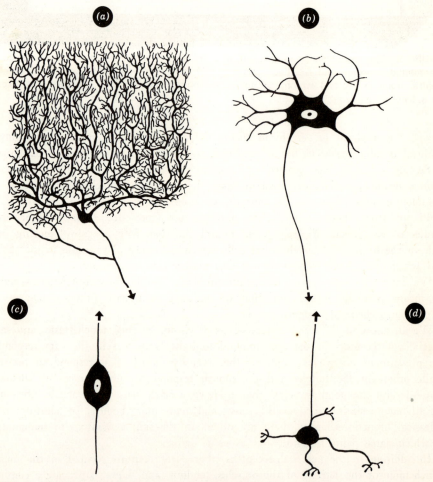

FIGURE 3   This figure serves to remind us how schematic the idealized neuron of the next figure is, by showing 4 of the thousands of distinct types of neurons. In each case, the arrowhead indicates the direction toward the axonal arborization, which is not shown. (a) A Purkinje cell of the cerebellum; (b) a motor neuron (the one closest to our schematic neuron); (c) a bipolar neuron of the olfactory system; (d) a granule cell of the cerebellum.

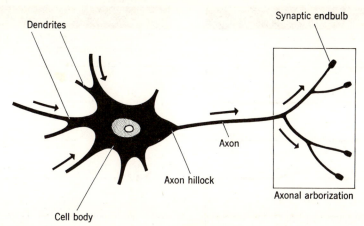

FIGURE 4   Schematic view of a neuron. Activity from receptors and other neurons modifies membrane potentials on the dendrites and cell body. The effects of these changes converge upon the axon hillock whence—for appropriate spatiotemporal patterns of incoming activity—a pulse of membrane potential will be propagated along the axon, branching out into the axonal arborization to activate the synaptic endbulbs which modify the membrane potential of other neurons, or of muscle fibers, in turn.

most neurons, while noting that this general picture must be modified for studies of many particular cases.

The basic scheme is shown in Figure 4, which is abstracted from a motoneuron of mammalian spinal cord. From the *soma* (cell body) protrude a number of ramifying branches called the *dendrites* (from the Greek *dendron*, a tree); these comprise a major part of the *input* surface of the neuron. There also extrudes from the cell body, at a point called the *axon hillock* (abutting the *initial segment*), a long fiber called the *axon*, which generally branches into the so-called *axonal arborization*. (*Arbor* is *Latin* for tree; note the cunning change of stem to avoid the monstrosity "axonal dendriticity." One may also speak of the dendritic arborization.) The tips or *endbulbs* (or *boutons*) of the branches of the axon impinge upon other neurons or upon effectors. The locus of interaction between an endbulb and the cell upon which it impinges is called a *synapse*, and we say that the cell with the endbulb *synapses upon* the cell with which the connection is made.

We can best imagine the flow of information as shown by the arrows in the diagram, for although "conduction" can go in either direction on the axon, most synapses tend to "communicate" activity to the dendrites or soma of the cell they synapse upon, whence activity passes to the axon hillock and then down the axon to the terminal arborization. The axon can be very long indeed. For instance, a neuron that controls the big toe is rooted in the spine and thus has an axon that runs the complete length of the leg. We may contrast the immense length of the axon of such a neuron with what must be the very small size of many of the neurons in our heads, which allows us to pack over ten billion of them into so small a space. For example, there exist small cells in the visual system called amacrine cells, whose branchings cannot appropriately be labeled dendrites or axons, for they are short and may well communicate activity in either direction, serving as local modulators of surrounding neurons.

To understand more about this "communication," we must consider the cell as a

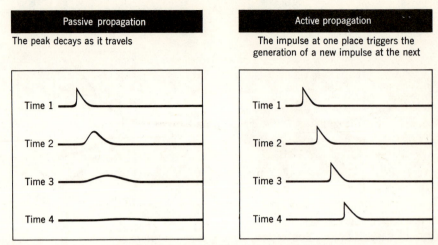

FIGURE 5   The two main modes of "communication" within the neuron. Passive propagation (analogous to the flow of heat in a metal bar) of changes in membrane potential is the usual mode for dendrites, the cell body, and very short axons; while active propagation (analogous to the propagation of the "ignition zone" in a fuse) is necessary for "communication" in long axons, and has been found in some dendritic structures, such as that of the Purkinje cell.

living creature enclosed by a membrane across which there is a difference in electrical charge. If we change this potential difference between the inside and outside, the change can propagate in much the same passive way that heat is conducted down a rod of metal—the change in temperature can propagate to other parts of the rod, but as it moves further and further away from the point at which heat is applied, so does the temperature change decrease (Figure 5). In the same way, a normal change in potential difference across the cell membrane can propagate in a passive way so that the change occurs later, and is smaller, the further away we move from the site of the original change.

For "short" cells (such as the rods, cones, and interneurons in the retina) this passive propagation suffices to signal a potential change from one end to the other; but if the axon is long, this mechanism is completely inadequate since changes at one end will decay away almost completely before reaching the other end.

Fortunately, cell membranes have the further property that if the change in potential difference is large enough (we say it exceeds a *threshold*), then in a cylindrical configuration such as the axon, a pulse can be generated which will actively propagate at full amplitude instead of fading passively. To understand this, think of a metal rod coated with gunpowder. If we heat the rod fairly gently, the gunpowder will not ignite, and the propagation of the temperature difference will be passive and fading. However, if we exceed the ignition temperature of the gunpowder coating in heating one end of our rod, then that segment of coating will burn spontaneously and will be hot enough to ignite the neighboring segment of gunpowder coating, and so on, all the way down the bar (Figure 5). Note that it is no longer a case of whatever heat we supply propagating passively along the tube. Rather, the heat we supply serves to trigger a "regenerative" process, a chain reaction which supplies its own energy so that once we have triggered the reaction at one place, it serves to unlock the energy stored in the next place, which can then trigger the following place, and so on and on. So it is with cylinders of membrane. Thus if the various potential differences on the dendrites and soma of a neuron yield, usually by passive propagation, a potential difference across the membrane at the axon hillock which exceeds a certain *threshold*, then a regenerative process is started—the electrical change at one place is then enough to trigger this process at the next place, to yield an undiminishing pulse of potential difference propagating down the axon.

In the example of the fuse, we can only obtain active propagation once, because once we have used it, the gunpowder is burnt up and there remains just the metal, which is capable of only passive propagation. Thus it is better to compare our axon with a *recoatable* metal bar—we are to imagine that after an impulse has propagated along the length of the axon, chemical processes take place which are the equivalent of recoating the fuse. (This *functional* equivalence does *not* mean that the change in the membrane actually takes the form of a recoating!) There is thus a short *refractory period*, a period during which a new impulse cannot be propagated along the axon, while the chemical restoration takes place.

If we were to start an impulse at any one place on the axon, it would propagate in both directions. However, if we start the pulse at one end of the axon (normally the axon hillock), it can only travel away from that end, since once a section has been triggered it becomes refractory until well after the impulse has passed out of range. An impulse traveling along the axon triggers off new impulses in each of its branches (or *collaterals*), which in turn trigger off impulses in their even finer branches (Figure 6). When an impulse arrives at one of the endbulbs, after a slight delay it yields a change in potential difference across the membrane of the cell upon which it impinges. The membrane on the endbulb is called the *presynaptic membrane*, and the membrane of the surface upon which the endbulb impinges is called the *postsynaptic membrane*.

Surprisingly, at most synapses the direct cause of the change in potential of the postsynaptic membrane is not electrical but chemical. There are some *exceptional* synapses which are so large, or have such tight coupling, that the impulse effects the polarization of the postsynaptic membrane without chemical mediation. However, the normal process is that the electrical pulse reaching the endbulb causes the release of a few little vesicles of a chemical called the *transmitter substance,* which

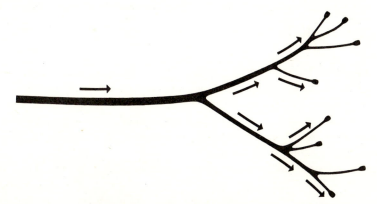

FIGURE 6 The normal direction of active propagation along an axon is from the axon hillock toward the axonal arborization. A spike arriving at a bifurcation is thought to normally trigger the generation of a spike in each of the branches.

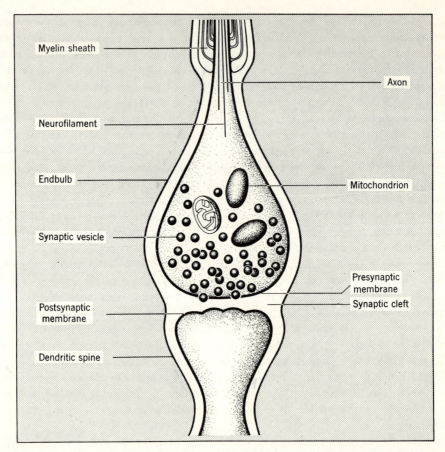

Myelin sheath

Axon

Neurofilament

Endbulb

Mitochondrion

Synaptic vesicle

Presynaptic membrane

Synaptic cleft

Postsynaptic membrane

Dendritic spine

FIGURE 7 There are perhaps a million billion sites of interaction within the CNS. A "typical" such synapse is shown here. We see that, for this type of synapse, a pulse arriving down the axon does not have a direct electrical effect on the neuron it impinges upon, but rather triggers the release of a number of synaptic vesicles (little packs of transmitter substance) through the presynaptic membrane, whence they migrate across the synaptic cleft to depolarize (or hyperpolarize) the presynaptic membrane. In this case the postsynaptic membrane forms the surface of a miniscule spine projecting from a dendritic branch to make synaptic contact. (The neurofilaments and mitochondria play a metabolic role. The myelin sheath, which surrounds most axons, serves—among other things—to increase the speed of spike propagation.)

then diffuses across the very small *synaptic cleft* (Figure 7) to the other side. It is the transmitter reaching the postsynaptic membrane that causes the change in polarization of this membrane. The transmitter substance may be of two basic kinds: either excitatory, that is, tending to move the potential difference across the postsynaptic membrane in the direction of the threshold, or, conversely, *inhibitory*, that is, tending to move the polarity away from threshold.

If there is any universal statement about the nervous system, it is that "There are no universal statements about the nervous system except for the universal statement that there are no universal statements except . . . ." However, many neurophysiologists believe Dale's law, which states that if we follow the axon of a neuron from a *mammal* through all its branchings, the synapses these branches form on other cells will either

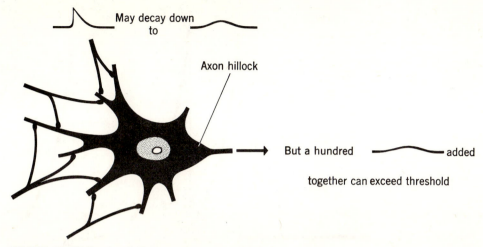

FIGURE 8 While the individual effect of synaptic activations may be small at the axon hillock, the combined effect—spatial and temporal summation—of hundreds of these synaptic activations may push the neuron above the threshold for pulse generation at its axon hillock.

be all excitatory or all inhibitory. This is not true for invertebrates; for example, Kandel et al. [1967] found opposite synaptic actions mediated by different branches of an identifiable interneuron in the mollusc *Aplysia*. In fact, the "law" may fail even for mammals since the Scheibels [1969] have found indirect evidence that some 30% of a certain class of fibers in cat spinal cord have both excitatory and inhibitory synapses (see also Scheibel and Scheibel [1970]). Of course, since they come from many different neurons, the synapses *on* a given cell may be of either kind, irrespective of the range of applicability of Dale's law.

The many little changes in potential difference across the membrane of a given cell, caused by the activity of all the synapses which impinge upon it, propagate passively (in most, but by no means all, cases) through the membrane of its dendrites and its cell body, decaying as they propagate. At the *axon hillock*, many different potential-changes will be converging, so that even though these changes are themselves very small, the total contribution by which excitation exceeds inhibition may be quite large (Figure 8).

In other words, the impulse arriving at the endbulb generally causes a subthreshold change in the postsynaptic membrane. Nonetheless, the cooperative effect of many such subthreshold changes may yield a potential change at the axon hillock which exceeds threshold—and if this occurs at a time when the axon has passed the refractory period of its previous firing, then a new impulse will be fired down the axon.

For simplicity, let us schematize the effect of a synaptic excitation to be to move the potential toward threshold with a time course like that shown in the first pulse of the graph of potential in Figure 9. (We shall not diagram the effect of inhibition, but it counteracts the move toward threshold whether by "making a negative contribution" or by "shunting off" excitation.) The changes in potential difference resulting from one spike arriving at a single synapse will almost invariably be far below threshold. However, these changes can have a cumulative effect in that one may arrive and add to the effect of another which has not yet decayed away. Thus, if we

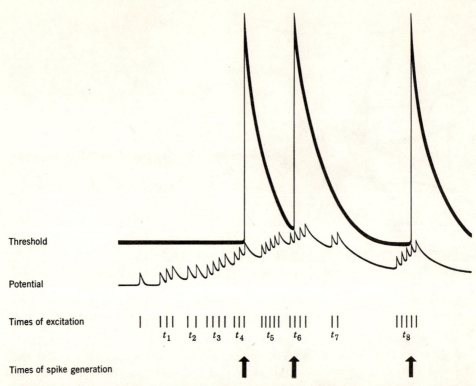

Threshold

Potential

Times of excitation

t_1 t_2 t_3 t_4 t_5 t_6 t_7 t_8

Times of spike generation

FIGURE 9   A more detailed schematization of temporal summation of pulses. We show each excitation as adding a small increment to the membrane potential, which rapidly decays back to its resting level. However, if the excitations are spaced sufficiently closely, they may summate sufficiently to reach threshold. The inability of an axon to propagate two spikes within what is called the refractory period of the neuron is schematized by the immense rise in threshold following the generation of each spike.

space subthreshold changes closely enough, they can accumulate and exceed threshold to yield a time course of potential change such as shown in Figure 9.

We may think of the neuron's threshold as being normally constant, but after we have fired an impulse down the axon, the threshold increases enormously and then takes quite a while to return to normal. Note that if, as at t_4, the changes accumulate to a level sufficiently far above *normal* threshold, it may exceed the *actual* threshold even before it has decayed back to normal. We thus speak of an initial *absolutely* refractory period, when it is too improbable that the changes could exceed the raised threshold, and the *relatively* refractory period when an exceptionally strong level of input can trigger an axonal impulse. Clearly, though, there is no sharp border between the absolute and relative refractory periods.

Note that the synaptic events which influence the axon may occur arbitrarily close together—if there were 10,000 synapses on a cell, it would not be unreasonable to expect a thousand of these to be activated in any one refractory period. Thus we get much interaction of events both within a refractory period and between refractory periods. For example, in Figure 9, we see that there are identical bursts of excitation at t_3 and t_6, yet only that at t_6 elicits a spike, even though it had to raise the potential

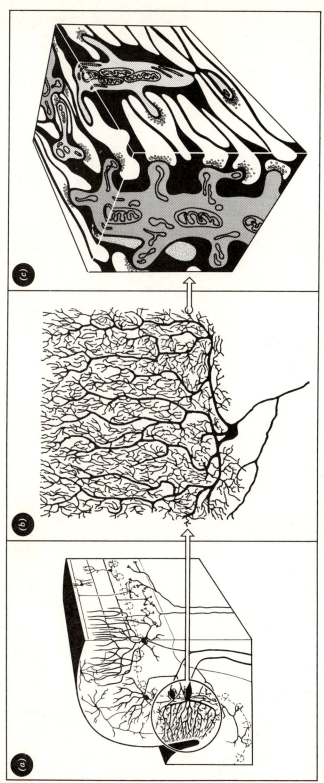

FIGURE 10 The three parts of this figure are meant to give the reader some idea of the complexity of the nervous system. In Figure 2 of Chapter 1 we saw the cerebellum (for further data on which see Eccles, Ito, and Szentágothai [1967]). The cerebellum can be divided into lobules, and each of these lobules is folded into a number of folia. In (a) we see a portion of just one of these folia, and have sketched a very few of the cellular components therein. In (b) we focus on one of these components. The Purkinje cell is about one third of a millimeter square in the orientation shown, but only about 1/30 of a millimeter thick. It is contacted by one climbing fiber, by up to 200,000 parallel fibers, and numerous axons from other cell types within the cerebellum. To emphasize the complexity, and incredibly fine detail, of its interconnections, we show in the front face of (c) a portion of one of the finest branches of a Purkinje cell. Off this branch we can see seven synaptic spines (five in the front face) protruding to make contact with passing parallel fibers. It is truly amazing that there are billions of cells in the brain; and yet when we focus on so small a part of the cell shown in (b) we can still find the richness of detail exhibited in (c). Brain theory (let alone experiment!) is still a long way from letting us fully understand the true use of such a richness of interconnections.

27

above the normal threshold because it occurred in the relative refractory period following the generation of a spike at t_4.

The range of effectiveness of synaptic interconnection in cells can well be illustrated by the Purkinje cell of the cerebellum (Figure 10), whose dendritic branching is spectacular indeed. Many types of cells synapse upon the Purkinje cells, and they do so in different ways. There are perhaps 200,000 fibers coming from other cells, called granule cells, which run essentially parallel to one another to pass through the dendritic tree of the Purkinje cell, and make synaptic contact there, one synapse per granule cell axon. In contrast, another fiber, called a climbing fiber, actually climbs over all the thicker branches of the Purkinje cell dendrites, making synapses time and time again. Thus, when a climbing fiber tells a Purkinje cell to "jump," it "jumps." The concerted action of many parallel fibers and other fibers may serve both to regulate how big that jump will be and to initiate Purkinje cell activity directly. This reminds us that synapses can differ in shape, size, and form.

The geometrical relationships between the different synapses impinging upon the cell determine whether different patterns of synaptic activation will yield the appropriate temporal relationships for the summed effect of the decaying potential changes arriving at the axon hillock to reach threshold, and so interactions between cells can vary greatly depending upon this synaptic geometry. In Section 2.4, we shall extend our feel for the subtlety of neural computation by examining the role of neurons in visual preprocessing. Here let us briefly relate the foregoing discussion of neurons to properties of receptors and effectors.

On the "input side", receptors share with neurons the property of generating potentials which are transmitted to various synapses upon neurons. However, the input surface of a receptor does not receive synapses from other neurons, but can transduce environmental energy into changes in membrane potential, which may then propagate actively or passively (many receptors, such as visual receptors, do not generate spikes). For instance, the rods and cones of the eye contain various pigments which can react chemically to light, and these chemical reactions in turn lead to local potential changes, called generator potentials, in the membrane. If the light falling upon the rod or cone is intense enough, then the potential changes will induce potential changes in interneurons sufficiently strong to fire the ganglion cells of the retina (Section 2.4) so that properties of the light will be signaled down into the nervous system as a train of impulses. Other receptors can transduce pressure intensities into generator potentials, and so on.

To discuss the "output side", we must first recall that a muscle is not a single unit, but is made up of many thousands of muscle fibers. The neurons which control the muscle fibers are called *motoneurons* (or motor neurons) and lie in the spinal cord, whence their axons may have to course vast (by neuronal standards) distances before synapsing upon the muscle fibers. The smallest functional entity on the output side (at least in mammals) is thus the *motor unit*, which consists of a motoneuron cell body, its axon, and the group of muscle fibers the axon influences.

A muscle fiber is like a neuron to the extent that it receives its input via synapses from other cells. However, its response to such activation is not to generate an impulse to be propagated down an axon, but simply to contract—and so the motor neurons which synapse upon the muscle fibers can determine, by the pattern of their impulses, the extent to which the whole muscle comprised of those fibers contracts, and can

Flexor muscle
contraction lessens
the joint angle

Extensor muscle
contraction increases
the joint angle

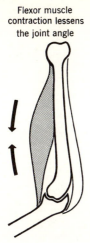
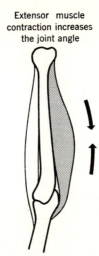

FIGURE 11   A schematic view of the elbow joint, showing the opposing action of the flexor and extensor muscles.

thus control movement. (Similar remarks apply to those cells which secrete various chemicals into the bloodstream or gut or which secrete sweat or tears.)

Since there is no command which a neuron may send to a muscle fiber that will cause it to expand—all the neuron can do is stop sending it commands to contract—the muscles of an animal are usually arranged in pairs (Figure 11). The contraction of one member of the pair will then act around a pivot to cause the expansion of the other member of the pair. Thus one set of muscles causes us to *extend* the elbow joint, while another set causes us to *flex* the elbow joint. If we wish to extend the elbow joint, we do not tell the *flexors* to expand, we just simply stop telling them to contract, and then they will be automatically expanded as the *extensor* muscles contract.

Synaptic activation at the motor *endplate* (i.e., synapse of a motoneuron upon a muscle fiber) yields a brief "twitch" of the muscle fiber. A low repetition rate of action potentials arriving at a motor endplate causes a train of twitches, in each of which the mechanical response lasts for longer than the action potential stimulus. As the frequency of excitation increases, a second action potential will arrive while the mechanical effect of the prior stimulus still persists. This causes a mechanical summation or fusion of contractions. Up to a point the degree of summation increases as the stimulus interval becomes shorter, although the summation effect decreases as the interval between the stimuli approaches the refractory period of the muscle, and maximum tension occurs, at which stage an increase in excitation frequency adds little more tension but does maintain the contraction. This limiting response is called a *tetanus*, and the tension (as distinct from amount of contraction) developed is about four times that of a single twitch (Figure 12). To increase the tension exerted by a muscle it is then necessary to recruit more and more fibers to contract.

At the receptors, increasing the intensity of stimulation will increase the generator potential. If we go to the first level of neurons which generate pulses, the axons "reset" each time they fire a pulse and then have to get back to a state where the threshold and the input potential meet. Thus the higher the generator potential, the

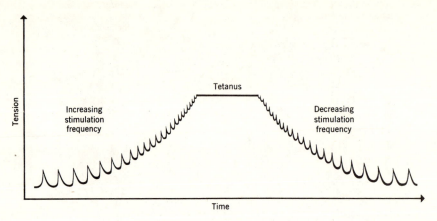

FIGURE 12   Tension in a single fiber held at constant length during increasing and decreasing stimulus frequency. The "twitches" at low frequency give way to prolonged steady contraction (tetanus) when the stimulus is maintained at a sufficiently high frequency.

shorter the time until they meet again, and thus the higher the frequency of the pulse. Thus at the "input" it is a useful first approximation to say that intensities of stimuli can be coded in terms of pulse frequency. As we leave the periphery and head toward more "computational" cells, we no longer have such simple relationships but rather interactions of inhibitory cells and excitatory cells, with each inhibitory input moving away from threshold, and each excitatory input moving it toward threshold. Then, to the extent that the frequency of excitatory impulses rises or the frequency of inhibitory impulses falls, so will the firing frequency tend to increase.

With this as background, we are now ready to discuss, in Section 2.4, the role of neurons in preprocessing visual input in the cat and the frog. However, some readers may first wish to consult Section 2.3, which shows (among other things) how the visual system fits into the overall anatomy of the brain.

2.3   AN ASIDE: SOME GROSS ANATOMY†

The brain is made up of many thousands of millions of neurons. In attempting to relate the overall functioning of the brain to the individual functioning of these cells, we are helped by the fact that visual inspection of a dissected brain allows us to identify various areas of the brain to which we may assign labels for easy reference. Further careful analyses, with the aid of microscopes to distinguish areas with different types of neurons, and chemical and electrical techniques to isolate differing properties, interconnections, and functions, allow us to refine these subdivisions.

A vast literature has grown up clarifying the subdivisions of the brain—which differ from species to species—and the connections between them. The subject of neuroanatomy is still in a state of flux—and the anatomy of many parts of the brain is as controversial as the theories of brain function we present in this book! However, as I repeatedly stress, we cannot expect to understand how the brain functions with-

---

† This section may be omitted at a first reading.

out relating function to underlying structure. Therefore, I have included two sections, this one and Section 5.2, which present some of the basic neuroanatomy readers will need if they wish to read further into the technical literature about the brain. Since many readers may find the concentration of new terminology in these two sections somewhat overwhelming, the book is so written that the reader can omit them without any loss of understanding of the other chapters. It should also be added that my own knowledge of neuroanatomy is limited and so I cannot claim any exceptional merit for the present exposition beyond its brevity. Much of the merit it does possess comes from the superb tutorial on Neuroanatomy, given by Walle Nauta at the 1966 Intensive Study Program of Massachusetts Institute of Technology's Neurosciences Research Program, which formed the basis for the first draft of these sections and which have since been published in revised form as the section "General Overview of the Vertebrate Brain" in Nauta and Karten [1970].

Three comments must be made about our schematic approach. First, while certain regions of the brain are clearly demarcated (no one argues about which part of the brain is the cerebellum) other regions merge gradually into one another. Just as it may be convenient to divide a strip of paper graded continuously from white to black into four areas labeled "white", "light gray", "dark gray", and "black", but would be foolish to argue about the location of the line separating "white" from "light gray", so must one treat the borders of such areas with circumspection. Second, just as some men have large heads but short bodies, while others are in reverse proportions, so may the relative shapes and positions of different areas vary from individual to individual. Third, the brains of different species, despite many similarities, can be very different—for example, our study of the different preprocessing in frog and cat retinae in the next section will make clear that just because part of a frog brain and a cat brain look grossly similar need not imply that they subserve the same function.

We are *vertebrates*—like all mammals (but also like birds and fish and frogs and crocodiles) we have a *spine,* a chain of hollow bones (*vertebrae*) running most of the length of the back, containing the mass of neurons that is known as the *spinal cord.* All sensory information from the skin, joints, and muscles of the trunk and limbs enters the central nervous system through the spinal cord; and all the *motoneurons* whose synapses control the muscles of the trunk and limbs have their cell bodies in the spinal cord. This is in distinction to the *cranial* nerves, for control of the head and intake of information from receptors in the head, which enter the nervous system via the brainstem. (Although we shall not consider them further here, we should note that the spinal cord also contains elements of the *autonomic* system, which are concerned with the innervation of glands, and the control of the muscles of piloerection and the smooth muscles in the walls of arteries, arterioles, and visceral organs.)

The neuroanatomy of invertebrates (spineless animals) is so varied—and so different from that of vertebrates—that we shall not consider it further. Rather, we shall study only vertebrate nervous systems, and in this section we shall place special emphasis on mammals, and especially on man.

First, the reader should refer back to Figure 2 of Chapter 1 (page 9) which shows how the structures that we shall now discuss are positioned in the human head. In part *a,* in which we see a side view as it might be revealed were we to slice the head in half, the so-called midbrain structures may be clearly seen. The brains of mammals, and especially of humans, are distinguished from those of other species by the "explosion" of new cortex—or *neocortex*—which comes, in man, to dominate the rest of the brain, as is clear, in the "outside" view of a human brain in part *b*, where the outfoldings of neocortex completely hide the midbrain from view. The human cerebral cortex is a sheet only 50 to 100 neurons in depth, but it contains so many billions of neurons that it must fold, and fold again, to fit into the space within the skull. As we shall see in Section 5.2, this great expansion of forebrain greatly modifies circuitry in the brainstem and spinal cord.

The cerebrum is usually divided into four lobes, the *frontal*, which is in the region of the forehead; the *temporal*, which is in the region of the temples; the *parietal*, which is at the top where the parietal bones form part of the skull; and the *occipital* lobe, from the Latin *occipitus*, meaning back of the head.

Grooves in the cortex may be called *fissures* or *sulci*, and the upfolded tissue between two sulci is a *gyrus*. Pathways connecting regions in the two halves of the brain are called *commissures*. The largest is the *corpus callosum,* which connects the two cerebral hemispheres.

The cerebral cortex is not a uniform structure, and it differs in composition from place to place. Certain areas of cortex can be dubbed *sensory* since they primarily process information from one modality—this includes not only the area labeled *somatosensory* in Figure 2 of Chapter 1 which receives information relayed via the spinal cord, but also the *visual, auditory,* and *olfactory* (shown in cut-away, since it is not on the outer surface) areas which receive information from the distance receptors in the head. The *motor* cortex is a source of fibers, some of which run down the spinal cord to control muscular activity. Phylogenetically, somatosensory and motor cortex are an indivisible amalgam, and in man (at least) there is not only sensory representation in motor cortex (hardly surprising—cells controlling movement should be responsive to appropriate external stimuli) but there also are cells in somatosensory cortex whose axons project† (as do those of neurons in motor cortex) to the motoneurons and interneurons of the spinal cord, thus influencing movement via at most two intervening synapses. It is thus common to refer to the area adjoining the central fissure simply as *sensorimotor cortex.* The rest of the cortex is called *association* cortex, but this is a misnomer, which reflects an erroneous nineteenth-century view that the job of these areas was simply to "associate" the different sensory inputs to provide the proper instructions to be relayed by the motor cortex. The absolutely false idea that 90% of the brain is "unused" probably arose from a layman's misinterpretation of the fact that the exact functions of much of these "association areas" are still not known.

The motoneurons which synapse upon muscles and thus control their contractions are *not* contained in the forebrain, though the neurons that relate to the *hypophysis* (or *pituitary gland*) are effectors, even if they do not control movement. (*Pitus* is the Greek for mucus, which is what the gland was thought to produce by the physicians of 300 B.C.) The hypophysis is the central gland for endocrine organs—it releases various subtle hormones which are broadcast through the bloodstream to control these organs. It is important to remember that this endocrine chemical messenger system is another "chain of command" in addition to the neural. We should complement this reminder of the variety of effector mechanisms by noting, similarly, that the sensory surface of the organism is *not* just the external surface. In fact, there are two sensory

---

† A region is said to *project* to another region if there is a neural pathway from the former to the latter.

surfaces in addition to the external (*exteroceptive*) inputs from the body surface and such sense organs as the eyes, ears, and nose. There are *proprioceptive* fibers providing feedback information on movement and orientation from muscles, joints, tendons, otoliths, and the semicircular canals; and there are *interoceptive* fibers bringing signals from the glands and viscera.

Before providing a further array of general terminology, let us provide some functional correlates for our anatomy by discussing two of the most important inputs to receptor arrays in the head. We shall not discuss smell and taste in this volume, but we do note that smell shares with vision and hearing the important property of registering data about distant regions of the environment. In Figures 13 and 14 we can gain some feel for the gross neuroanatomy of the visual and auditory systems which undertake the peripheral processing of the responses of rods and cones to the light patterns reflected from the environment, and of the responses of hair cells in the inner ear to the vibrations set up by sound waves impinging upon the ears.

In the schematic side view of a mammalian visual system in Figure 13 we see that *rod and cone* activity, after being preprocessed by two layers of cells within the *retina*, passes up the *optic tract* (the array of axons of the retinal *ganglion cells*) and branches into a number of pathways. Two of these lead to midbrain structures, the *superior colliculus* and the *pretectum*. We shall have much more to mention about the superior colliculus (and the *tectum*, its homolog, i.e., the structure with the corresponding anatomical location and evolutionary history, in the frog) in Sections 5.5 and 7.2, stressing its role in controlling the gaze of the animal. A third destination for the optic tract—and the dominant one in man—lies in the *thalamus* and is called the *lateral geniculate nucleus* because it is the lateral part of two structures bent or angled like a knee (think of *genu*flection, bending the knee), where signals are further preprocessed en route to the region of cortex at the rear of the head. This *visual cortex* is somewhat striated (striped) in appearance, and so is referred to as *striate cortex*. (Striate cortex is completely different from the corpus striatum, which we shall discuss in Section 5.2.) This visual cortex is also called area 17 because it was the seventeenth area that a man named Brodmann put a number on. The optic radiation —the axons from the lateral geniculate—also projects to the surrounding prestriate cortex in areas numbered 18 and 19. In addition to a two-way communication (not shown in our figure) between visual cortex and superior colliculus, there are also pathways from visual cortex to other areas of cortex, of which the *frontal eye field* (involved in monitoring of eye movements) and *infratemporal* (i.e., on the underside of the temporal) cortex are shown here.

To complement this schematic side view, we show, in Figure 13*b*, a "top view" of a human visual system, in which we represent the pathways from retina to superior colliculus and lateral geniculate. The important feature shown here is that the optic tracts from the two eyes meet in the *optic chiasm* [named for the Greek letter χ (chi), whose shape it resembles] in such a way that all axons whose receptive fields lie in the right visual field pass on toward the left half of the brain, whereas the left visual field reports to the right hemisphere.

The reason that we are not possessed of two separate consciousnesses of the left and right visual fields, then, is due in part to the midbrain structures, but even more so in man to the presence of the *corpus callosum*, an immense tract of axons whereby the two cerebral hemispheres intercommunicate. Fascinating experiments by Sperry and his co-workers have shown that if its brain is "split" by sectioning the corpus collosum

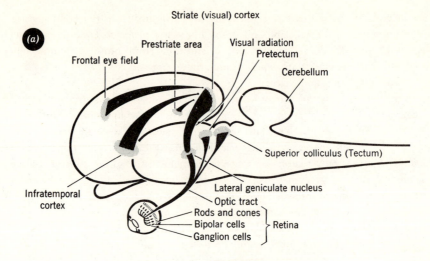

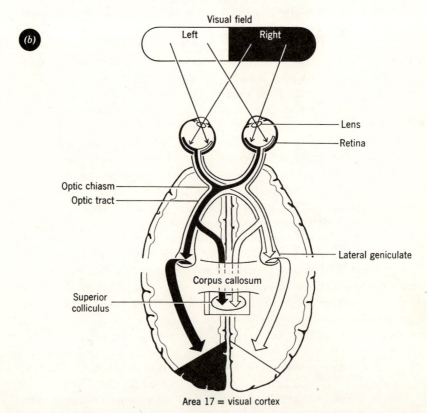

FIGURE 13 Two schematic views of the visual system of a mammal. The main thing to note—both in the side view (a) and in the schematic horizontal section of the human visual system (b)—is that there are visual pathways both to neocortex (via the lateral geniculate bodies of the thalamus) and to the midbrain (pretectum and superior colliculus).

and other commissures, an animal acts as if there were two separate consciousnesses in the two hemispheres. A man with a split brain may be reading a newspaper with his left brain only to have it put down by the hand controlled by his right brain!

Turning to Figure 14, we can at last answer the burning question "To what is the lateral geniculate lateral?" The answer is, as a respite from more and more new terminology, the *medial* geniculate nucleus, which plays for audition the role played by the lateral geniculate for vision, for it is the last "way station" en route to the auditory cortex. The superior colliculus is so called simply because it is above (i.e., superior to) the inferior colliculus. The crossed input to cells in the superior olive allows them to pool information from the two ears to obtain spatial location of sounds. The projection of fibers upon the auditory cortex has in part been found to

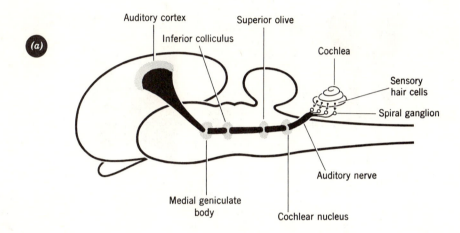

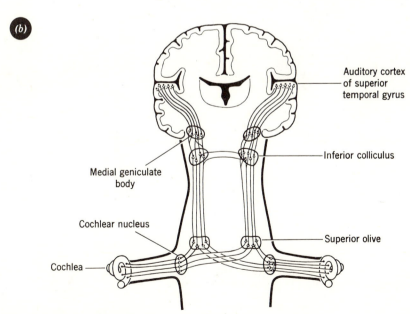

FIGURE 14 Two schematic views of the auditory system: (a) gives a schematic side view, while (b) shows a section of the human brain as seen from the front.

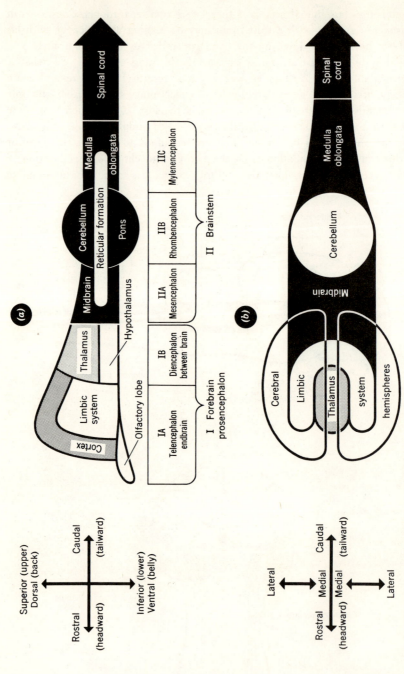

FIGURE 15 Two schematic views (after Nauta) of the central nervous system of a nonmammal. The side view (a) shows the three main subdivisions of forebrain, brainstem, and spinal cord, and suggests a number of further subdivisions. The subdivisions of the forebrain and brainstem are shown from another angle in the view from above (b). Note that these views are highly schematic indeed—the next figure is designed to indicate how variegated are the forms these structures take in different species.

36

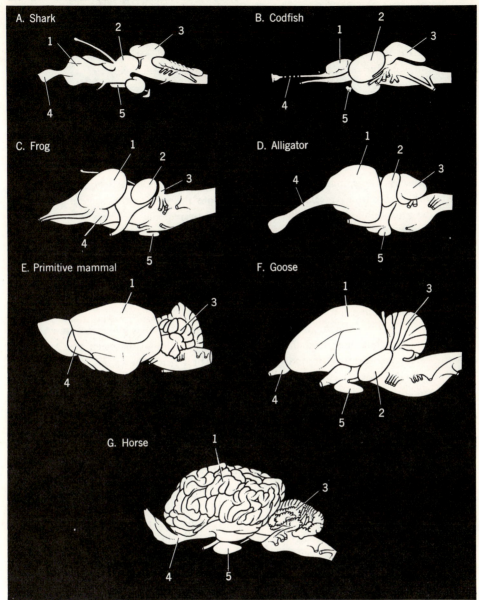

FIGURE 16 Side views of various brains to show how the basic groundplan of Figure 15 differs greatly between species. (After Romer.) (1) Cerebrum, (2) optic lobe, (3) cerebellum, (4) olfactory system, and (5) pituitary.

be tonotopic—that is, place corresponds to tone or pitch—but the discovery of "miaow detectors" and "click detectors" in the auditory cortex of cats has complicated the picture. There is also an auditory input to the superior colliculus, so that a sudden noise can alert the visual system to scrutinize its source. (In fact, superior colliculus receives input from all modalities.) Since the auditory system is not treated in further detail in this book, we refer the interested reader to Whitfield [1967] for a fuller account of *The Auditory Pathway*.

In the remainder of this section, we reexamine the various parts of the brain, using the schematic "groundplan" of Figure 15. (Figure 16 will show how the relative proportions of the various subdivisions vary greatly from species to species.) As we move from "head" to "tail" the three main subdivisions are the following:

1. *The forebrain*, which comprises the *endbrain* and the *diencephalon*.
2. *The brainstem*, which comprises the *midbrain*, *pons* (but not the *cerebellum*), and *medulla oblongata*.
3. *The spinal cord*, which contains various reflex mediating pathways as well as other channels relating different segments of the cord, and other levels of the brain.

We shall discuss the spinal cord in Section 5.1, and then see in Section 5.2 how its basic motor mechanisms are elaborated. We devote the rest of this section to a quick tour of the gross subdivisions of the forebrain and brainstem.

The ENDBRAIN [also called the *telencephalon* (Gr. *telos*, end; *enkephalos*, brain)] is the most headward portion of the brain in vertebrates; it comprises the cerebral hemispheres, which in mammals undergo a unique enlargement to form the neocortex, or new cerebral cortex (*cortex* is Latin for the bark of a tree). The lobes are richly interconnected, and their integration with midbrain structures is required for proper functioning.

The *limbic system*, shown as part of the telencephalon, has no direct relationship to arms and leg, but gets its name because it lies "in limbo" between the brainstem and the cerebrum, forming the margin of the cerebral hemispheres and containing the *allo* (i.e., old) *cortex*. It is *multimodal* in that it combines information from different sensory modalities, and it is especially concerned with the behavioral reactions of the individual toward survival of self and species (the four F's of feeding, fleeing, fighting, and reproduction), its responses being mediated through the lower centers of the diencephalon. It includes the hippocampal formation and the amygdaloid nucleus. It is also intimately involved in visceral activity, the physiology of emotions, and the reception of olfactory stimuli. [It has also been called the *rhinencephalon* ("smell brain") because of an undue emphasis of this last function.]

Olfactory neurons are very like epithelial (skin) cells. They synapse in the *olfactory bulb* (a primitive outpost of cortex), messages then passing to olfactory cortex via the olfactory nerve (we here use "nerve" in the sense of a bundle of axons).

If we cut through a cerebral hemisphere we find that the cortex (surface) is *gray matter* (i.e., is rich in cell bodies), whereas the interior comprises both regions of *white matter* (i.e., is formed largely by cell processes or axons) and well-demarcated regions of gray matter. These latter regions of gray matter lie at the base of the hemisphere. Of these, the ones which lie in the forebrain are called the *basal ganglia* (or *corpus striatum* because of their striated appearance) and play an important role in the control of movement (Section 5.2). The remaining regions are the thalamus and hypothalamus of the diencephalon, to which we now turn.

The DIENCEPHALON (Gr. *dia,* through or between) comprises the thalamus and hypothalamus. Portions of the *thalamus* process sensory information en route to cerebral cortex, as well as receiving some projections from cortical areas. One part of the dorsal thalamus modifies the nature of motor stimuli being sent to the musculature so that the message which reaches the lower nerve cells will produce an organized response. The medial and lateral geniculate bodies which we have already seen to transform auditory and visual information also form part of the thalamus.

The *hypothalamus* is concerned with the chemical state of the body: salt regulation, blood pressure, respiration, temperature regulation, water conservation, hunger and satiety, regulation of the endocrine system, and—with the limbic system—has its predominant role in emotional and motivational expression.

We now turn to the brainstem and cerebellum.

The MIDBRAIN [or *mesencephalon* (Gr. *mesos,* middle)] is involved in visual, auditory, and total body reflexes. It contains many ascending and descending long fiber systems pertaining to somatic sensation and the primitive motor systems. It also contains nerve cell complexes in its reticular formation maintaining antigravity, homeostasis, and the sleeping-wakefulness cycle in man.

The RHOMBENCEPHALON (so called because of its rhombic shape in mammals) contains the pons and cerebellum, as well as many ascending and descending tracts. The *pons* contains many scattered nuclear groups as well as descending fiber tract systems. It sends fibers *contralaterally*† informing the cerebellar cortex as to the nature of the impulses sent via tracts in the spine to lower motor cells, and contains brain stem nuclei for cranial nerves as well as reticular nuclei and ascending (sensory) and descending fiber (primitive motor) systems. The *cerebellum* has outputs to both higher and lower centers and appears to deal with tonus of muscle groups and with synergic regulation of opposing muscle groups to promote the most coordinated movements. It may achieve this by connections with the midbrain reticular substance or by projections via thalamus, which relays the cerebellar influence to motosensory cortex, thus modulating its control of the motor sequence.

The MEDULLA OBLONGATA [L. *medulla*, marrow, *oblongata*, extended, also known as the *myelencephalon* (Gr. *myelos*, marrow)] is the extension within the head of the spinal cord, which forms the marrow of the bones of the spine. It is concerned with the reflex control of the cardiovascular system, respiration, emetic reflexes, and equilibrium. Long ascending and descending tract systems must of course run through the medulla. Ascending sensory bundles, arising partly from the spinal cord, project information concerned with position of body parts and muscle tonus to the cerebellum.

We close by reminding the reader that the brains of different animals are as varied as their outward appearances. Some indication of this is given in Figure 16, and we shall reinforce the point with our comparison of the visual systems of the frog and the cat in the next section.

2.4 VISUAL PREPROCESSING IN CAT AND FROG

Attneave [1954] noted that whenever we have a priori information about an ensemble of "messages," we can use this to achieve an economy of description that would otherwise be unobtainable. For example, were arbitrarily complicated patterns of black and white dots to be equally meaningful patterns of visual stimulation in our everyday lives, there would be no way of representing a visual scene more economically than by giving the light intensity at every point of the scene. However, as the success of caricatures of political figures attests, much of the information about a visual scene

---

† The fibers starting on one side of the midline project to the other (contrary) side of the body. Similarly, an *ipsilateral* projection is one that stays on the same side of the body throughout its course.

FIGURE 17 Attneave's sleeping cat: a recognizable outline is obtained by replacing curves by straight lines joining points of maximal curvature.

can be given by a few contours. Further, these contours are usually made up of relatively few segments—the intricate wiggles due to the presence of fur which perturb the curve of a cat's back are irrelevant to our recognition of the outline of a cat, although our separate recognition of the texture of fur may add to our perception. Attneave thus suggested that the points of most importance in our recognition of form are those where a contour changes or comes to an end. For example, he constructed Figure 17 by finding the 38 points of maximum curvature from the contour of a picture of a sleeping cat and connecting appropriate points by straight lines.

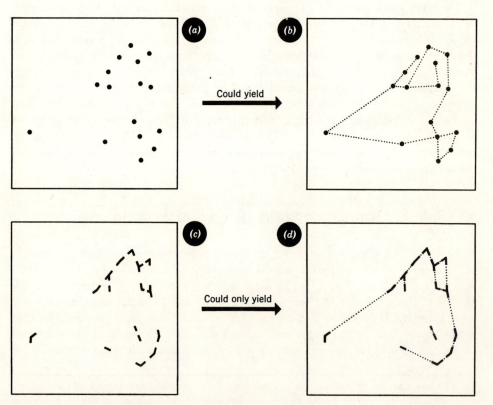

FIGURE 18 On the virtues of angle information.

However, he did not consider how we would tell which pairs of points it would be appropriate to join. A simple resolution would seem to be that shown in Figure 18 —rather than just give points of maximal curvature as in Figure 18a, which can yield inappropriate connections as in b, we give the angle at each point as in c, which yields the correct connections unambiguously as shown in d.

This suggests that a useful preprocessing scheme for visual stimuli might proceed in two stages: first, reduce the pattern of light and shade to essential contours; second, reduce the contours to a specification of the angles at positions of contour change.

Barlow has approached the problem of visual preprocessing in terms of more strictly neural considerations. Given that the receptors are transducers—energy converters transducing level of environmental energy into, say, frequency of axonal firing —Barlow [1959] asked how further layers of preprocessors (Figure 19) might so

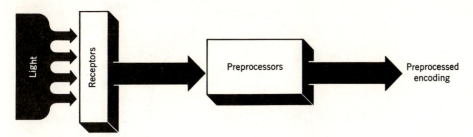

FIGURE 19 Schematic view of visual preprocessing. Receptors transduce light patterns into graded changes of membrane potential. Further layers then preprocess these potentials to yield the encoding of the visual scene, as a spatiotemporal pattern of axonal spikes, that reaches the brain.

recode the input, making use of regularities in the normal environment, to "minimize the neural traffic"—that is, to ensure that a neuron's activity would only depart from its resting level if by doing so it would signal some property of the environment of potential importance to the animal. As Barlow [1969] has pointed out, Attneave's work suggested that an appropriate set of preprocessors would signal points of maximal curvature; our discussion of the problem of joining such points has suggested that angle detectors would be appropriate for each such region.

To learn the fate of these general considerations, it will prove useful to contrast the visual systems of cat and frog: In all vertebrates, be they frog, cat, or man, light enters the lens and passes to the back of the eye, where it traverses the retina, passing through layers of transparent cells to reach the *rods* and *cones* (Figure 20). When sufficiently stimulated by light, the rods and cones produce generator potentials (continuously variable dc potentials) which elicit impulses from the *ganglion cells* via the *interneurons* whose axons impinge on the ganglionic dendritic trees. The optic fibers are the axons of the ganglion cells and course across the retina to come together to pass through the retina at a region which is consequently a *blind spot*, thence coursing back up the *optic nerve* to the brain.

Since, as we shall see in more detail later, the output of the ganglion cells is quite different from the light intensity encoding of the receptors, we may say that the retina *preprocesses* the visual input. To recapitulate the essence of our discussion in Section

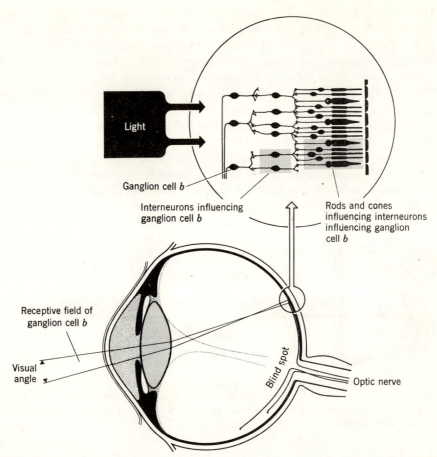

FIGURE 20 A side view of an eye showing how light is focused by the lens upon the retina. The insert shows (in very schematic form) that light passes to the rear of the retina to affect rods and cones, which in turn affect the neurons that affect any given ganglion cell. Tracing the light cone back from the receptors that affect a given ganglion cell through the lens, we find the region of the environment—the receptive field of the cell—in which light can affect the firing patterns of the ganglion cell. The ganglion cell axons course across the retina, coming together at the blind spot where they pass through to travel up the optic nerve to the brain.

2.3, we have that in mammals—for example, cat and man—the preprocessed messages are sent up to the lateral geniculate nucleus (see Figure 21a) the optic tract's "way-station" in the thalamus, which after further processing sends signals to various cortical cells for the processing involved in pattern recognition, while a subsidiary (but older in terms of evolution) pathway feeds the orienting (i.e., head and body turning) mechanisms of the superior colliculus (Section 5.4).

In the frog, we have the situation shown in Figure 21b where the optic nerves proceed back from the eyes to innervate mainly the optic tectum. The arrows give some idea of how the visual stimulus is mapped back to the tectum which—in the frog, as distinct from the mammal—plays a primary role in pattern recognition ("How to relate") as well as orientation ("Where"). The fact that the frog's tectum is anatomically similar to superior colliculus may indicate some gross similarities of func-

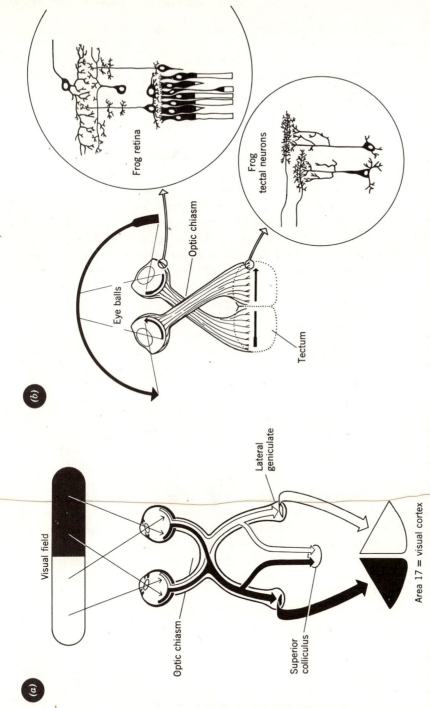

Area 17 = visual cortex

FIGURE 21 A comparative view of the visual systems of a human and a frog. In the human visual system (a) we see the predominance of messages going via the lateral geniculate nucleus of the thalamus up to cortex with relatively little going to the superior colliculus; while in the frog (b) it is the connections to the tectum (which is the amphibian analogue of the mammalian superior colliculus) that predominate. Note also the splitting of the two halves of the visual field so noticeable at the human optic chiasm, yet absent in the frog. We also augment the reminder of Figure 3 that there is no such thing as a typical neuron.

tion but, as will become abundantly clear below, this does not indicate identity of detailed function.

We define the *receptive field* of a ganglion cell—be it in cat or frog—to be that region of the visual field in which stimulation can affect the activity of the ganglion cell. As indicated in Figure 20, it can thus be defined as the truncated cone of space from which light can impinge upon the rods and cones which influence the interneurons affecting the given ganglion cell. The visual angle of the receptive field is then defined by the angle at the vertex of the cone.

A question of interest, then, is what sort of light pattern does a ganglion cell *detect*? In other words, what type of pattern is correlated with the greatest signaling from the cell? Intriguingly, although all vertebrates share the fundamental retinal architecture shown in Figure 20, the actual function of the ganglion cells differs greatly from species to species. For example, Lettvin, Maturana, McCulloch, and Pitts [1959] found that most frog ganglion cells could be classified as being of one of four types—such as "moving spot detectors" and "large moving object detectors"—none of which is found in the *cat,* whose retinal ganglion cells may better be characterized as "contrast enhancement devices." This ties in with our action-oriented point of view—a frog with little visually guided behavior beyond snapping at "wiggles" and jumping away from "enemies" has a retina which "throws away" most aspects of the visual input not related to these features, whereas a cat, leading a subtle life (such as watching a mouse-hole intently and springing only when the mouse pokes his head out far enough), cannot function with so specialized a retina. Let us examine these experiments on pre-processing more carefully.

A frog does not normally move its eyes save to compensate for head or body movements—say when on a rocking lily pad—to maintain a stabilized image on its retina. Thus, though frogs detect their prey solely by vision, they do not track their prey or search the visual field for items of interest. They prey only on moving insects, and their attention is never attracted by stationary objects. A large moving object provokes an escape reaction toward whatever region is darkest—the frog being equally at home in land and water, choosing a landing site is not important. For them, a form deprived of movement seems to be behaviorally meaningless. They seem to recognize their prey and select it for attack from among all other environmental objects because it exhibits a number of features such as movement, a certain size, some contrast, and perhaps also a certain color. They will thus treat the wiggling toe of a fellow frog scratching its back as if it were a moving fly; but they will not snap at a dead fly even when they are starving. This ability of frogs to recognize their prey and snap at it is not altered by changes in the general environment, for example, changes in illumination. Their sex life is conducted by sounds, touch, and smell.

Lettvin, Maturana, McCulloch, and Pitts [1959] addressed themselves to an investigation of the frog visual system designed to locate those properties of the system, if any, which assist the frog in recognizing prey and enemy. Whereas Hartline [1938] had grouped the ganglion cells into three classes, according to their response to a small spot of light on their receptive fields, Lettvin et al. noted that spots of light are not the natural stimuli for the frog that flies or worms are (unless it feeds on fireflies) and thus sought to find more "naturalistic" functions of the ganglion cells by studying their response to objects. They argued that the behavior of the frog seems to demand the presence of some functional invariants in the activity of the components of its visual system so that the retina might carry out computations on the visual image which serve to reveal crucial properties, such as the presence of a prey or an enemy.

Here we shall report their findings on the visual correlates of the activity signaled by retinal ganglion cells to the frog tectum. In Section 7.2 we shall return to these data to build a model of how activity in the frog tectum might be converted into action— thus we shall build on "what the frog's eye tells the frog's brain" to suggest "what the frog's eye tells the frog". Lettvin et al. studied the common American frog, *Rana pipiens*. The frog was placed so that one eye was in the center of a hemisphere (see Figure 22) 14 inches in diameter (so that 1° corresponds to about 1/8 inch), which formed the experimental visual field. An electrode was so inserted into the frog that it could respond either to the activity of a single ganglion cell (by placing the tip of the electrode on the axon of the cell in the optic nerve) or to that of a cell in the tecta. The aluminum hemisphere represents about two-thirds of the visual field of one frog eye. By proper orientation of the animal, one could cover any desired part of the visual field and could entirely control the receptive field of the cells under study. The stimulating objects were moved on the inner surface by means of a magnet moved on the external surface. Numerous shapes and kinds of objects were used, for example, dark disks, dark strips, and dark squares.

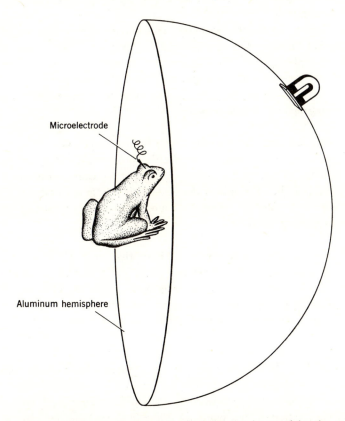

FIGURE 22 A magnet outside an aluminum hemisphere can be used by the experimenter to move visual stimuli inside the hemisphere. The frog's responses to the stimuli can then be monitored by microelectrodes inserted into its optic tract or tectum.

It was found that the responses of ganglion cells fell into four groups (and possibly a fifth, which we shall not mention). Each ganglion cell belongs to only one of these groups, and the cells of each class are uniformly distributed across the retina. In any small retinal area, one finds representatives of all groups in proportion to their general relative frequencies. There are 30 times as many of types I and II as there are of types III and IV.

GROUP I. THE BOUNDARY DETECTORS.   (Receptive fields 2 to 4° in diameter.) They respond to any boundary between two shades of gray in the receptive field at any orientation provided it is sharp. Sharpness of boundary rather than degree of contrast seems to be what is measured. The response is enhanced if the boundary is moved and is unchanged if the illumination of the particular contrast is altered over a very wide range. If no boundary exists in the field, no response will result from change of lighting, no matter how sharp the change. Another property of the group I cells is that if a boundary is brought into the receptive field in total darkness and the light is switched on, a continuing response occurs after a short initial delay.

GROUP II. THE MOVEMENT-GATED, DARK CONVEX BOUNDARY DETECTORS.   (Receptive fields of 3 to 5°.) They too respond only to sharp boundaries between two grays, but only if that boundary is curved, the darker area being convex, and if the boundary is moved or has moved. Again, the responses are invariant over a wide range of illumination, roughly that between dim twilight and bright noon. One interesting experiment used a large color photograph of a frog's natural habitat of flowers and grass. Waving this around in the receptive field of a group II fiber elicited no response. Moving a fly-sized object relative to the photograph yielding an excellent response, although moving it with the photograph yielded no response.

GROUP III. THE MOVING OR CHANGING CONTRAST DETECTORS.   (Receptive fields 7 to 11° in diameter.) They respond invariantly under wide ranges of illumination to the same silhouette moved at the same speed across the same background. They have no enduring response, but fire only if the contrast is changing or moving. The response is better (higher in frequency) when the boundary is sharp or moving fast than when it is blurred or moving slowly.

GROUP IV. THE DIMMING DETECTORS.   (Receptive field 15° in diameter.) They respond to any dimming in the whole receptive field weighted by distance from the center of that field. Boundaries play no role in the response. The same percentage of dimming produces the same response, more or less independent of the level of lighting at the beginning. The response is prolonged if a large dark object stops within the field.

The axons of the cells of each group end in a separate layer of the tectum. Each of these four layers of terminals in the tectum forms a "continuous" map of the retina with respect to the operation performed by the corresponding ganglion cells. The four layers are in registration in that points in different layers which are stacked atop each other in the tectum correspond to the same small region of the retina (Figure 23).

Thus the function of the frog retina is not to transmit information about the point-to-point pattern of distribution of light and dark in the image formed on it. On the

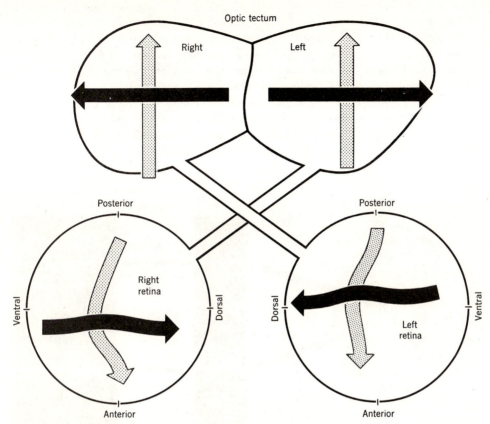

FIGURE 23 The retinotectal projection of an adult toad, showing how a direction upon the retina is mapped to a corresponding direction upon the tectum.

contrary, it is mainly to analyze this image at every point in terms of four qualitative contexts (boundaries, moving curvatures, changing contrasts, and local dimming) and to send this information to the tecta where these functions are separated in four layers of terminals.

The point is that (Lettvin et al., p. 1950) "the eye speaks to the brain in a language already highly organized and interpreted, instead of transmitting some more or less accurate copy of the distribution of light on the receptors." Further, the encoding is such as to aid the frog in finding food and evading predators—in recognizing the universals *prey* and *enemy*—as suggested in their closing paragraph (p. 1951):

The operations thus have much more the flavor of perception than of sensation if that distinction has any meaning now. That is to say that the language in which they are best described is the language of complex abstractions from the visual image. We have been tempted, for example, to call the convexity detectors "bug perceivers." Such a fiber (operation 2) responds best when a dark object, smaller than a receptive field, enters that field, stops, and moves about intermittently thereafter. The response is not affected if the lighting changes or if the background (say a picture of grass and flowers) is moving, and is not there if only the background, moving or still, is in the field. Could one better describe a system for detecting an accessible bug?

Turning from the ganglion cells to cells of the tectum, Lettvin and his colleagues found several kinds of cells. They were not able to define the subgroups at all well, but there are two extremes of the populations which they have named "newness neurons" and "sameness neurons." The former is concerned, it seems, with detection of novelty and visual events; the latter with continuity in time of interesting objects in the field of vision. At least one of them sends lines back to the retina and may affect the activity of ganglion cells significantly.

Let us now contrast the frog's preprocessors with those in the visual system of the cat. We turn to an examination of Hubel and Wiesel's work on the cat visual system: The receptor cells will tend to excite various interneurons. The bipolar interneurons can in turn excite retinal ganglion cells, while inhibitory interactions seem to be

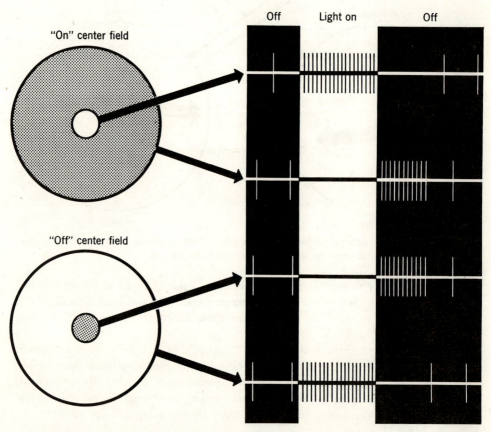

FIGURE 24 Response characteristics of two types of ganglion cell in the cat. The top half represents a cell with an on-center field and an inhibitory surround; the bottom shows a cell with an off-center and an excitatory surround. To the right-hand side of the figure we see a record of the impulses that a typical experiment might show traversing the axon of such a cell. The left-hand column shows the low level of spontaneous firing one might see from such a cell when it has been sitting in the dark for a while. The middle column indicates the level of firing that we get when a small spot of light is switched on in the indicated area. For instance, turning a spot of light on in an on-center field will greatly increase the rate of firing; while turning a spot of light on in an off-center field will greatly reduce the rate of firing. The third column indicates the transient change in the firing level that occurs when the light is first turned off before the return to normal.

provided by another population of interneurons, called horizontal cells. Each retinal ganglion cell is thus influenced by quite an array of receptor cells. Kuffler found that ganglion cells in the cat retina have dendritic fields which to a first approximation are circular, with two regions. The rods and cones that influence the central region via interneurons tend to have an excitatory effect (i.e., increasing the intensity of light falling on rods and cones connected to this central region will tend to increase the firing rate of the cell) ; while the surrounding annulus is so connected that if we turn up the intensity of light on the corresponding receptors here, then that will tend to turn down the activity of the cell. The strength of the synapses in the overall area of connections is such that if we uniformly illuminate the whole receptive field, excitation from the central area will slightly exceed the inhibition from the annulus so that the cell will have a spontaneous, fairly low level of firing which signals the overall level of a uniformly illuminated field. Significant departures of firing rate from the resting level so established will then signal any important nonuniformities in the illumination of the cell's receptive field.† There also exist cells with off-centers and on-surrounds.

A highly simplified example should clearly show how the properties of nervous tissue presented in Section 2.2 would indeed allow a simple neuron, by its very dendritic geometry, to compute some useful function. We shall first model a neuron that signals temporal pattern, and then analyze a cell like the cat's ganglion cell "contrast detector." First, consider a neuron with four dendrites (cf. Rall [1964, p. 90]), each receiving a single synapse from a visual receptor, arranged as in Figure 25 so that synapses A, B, C, and D are at increasing distances from the axon hillock.

We assume that each receptor reacts to the passage of a spot of light above its surface by yielding a generator potential which yields in the postsynaptic membrane the time course of depolarization shown in Figure 25a which is superimposed on the resting potential. This time course is propagated passively, and the further it is propagated, the later and the lower is its peak, as shown in Figure 25b where we graph the time courses for locations further and further removed from the synapse. The effect at the axon hillock of an input at D is later and less than that of an input at A, B, or C. Now consider the effect of the arrival of inputs at A, B, C, and D upon the axon hillock. If four inputs reached A, B, C, and D simultaneously, their effect at the axon hillock might approximate the sum of their separate effects (Figure 25c) and yet be less than the threshold required to trigger a spike there. At this stage, one might imagine the cell to be useless since it will not respond to what is apparently maximal stimulation—all four inputs being activated simultaneously. However, if an input reaches D before one reaches C, and so on, in such a way that the peaks of the four resultant time courses at the axon hillock coincide, we could well pass threshold, as shown in Figure 25d. This then is a cell which, although very simple, can detect direction of motion across its input.

If we imagine the lines feeding the synapses to be axons of photoreceptors which respond with a generator potential to the passage of a moving spot, then our cell responds only if that spot is moving from right to left, and if the velocity of that

---

† Incidentally, Hubel and Wiesel find in monkeys that just as there are rods and cones that are sensitive to different hues, so that some fire maximally to red light, others to green light, and others to blue light, so there will be ganglion cells in here which can detect color boundaries (e.g., green center and red surround). However, we shall consider only monochromatic illumination here.

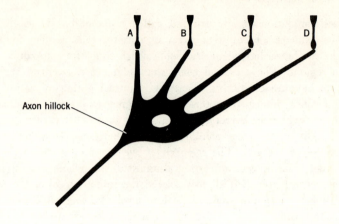

Axon hillock

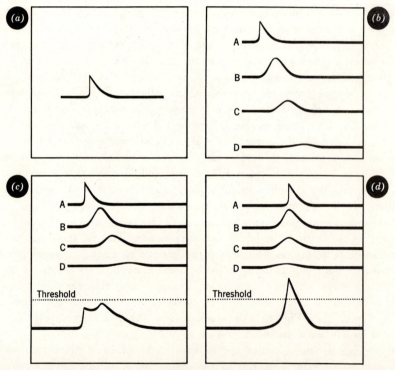

FIGURE 25 In this figure, we study how the neuron shown could function as a motion detector because of its dendritic geometry. A potential change (*a*) occurring at a synapse is increasingly degraded, and its peak increasingly delayed, the further it has to travel, as shown (*b*) in the decreasing effects at the axon hillock of stimulation at A, B, C, and D. We thus see (*c*) that if four stimuli reach A, B, C, and D simultaneously, their combined effect at the axon hillock does not reach threshold; but that if the synapses are activated in the order D-C-B-A, so that the peaks reach the axon hillock simultaneously, the combined effect will exceed threshold.

50

motion falls within certain limits. Our cell will not respond to a stationary object, or one moving from left to right. We see, then, that the geometry of the cell can have a great impact upon the function of the cell. In this case, the asymmetry of the placing of the dendrites on the cell body yields preference of one direction of motion over others. A whole area of research lies here—the study of form-function relations in neurons (for a recent review, see Rall [1970]). When we recall that many neurons in the human brain have 10,000 synapses upon them, we see that the potentialities of functions of single neurons are—depending on our mood—either very exciting or very frightening. As Bullock puts it, "Neurons are people." Sociology sometimes yields good metaphors for brain function, and vice versa.

Considering the visual world of an animal, most crucial information is contained in change—change in space and change in time. Note, again, success of caricature in reminding us of our favorite politicians† or the way in which moving objects catch our attention. Thus much "preprocessing" in the early stages of the sensory systems serves to enhance spatial and temporal contrast by signaling most strongly for changes in the receptive field over time, or changes within the space of the visual field. Having seen a moving spot detector, let us now look at a spatial change detector similar to that we saw to occur among the ganglion cells of cat retina.

It is not of much interest, generally, that points such as A, B, C, and D have a particular intensity in Figure 26; the important thing is that there is a sudden change in going from C to D. Let us thus give another example of "neuron design," this time making use of inhibitory as well as excitatory synapses to approximate the cat's on-center off-surround ganglion cell, for one way of extracting boundary information is to use a cell which is connected as in Figure 28 to a circular field of cells, being excited by those in the center and inhibited by those at the periphery. If we denote by r_0 the resting firing level the cell emits when fed by photoreceptors in a uniformly illuminated field we might get the chart of responses shown in Figure 27 from cells whose receptive fields are positioned as shown with respect to a boundary in the visual field. The activity of the cell thus departs from r_0 in the region *surrounding* the boundary.

Moving, now, from the cat's retina up to visual cortex (without discussing the character of cells in the lateral geniculate, which seem to be contrast detectors "only more so") we note that Hubel and Wiesel found both "simple" cortical cells (responsive to lines at a specific orientation in a specific place) and complex cells which respond to lines of a given orientation in varying locations. Connection schemes which they suggested might give rise to the behavior of simple cortical cells are explained in Figure 29. Presumably the response of complex cortical cells can in turn be explained in terms of relatively simple connections from an appropriate array of simple cortical cells. Hubel and Wiesel [1965] also found "hypercomplex" cells in areas 18 and 19 (which adjoin the primary visual cortex) which respond to angles of specific size and orientation in varying locations.

We see then that the angle detectors "predicted" by our discussion of Figure 18 have indeed been found in the visual cortex of cat (Hubel and Wiesel [1962]) with the contrast enhancement cells (Kuffler [1953]) and lateral geniculate presumably providing the preliminary preprocessing appropriate to contour extraction. Angle

---

† But in reading what follows, bear in mind that we *can* distinguish the caricature from the real thing.

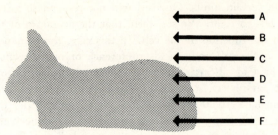

FIGURE 26   It is not of as much interest that points such as A, B, C, D, E, and F have a particular intensity as it is that there is a relative change in going from C to D.

detectors have *not* been found in the frog's visual system. Why does our "prediction" fail for the frog? The following explanation seems to be plausible. The frog has very simple visumotor behavior—the frog is irresponsive to visual stimuli, save that it will snap at, or orient toward, an object moving in flylike fashion, and will avoid a large moving object. In short it responds to a localized feature of the environment, rather than needing to utilize information from a large region of its visual field to integrate a course of action. Thus, where an animal such as the cat may make use of angle information to strip a contour to its bare minimum—so that it is only from higher level integration that action-oriented patterning can emerge based on "global" properties of the visual stimulus—the frog can use "local" properties to commit itself to action [although (see Section 7.2) global computations are required to determine

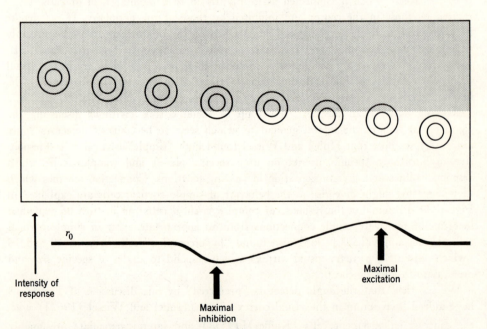

FIGURE 27   Each on-center contrast detector fires at a rate proportional to the difference in stimulation received between center and surround. The detectors thus accentuate a boundary by signaling it with a "doublet" of departure from the resting level. Cells just outside the boundary yield maximal excitation; while cells just inside the boundary yield maximal inhibition.

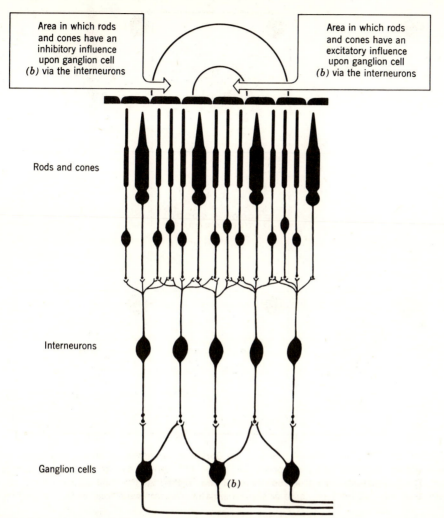

Area in which rods
and cones have an
inhibitory influence
upon ganglion cell
(b) via the interneurons

Area in which rods
and cones have an
excitatory influence
upon ganglion cell
(b) via the interneurons

Rods and cones

Interneurons

Ganglion cells

(b)

FIGURE 28   This is a highly schematized drawing of a section of retina, omitting such crucial interneurons as amacrine and horizontal cells. However, the point is not to convey the richness of retinal microanatomy, but rather to emphasize that rods and cones may affect ganglion cells in different ways. In this case, we suggest a central region of receptors serving to excite b, and a surrounding annulus serving to inhibit b.

which local feature to act upon] and it is thus appropriate that the outputs of the preprocessors can be action-coded, so that it makes sense to talk of one population of cells in the frog retina as being "bug detectors." We shall suggest that the control of eye movements in mammals has a great deal in common with the control of overall movements in the frog.

Note that we are thus saying that while preprocessing at the ganglion cell level in the frog is already "action-oriented", preprocessing even as "late" as the angle detectors of areas 18 and 19 of cat is "action neutral", and is only predicated on the fact that regularities of the environment permit objects to be well delimited in terms of the points of maximal curvature of their contours. We defer a discussion of higher-level "pattern recognition" to Section 4.3, but here let us note the discussion by Arbib

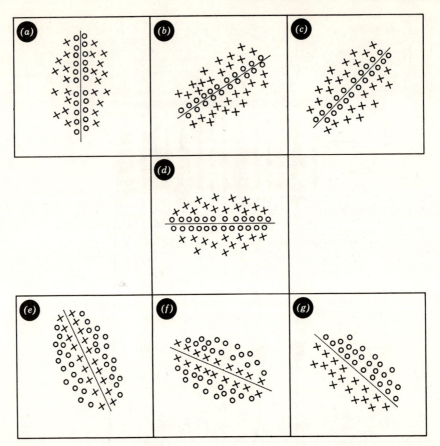

FIGURE 29 Hubel and Wiesel found in cat cortex a population of cells they called simple cells whose receptive fields comprise "on" and "off" areas separated by straight boundaries. The orientations vary from cell to cell, and in the cat the total size of the receptive field is about 4 degrees of visual angle in diameter. Circles mark "on" areas; while crosses mark "off" areas.

[1972] of complexity and evolution, which suggests ways in which different functions for a network can favor different encodings of information. This provides another line of support for our contention that "action-oriented coding" may well play an important role in perceptual networks.

  Having established some support for our contention that perception is action-oriented, and having gained some basic acquaintance with neurons and neuroanatomy, we now foresake the brain for two chapters to study the contributions that system theory and the artificial intelligence approach can provide to our study of thought and behavior.

System Theory and
Artificial Intelligence

3 | An Introduction to System Theory

Engineers concerned with the control of spaceships, chemical processing plants and related systems have refined the everyday formulations of such crucial concepts as those of state, algorithms, feedback, and adaptation. Since their formulations have proved immensely helpful in analyzing the behavior of complex man-made systems, it seems reasonable to hope that they will aid us in understanding complex natural systems too. Thus we devote this chapter to an exposition of these ideas which places them firmly in a cybernetic framework.

In Section 3.1, we note that just as a person's state of knowledge will influence how he answers a question, so must we, in analyzing any system, specify some internal state if we are to relate its current inputs and outputs. In Section 3.2 we see how the study of algorithms lets us understand how complex patterns of behavior may be explained by series of relatively simple operations controlled by current testing of the state of the system; and in Section 3.3 we give explicit attention to that form of testing known as feedback. Finally, in Section 3.4 we see how the structure of a system may change adaptively to allow it to cope more adequately with its environment, citing the ability of a computer to play championship checkers as a dramatic example of the extent of machine learning. Although, in this volume, we stress the application of these ideas to artificial intelligence and brain theory, the reader should appreciate their power and general applicability. Such diverse fields as history, biology, sociology, philosophy, psychology and economics can all be illuminated by the system theoretic ideas of this chapter.

3.1 STATES

Consider an *organism* interacting with its *environment*. The behavior of the organism will be influenced by aspects of the current activity of the environment—we speak of these aspects as constituting the *input* to the organism—whereas the activity of the environment will be responsive to aspects of the current activity of the organism—we speak of these aspects as constituting the *output* of the organism (Figure 1). Though our current models may not sufficiently stress this fact, our long-range theories must not fail to emphasize that we do not have

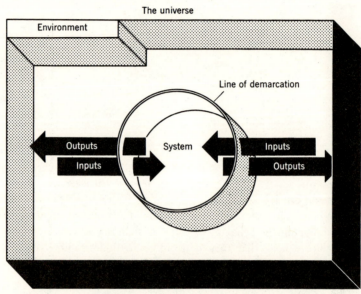

FIGURE 1   Here we see how any "universe" can be divided into two parts—the "system" that is our primary object of study and the "environment" that comprises all those aspects of the rest of the universe which will impinge upon the system.

isolated passive organisms upon which inputs just impinge from the outside, but rather organisms and environment in mutual interaction. The outputs of the organism may be construed as inputs to the environment, and vice versa.

The inputs and outputs that actually enter into a *theory* of a system are a small *sampling* of the flux of interactions between the system and the rest of the universe that the scientist expects to play an important role in the observed behavior of the system. For example, an analysis of a vending machine would normally limit the input pattern to the coins we insert and lever we pull—to the exclusion of kicks or electricity supply. Similarly, possible electric shocks from the machine will not usually be listed in the repertoire of outputs, but whether it produces no object at its output or an object and change will form an important part of our description.

There is essentially no limit to how many variables one could include in the analysis —the art of good theory is to select the variables that really matter. A theory of human cognition might take into account wind gusts and the temperature of the left armpit, but one has no reason to expect the inclusion of such whimsical variables to yield a better theory. A crucial task in any theory-building is to pick the right variables.

No matter how fortunate our choice of inputs and outputs to enter into our description of a system, we cannot expect them to constitute a complete description. We cannot predict how someone will answer a question unless we know her state of knowledge; nor can we tell how a computer will process its data unless we know what program of instructions (see Section 3.2) is controlling its computation. In short, we cannot expect a full understanding of human mental processes if we follow those psychologists who view the organism as responding passively to a series of stimuli in a way which can be manipulated by some schedule of reinforcement. Rather, we must include a description of the internal state of the system which determines what the organism will extract from its current stimulation in determining its current actions and modifying its internal state. Again, the theories which extend those presented in this volume must include similar constructs for the environment.

To spell out the role of the internal state, let us examine the vending machine (Figure 2) in more detail. If we insert enough money and pull the lever under a picture of an object, then this "stimulus" will usually elicit only one "response," namely, the vending of the pictured object and the correct change. Actually, the machine vends the bottom object of the stack above the lever. It is only if there are still quantities of the object we desire correctly stacked inside the machine that it can continually vend the object we want. The details of the coins inside the machine will determine whether or not the machine makes change. Thus, the output of a vending machine cannot always depend only upon the stimulus we present to it. If we were to start the machine at the beginning of the day with a full selection of small change and with all its hoppers correctly stacked, the "normal" stimulus-response description would work awhile—but eventually candy or change would be depleted and the description would become misleading. To specify the machine's next output, for any input, we have to know what object is at the bottom of each of the stacks and what change is in the hopper. However, knowing what object is at the bottom is not enough to predict still later outputs because if we now extract an object, then the object above it will affect future output. Thus in this very simple example we see that the complete internal state of the system must include the complete ordered list of objects in each stack and a complete listing of change.

To summarize, then, our description of any real system will contain the following five elements, and our choice of these will depend upon the aspects of the system of most interest to us:

1. The set of *inputs*: those variable parameters of the environment which we believe will affect the system behavior of interest to us.

2. The set of *outputs*: those parameters of the system which we choose to observe, or which we believe act upon the environment at any time in such a way as to yield observable changes in the relationship between the system and its environment.

3. The set of *states*: those *internal* parameters of the system—which may or may not also be output parameters—which determine the relationship between input and output. The state of a system is the system's "internal residue of the past"—when we know the state of a system, no further information about the past behavior of the system will enable us to refine our predictions about the way in which future inputs and outputs of the system will be related.

4. The *state-transition function*: which determines how the state will change when the system is provided with various inputs.

The vending machine as seen from outside

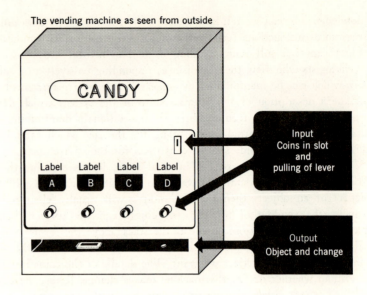

The vending machine with internal state revealed

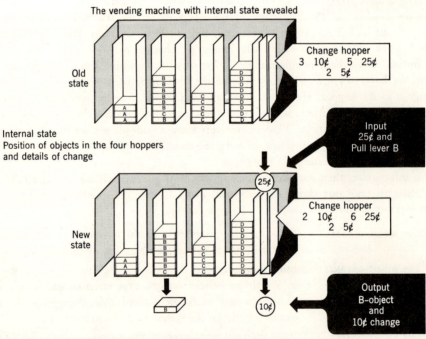

FIGURE 2 Two views of a vending machine. In the top view we see the vending machine from the outside—if we put in coins and pull a lever, out comes an object and change. However, the bottom view emphasizes that the relationship between input and output must depend on the internal state of the system, and that applying an input not only yields an output but also serves to update the state. (Question: If, given the machine in the new state shown, we repeat the input "25¢ and pull lever B", what will the next output be?)

5. The *output function*: which determines what output the system will yield with a given input when in a given state.

We stress, again, that while such a model may suffice to explain how the system will behave with stipulated inputs over a short period of time, more subtle theories must incorporate similar models of the environment to account for long-range interactions. This can be exemplified by the system A of Figure 3a. It has the set of numbers for its input, output, and state sets. Whenever it receives n for its input, its next state and output will be $n + 1$. Thus if we were to isolate it, we would conclude that its function was to add 1 to any input. However, if we were to come upon a copy A_1 of A connected to another copy A_2 in the manner shown in Figure 3b, we might view their tasks quite differently—for we might then find A_1 "counting out" the even numbers in sequence, while A_2 performed the same service for the odd numbers. It is in this sense that "the whole is more than the sum of its parts"; even if we have a complete understanding of the parts (as in Figure 3a), we may not perceive the crucial patterns in their behavior unless we can integrate them into the right totality (as in Figure 3b).

Any system in which the state-transition function and output function *uniquely determine* the new state and output from a specification of the initial state and subsequent inputs is called a *deterministic system*. Although this is the case of most interest to us in this volume, it must be noted that there are cases in which no matter how carefully we specify subsequent inputs, we cannot specify exactly what will be the subsequent states and outputs. If we are lucky, we can give tight probabilities on the new states and outputs—and in that case, we have a system which is called *stochastic*.

Let us see, briefly, that a stochastic treatment may be worthwhile either because we are analyzing systems at the quantum level, or because we are analyzing macroscopic

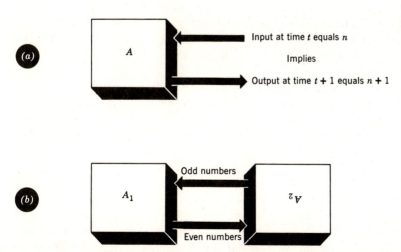

FIGURE 3 "The whole is more than the sum of its parts": When system A receives n for its input, its next state and output will be n + 1. Thus, if we were to isolate it (a), we would conclude that its function was to add 1 to any input. However, given the interconnection (b) of two copies of A we might view their tasks quite differently—for we might then find A₁ emitting the even numbers in sequence, while A₂ emitted the odd numbers.

systems which lend themselves to a stochastic description by ignoring "fine details" of microscopic variables.

For example, it is usually more reasonable to describe a coin in terms of a .5 probability of coming up heads, than to measure the initial placement on finger and thrust of thumb in sufficient detail to determine whether the coin will come up heads or tails in any particular case. Thus, in analyzing a system, it often proves not worth introducing extra detail into the input or state variables, and so we describe the system at a grosser level that involves the measurement of relatively few variables, on the basis of which one can only predict what the probabilities of various outcomes are.

The most widely received interpretation of quantum mechanics takes this one step further by claiming that there are certain probabilities that are not resolvable even by making arbitrarily fine measurements and that, in some sense, the action of the universe is inherently stochastic. Whereas in Newtonian systems, the state of the system comprised the positions of its components, which are directly observable, and their velocities, which can be estimated from the observed trajectory over a period of time, the states become much more abstract in quantum mechanics, and there the state is what is called a wave function, which determines only probability distributions on the outcomes of observations of positions and velocities. Interestingly, the updating of the state in quantum mechanics is still a deterministic process, but the state no longer gives precise predictions—the state only allows determination of *probabilities* of different outcomes.

Many psychologists have studied learning tasks under the heading "stochastic learning theory" in a way which suggests the brain has but two states—"task learned" and "task unlearned"—with nothing but random transitions to tie behavior together. Of course, the actual learning process in the real brain proceeds by numerous subtle changes—it is only the output which forces a binary value, masking the neural continuum. This is like the above situation in quantum mechanics, where the state of a system is now described by a function which contains information about the probability distribution of results of measurement. No finite set of measurements of a quantum-mechanical system has the property which this infinite-dimensional function possesses to meet the system theorist's definition of state: "Information about the system with the property that in estimating the future activity of the system, no further information about the past of the system will help." In coming to describe the activity of the brain, we will have to evolve state-descriptions as alien to present-day psychological jargon as the quantum state is to the classical position and velocity description of Newtonian physics. Of course, Newtonian mechanics is perfectly adequate for a wide range of phenomena, and so may be much of conventional psychology, but as our powers of observation become more sophisticated, so must the inadequacies of the classical approach become more apparent.

A suggestive illustration (discussed at greater length in Section 7.1) comes from the reticular formation (RF) of the brain stem (Figure 2 of Chapter 1). In mammals, RF functions in complex interaction with higher brain centers. However, in lower animals, a case may be made for viewing the RF partly as a "redundancy of potential command" device for committing the whole organism to an overall mode of action—in higher animals, the RF has, among others, the related responsibility for switching the organism from sleep to waking and back again. Certain anatomical considerations suggested a poker chip analogy, in which local computations take place in thin sections normal to the direction of the spinal cord, and with connections between these sections or "modules" running up and down the RF. Each module receives a variegated sample of sensory information. The question is: How can these modules interact in such a way as to reach a common decision to cause the animal to change into a suitable mode? Kilmer and McCulloch set forth a scheme of interconnections which, when simulated on a digital computer, yields satisfactory switching characteristics. The observation here is that the subsystems make tentative decisions on the basis of partial information, then slowly change under mutual interaction until sufficient consensus is reached to commit the organism to an overall mode of action. At no time would an "it's in this mode or that" description suffice to specify the *dynamics* of the model even though it describes the external appearance.

With this general discussion as background, let us turn to Figure 4 for the form taken by our general system description when applied to a neural network. One of the central problems for our study will be to understand to what extent neural mechanisms can be found to account for phenomena at the psychological level, but it must be realized that no simple reduction may be possible. Two different psychological stimuli —a light moving toward the subject, or a stationary light toward which the subject is moving with the same relative velocity—can yield identical neural input, which attains distinctiveness only in terms of differences of the internal state in the two cases. Thus the psychological input may correspond to not only the input, but also aspects of the state at the neural level (Section 6.3). Conversely, the pushing of a button could be accomplished by many different patterns of muscular activation, and so there is no simple one-to-one correspondence between neural and psychological descriptions. Nonetheless, as this book attests, though a naive reductionism does not apply, many psychological phenomena can be explained in neural terms.

Here let us give a simple network of formal "neurons" which may help us gain a little more feel for the dynamics of a system described at the neural network level. We

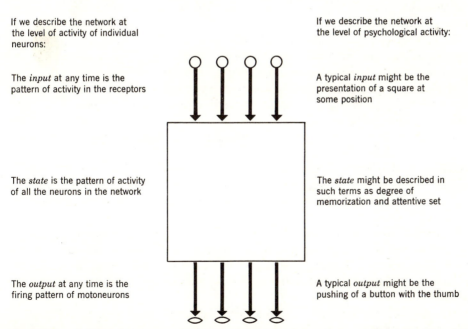

If we describe the network at the level of activity of individual neurons:

The *input* at any time is the pattern of activity in the receptors

The *state* is the pattern of activity of all the neurons in the network

The *output* at any time is the firing pattern of motoneurons

If we describe the network at the level of psychological activity:

A typical *input* might be the presentation of a square at some position

The *state* might be described in such terms as degree of memorization and attentive set

A typical *output* might be the pushing of a button with the thumb

FIGURE 4 Two forms of state-variable description for a network—at the level of activity of individual neurons and at the level of psychological activity.

shall, in fact, give an example, useful for our discussion of hierarchical control in Chapter 5, of how a circuit might be simply triggered by higher centers to yield useful sequences of action. Consider the highly simplified model of a leg (adapted from Weiss [1941]) whose single ball joint is operated by four muscles.

We imagine a rigid "leg" attached to the joint as shown in Figure 5. The leg may be moved forward by contracting the abductor (Ab) and backward by contracting the adductor (Ad); while the foot is raised by contracting the elevator (El), and pressed to the ground by contracting the depressor (De). Thus the following sequence of muscular contractions yields a reasonable parody of the contribution of one leg to the forward progression of a four-legged creature, the cycle starting with foot firmly on the ground, far forward with respect to the body:

1. De, Ad.   With foot firmly on the ground, attempt to pull the leg back; instead, friction of foot on ground yields forward motion of body.
2. El.   When foot is as far back as possible, raise it from the ground.
3. El, Ab.   Keeping foot off the ground, move leg fully forward.
4. De.   Then lower it to ground, ready to repeat cycle.

The reader interested in seeing a more detailed account of the form such "motor scores" may take in actual animals is referred to Weiss [1941], Roberts [1967], and Gray [1968]. Here we merely note how simple sequencing of muscles can yield biologically useful behavior.

One can certainly devise a neural network which could yield the sequence (*) of muscle contractions. For simplicity of diagraming we replace the pool of motoneurons controlling each muscle by a single formal neuron, and we draw the setup as if a single pulse arriving at the motoneuron would yield a contraction of its muscle of appropriate duration (Figure 6). Here (cf. the cells of Figure 1a of Chapter 1) a cell fires at time $t + 1$ if at time t an input marked 1 fires but none of the negative inputs fires.

An ON signal from "higher centers" initiates a pulse in the control loop, an OFF signal annuls all activity in the loop. As the four control neurons are activated by the circulating pulse, they trigger the appropriate combination of muscular contractions. In this case, the input is given by the firing pattern of the two input lines "from higher motor centers" and the output is given by the firing patterns of the four output lines "to the muscles." However, the input clearly does not determine the output without further specification of the state, that is, the pattern of firing within the loop.

EXERCISE.   Modify this circuit to prevent the ON signal from triggering a new pulse in the control loop if one is already circulating there, and to ensure that the OFF signal does not take effect until the foot is on the ground.

The crucial point of this discussion of the state of a neural network is that the *current output of the network need in no sense be a response to the current input regarded as stimulus*. Rather, the firing of those neurons which feed the output can be influenced by activity within the network reflecting quite ancient history of the system.

We can make this last fact very clear by an extremely simple example (Figure 7). We consider a formal "neuron" with two inputs, one from the outside and one taken as a branch of its own output. The numbers are so chosen that the output will fire

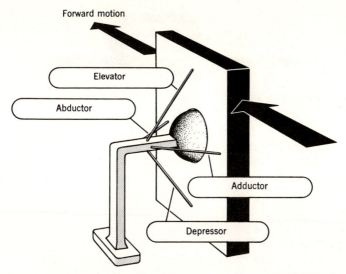

FIGURE 5   A simplified model of a leg, with ball and socket joint and rigid "knee". The "thigh" is controlled by four muscles—the abductor pulls the leg forward when it contracts, the adductor pulls it back, the depressor contracts to press the leg down, and the elevator elevates the leg upon contraction.

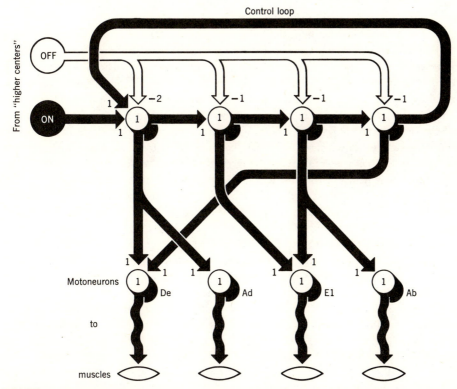

FIGURE 6   A simple circuit for the rhythmic control of walking in the "leg" of Figure 5. An ON signal "from higher centers" initiates a pulse in the control loop; an OFF signal annuls all activity in the loop.

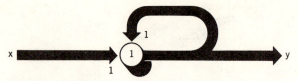

FIGURE 7   A formal neuron which "remembers" if its input line has ever been activated, as a result of a pulse "reverberating" around the loop.

at time $t + 1$ if either input fires at time t. Suppose the neuron is initially quiet —$y(0) = 0$. Then if the input x stays off, the neuron will stay off. But as soon as $x = 1$, y will be turned on, and a pulse will "reverberate" around the loop, keeping the neuron permanently on. Thus the neuron "remembers" indefinitely that its input line has ever been switched on. [Exercise: Note that it can then remember nothing else. Consider how an OFF input might be added to allow it to "start its vigil afresh."]

In our Figure 7 example, one might imagine that, rather than have the memory of the input stored only in the "reverberating loop," each activation drops the threshold somewhat, so that if the neuron fires repeatedly, its threshold may eventually drop to zero to allow spontaneous firing irrespective of input. "Memory" is then stored in the threshold value and is insensitive to the loss which would result from the random failure of a single pulse to traverse the reverberation loop.

A notable limitation of our system model, then, has been the assumption that the transition function is fixed. In fact, we must also study how the next-state function may change in time. Here, a hierarchical approach is useful—at one level and on one time scale we study the immediate activity of the system, whereas at another level of the hierarchy and on a longer time scale we see how the processes underlying that activity *adapt*. We shall discuss some strategies for adaptation in Section 3.4.

In describing the way in which a system such as the brain adapts over time, one could introduce a huge state-space to encompass not only the state of its activity, but also the state of its adaptation or learning. However, this multiplicity of states obscures that essence of the computational process which can be revealed by considering a smaller state-space—activity in which changes the dynamics over time. When we treat a system as an *adaptive system* we are usually saying that we have a deterministic system whose state can conveniently be decomposed (Figure 8) into two parts, one changing quickly, which we loosely refer to as *"the" state* of the system, and the other changing slowly, which we speak of as composing the *adaptation parameters* of the system. In psychological jargon, we may speak of *short-term memory* and *long-term memory*.

Such a decomposition may give us much insight into the *function* of a system yet do gross insult to its structure; for example, *"the" state* of a neural network might be given by the firing patterns of its neurons, while the *adaptation parameters* might be the pattern of synaptic weights and thresholds of those same neurons. Thus (cf. our Figure 1 of Chapter 1) placing the two components in separate boxes may have no physical meaning, though it may aid our understanding of the psychological processes involved, and may yield a useful mathematical model for our study of function. Nothing limits us to only two levels.

Some psychologists have made the distinction between short-term and long-term memory using the criterion that the latter persists after activity in the neural network has been interrupted. We shall briefly discuss experimental evidence for this distinction now. Then in Section 3.4 we shall build upon our simple example of parameter adjust-

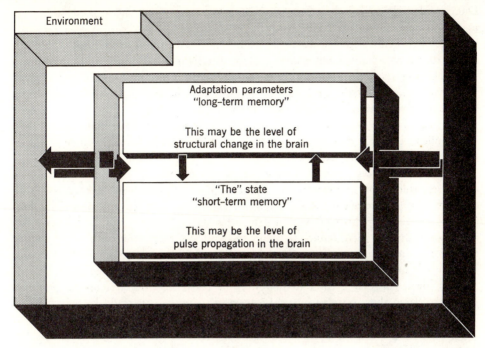

FIGURE 8 A *functional* decomposition of an adaptive system into two levels of "long-term memory" and "short-term memory" (cf. Figure 17).

ment in Figure 7 to briefly discuss the *identification problem* of control theory, which requires a controller to adjust the parameters it uses in controlling some other system.

In the neural nets of Figures 6 and 7, the state of the system was encoded in the activity of the formal "neurons." If this activity were to be interrupted, the "memory" of the system would be lost unless some other mechanism—such as the threshold drop hypothesized for Figure 7—of storage existed. Experimental evidence does indeed suggest that electrical activity in the brain is required to "store information" in the short run, while other mechanisms are involved in long-term memory. Here we shall content ourselves with a brief description of three early experiments. Many related experiments are reviewed by John [1967] and Gurowitz [1969]. Suffice it to say that all too many of them are striking evidence for the need for the cybernetic approach, naively viewing the task of memory as storing a few stimulus-response pairings at ready-made synapses rather than helping an organism adapt its interactions with a complex environment.

Taking advantage of the fact that hibernation can be induced in hamsters, Ransmeier and Gerard [1954] taught the animals a maze and then cooled them down to 5°C, effectively abolishing neural electric activity. The hamsters were then allowed to recover to normal temperature and were retested in the maze. No loss of memory was noticed. Ransmeier and Gerard concluded that a material change had taken place to store information without electrical activity.

Other experiments suggest that electrical activity may play a role in short-term memory and in the transfer of information to a more enduring form, and attempts have been made to measure the time required for such consolidation to take place.

Duncan [1949] studied the effect of ECS (electroconvulsive shock),† which serves to disrupt ongoing electrical activity in learning in rats. A box was divided into two equal compartments with one having a grid floor that could be electrified. The other compartment was painted white and contained a lighted 100-watt bulb to keep the rats from preferring this "safe" area. After the rat had explored both compartments (and had returned to the grid floor) the grid was charged with a stimulus strong enough to drive the animal into the other compartment. He was allowed to stay there for 10 seconds and then was taken out. After a prescribed time interval, an ECS was applied. The experiment was repeated for different rats with the time lapse between the grid shock and ECS being varied.

This procedure was repeated, giving the rat 10 seconds to get from the grid side to the safe side before the electric shock was applied. It was then observed how well the rats "learned" to avoid the electric shock by passing into the safe side of the box. Those rats receiving the ECS within 4 minutes suffered considerable loss of memory as demonstrated by their failure to avoid the grid shock by running into the lighted box. If the time lapse was an hour or greater, no difference was noticeable between the behavior of the rats receiving ECS and control rats which received no ECS.

This, then, suggests a consolidation time of between 4 minutes and 1 hour for "transfer" from short-term to long-term memory. However, it could be objected that ECS had not destroyed a short-term memory but had taught the animal that the shock in the first compartment was not so bad after all! To counter such objections, Quartermain et al. [1965] placed a rat on a small elevator, which was then lowered to the ground, at which time the rat usually jumps down. If a rat did so, it received a punishing shock. ECS tends to block the rat's tendency not to jump a second time if it is administered within 15 seconds. Quartermain administered an ECS to certain rats in a black bag—to avoid the rat's learning an avoidance response to the place where ECS occurs. The behavior of these rats was essentially the same as that of their counterparts. This supports the theory that lack of retention after ECS is due to a true amnesia brought about by physiological change rather than its being caused by a learned interference. To reconcile Quartermain's 15-second consolidation time for his learning task with the 15-minute or so consolidation time observed by Duncan is an as yet unresolved problem. Other experiments—reviewed in the books cited here —show that even longer interference results from the application of chemicals which disrupt the cell's biochemistry. This simply reminds us that there are not two distinct compartments labeled long- and short-term memory, but a more continuous transformation from one form to the other. We can only hope that the elaboration of sufficiently sophisticated models of memory structures, perhaps along the lines suggested by our slide-box metaphor (Section 4.1), will provide new concepts to guide the construction of clarifying experiments.

3.2 ALGORITHMS

An *algorithm* is like a recipe—it tells us how an apparently complicated operation may be broken down into a sequence of simple steps. A computer is a system which

---

† The ECS therapy used for mentally disturbed humans may be compared with the kicking of a recalcitrant machine: both imply a profound ignorance of the underlying mechanism, but they sometimes work.

can take an algorithm and use it to process the data it is given to obtain desired results. Before World War II, a computer was a person (possibly operating an abacus or desk calculator) adding together various numbers, multiplying them by other numbers, and so on, be it to compute the weekly paychecks of the employees of some firm, or to determine the best aerodynamic shaping of an airplane wing. But now we normally think of a computer as a man-made machine which, given a *program* (i.e., an algorithm in suitably encoded form), can take in data through its input channels and subject them to millions of basic operations per second, to produce not only the results a human computer could produce, but results involving so many millions of operations that assigning such tasks to teams of even hundreds of human computers is practically unthinkable.

The success of the computing machine is in part due to the speed of its circuitry. Where a human computer can add at most a few digits in a second, a modern electronic adder can add millions of numbers in the same time. Interestingly, the "cycle time" of a neuron is "midway" between that of a human and an electronic circuit—the refractory period of a neuron lasts the order of a millisecond—and it is worth pondering the fact that while a human computer adds a few digits together, ten billion neurons in his head carry out a thousand operations of, if anything, greater complexity. This suggests that the human brain has not evolved as an adding machine—I would suggest that it is only the use of internal models to plan and resolve conflicting possibilities for action in interacting with a complex environment that can come close to "justifying" the brain's power as a computer.

A deeper reason for the success of computing machines has nothing to do with their circuitry, but rests on a basic logical property of algorithms, namely, that an algorithm can be *specified* in far fewer steps than it takes to *execute* it (i.e., carry it out with particular data). At first this seems paradoxical, for one can imagine leaving out a few instructions on a given execution, but may be hard put to imagine where new ones can come from! The resolution is simple—algorithms often contain sequences of instructions which may be paraphrased as "keep repeating the following steps until you've gone far enough." To make this quite literal, consider the following algorithm for telling a human how to find the door of a totally dark room. (For simplicity, we shall assume that all furniture is obligingly removed from our path, and that the door is closed.) The verbal instructions we might give a human would be: "Walk to the wall, then walk along the wall until you find the door." This might then be broken down into the following sequence of "unit operations":

1. Extend left hand in front of you.
2. Does hand touch the wall or door?
   If answer is YES: Go to instruction 5.
   If answer is NO: Go to instruction 3.
3. Take one small pace, advancing the left and right feet equally.
4. Go to instruction 2.
5. With left hand still touching the wall or door, turn till it is to your left.
6. Does hand feel a door?
   If answer is YES: Go to instruction 9.
   If answer is NO: Go to instruction 7.
7. Take one small pace, advancing the left and right feet equally.
8. Go to instruction 6.

9. STOP (or: transfer to next program of action appropriate to having found doorway).

This program clearly exhibits the property of normally having a shorter specification than execution. If the walker starts 12 paces from the wall, and must then advance 8 paces along the wall to find the door, then he must execute a total of 63 instructions, seven times as many as were required to specify the program. [The perceptive reader may have noted that this "program" works only if the door is in the first wall. How would you handle the case in which the door might be in *any* wall of a rectangular room? What extra instructions are required if the wall is irregularly shaped?] We should add that this example, while making clear the economies of specification over execution, is *not* intended as an example of speed of operation. A robot cannot take a million steps a second any more than a man can. It is only when the basic steps can be performed by electronic circuitry within the machine, rather than being performed in "whole body" interaction with the environment, that the computer's full speed can be tapped.

It would avail us little that the machine could add a million numbers in 1 second if we had to individually instruct it for each of those additions. But if we need to specify a thousand instructions to cause it to execute a million instructions, then the speed of the circuitry can be well used indeed, provided that:

1. The computer can store the program and data, and it is not limited by the speed of its input and output equipment.
2. The computer has circuitry for executing all the basic operations.
3. The computer has circuitry for conducting the necessary tests and automatically transferring control to the instruction specified by the result.
4. The computer can read in material from its receptors and send out commands to its effectors.

A computer "fresh from the factory" has wired into it the ability to respond to a repertoire of strings of numbers which encode (in a form which humans do not find at all natural) very simple instructions such as "add the numbers at two specified locations in storage" or "test to see whether or not a certain number is positive" or "read in the next chunk of data and store it at such-and-such an address." Usually, humans specify problems in a blend of mathematics and English and must exercise great skill in rendering the specification into an appropriate sequence of instructions to the computer in *machine language*. To ease this programing task, people have devised languages which are still rather formalized, but in which it is far easier for a human to specify the steps by which the computer should solve the given problem. It is then necessary to give the computer a special program called a "translator," which enables the machine to accept a program written in this new language and translate each "high-level" instruction into a sequence of machine language instructions. (We often refer to such "little programs" which can replace "high-level" instructions as *subroutines.*) We call the translator an *interpreter* if it translates one instruction at a time, executes it, and discards the translation before going on to the next instruction; we call it a *compiler* if it translates the whole program straightaway, and then only refers to the machine-language translation while actually processing data.

For example, if we are programing the motion of a robot, which has two drive wheels, the "machine language" might include three instructions:

L: locking right wheel, advance Left wheel one step.
R: locking left wheel, advance Right wheel one step.
B: synchronously advance Both wheels one step.

It might also include the control and logic instructions we shall use below.

However, we might want to use instructions like "Advance 5 feet" or "Turn 30° to the right." Suppose, then, that with one wheel locked, the robot will turn a full 360° with 72 steps of the other wheel, while synchronous steps of both wheels will advance the robot 2 inches.

EXERCISE. How wide is the robot?

We might then equip the robot with an interpreter which will make the following translations:

Advance N feet
1. Set $x = 6N$
2. Does $x = 0$?
   YES: go to 6.
   NO: go to 3.
3. B.
4. Replace x by $x - 1$.
5. Got to 2.
6. Stop.

Turn $\theta°$ to the right
1. Set $x = \theta/5$ (rounded up to the nearest integer).
2. Does $x = 0$?
   YES: go to 6.
   NO: go to 3.
3. L.
4. Replace x by $x - 1$.
5. Go to 2.
6. Stop.

Before closing this section, we should note that the algorithms we have exhibited above are all *serial*—that is, they all have the property that only one unit operation is executed at a time. The brain, on the contrary, seems to be highly *parallel* in that each neuron is continually "testing" the neurons which synapse upon it, so that billions of unit operations take place at any time. Nonetheless, specifying the connectivity of a network to perform a task yields an algorithm for that task just as surely as does the specification of a sequence of instructions. Most work in artificial intelligence seeks any algorithm that will yield an "intelligent" function—and usually settles for a serial one, since that is the type handled by most present-day computing machines. However, when we turn to brain theory in Part III we shall be more interested in parallel algorithms whose structure reflects that of the brain. Ironically, though, we shall usually test our theory by simulating our model on a computer, in other words, by translating our parallel algorithm into a serial algorithm. The trivial example of Figure 9 should make clear the strategy involved: We write a whole sequence of instructions to indicate what will happen in one single step of operation of the parallel system. If we only look at the state of the serial computation at the end of each

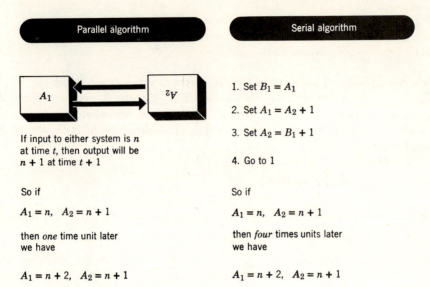

Parallel algorithm	Serial algorithm
A_1 A_2	1. Set $B_1 = A_1$
	2. Set $A_1 = A_2 + 1$
If input to either system is n at time t, then output will be $n + 1$ at time $t + 1$	3. Set $A_2 = B_1 + 1$
	4. Go to 1
So if	So if
$A_1 = n, \quad A_2 = n + 1$	$A_1 = n, \quad A_2 = n + 1$
then *one* time unit later we have	then *four* times units later we have
$A_1 = n + 2, \quad A_2 = n + 1$	$A_1 = n + 2, \quad A_2 = n + 1$

FIGURE 9   An example of a parallel algorithm which can be simulated by a serial algorithm, using an extra state variable and a slowdown by a factor of 4 (cf. Figure 3).

"cycle" of simulation, we may then obtain, as it were, a "slow-motion picture" of the parallel computation.

With this as background, we now have a general feel for the way in which complex functions may be reduced to patterns of simple operations.

3.3   FEEDBACK

Instructing a robot to turn 30° by locking one wheel and advancing the other six steps will only be effective if, for example, the wheels do not slip. Should they slip, the controller would have to issue extra stepping instructions to cause the robot to point in the desired direction. Thus in controlling any interactions of a system with its environment in which there is a possibility of unexpected disturbances, such as slippage, it is clearly important that information be continually *fed back* from peripheral receptors to tell the controller how effectively it is controlling the interactions. For example, it is easier for a human to grasp a moving object if she can see how far her hand has to move—that is, if the brain has "visual feedback" from receptors (in this case the eyes) as to the position of the effector (in this case the hand). The brain can then compute appropriate instructions to cause the muscles to reduce the difference between the actual position of the hand and its desired position on the object. Again, when walking we make crucial use of "feedback" from the pressure receptors of the soles of the feet, as is well illustrated by the common experience that if we have "pins and needles" and so have to walk without such feedback, our leg movements are clumsy and ill coordinated.

Thus *feedback*—comparison of actual performance with some "desired" performance —must play an essential role in the control of an organism or a robot. The general scheme of such feedback control is shown in Figure 10.

The controller, being able to continually monitor the outcome of previous control

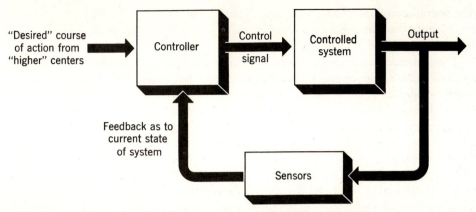

FIGURE 10   General setup for a system that uses feedback as to the current state of the controlled system in computing the control signal.

signals, can modify them should the resultant behavior of the system be somewhat unsatisfactory, say because of unexpected environmental disturbances. For example, when driving a car, we can maintain a desired speed despite variations in the slope of the road if we monitor the speedometer to determine whether an "accelerate" or "decelerate" signal is appropriate at any time.

In Figure 11 we diagram a special case of the feedback control scheme—a so-called *negative feedback system* in which a quantity θ_d indicating the *desired* output, and the *actual* output's measure θ_a are constantly fed into the error detector, which takes their difference

$$e = \theta_d - \theta_a$$

and supplies this error signal to the controller. For any particular such system, the problem is to so design the controller that the error e can be kept satisfactorily small.

Suppose the controller malfunctions by *overcompensation* for the error. If e is initially positive and the controller overcompensates, then e becomes large and negative; another overcompensation and e becomes large but positive; and so *ad infinitum* as

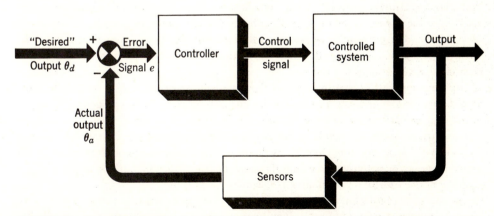

FIGURE 11   A negative feedback system in which control is based on a signal $e = \theta_d - \theta_a$ as to the error between the desired and actual output of the controlled system.

the system goes into wild oscillations. Thus in constructing a controller, we must so design it that the resultant system is stable, in that the error soon settles down to a small value if the input is relatively steady.

A negative feedback system of the type given in Figure 11 is often called a *servomechanism*. It is the steering mechanism of a ship—an example of a servomechanism—which yielded the etymology of "cybernetics," for "χυβερνητης" is the Greek word for "helmsman." We have now seen that an important property of a servomechanism is that if it is not properly designed the error may oscillate wildly rather than diminishing. One of Norbert Wiener's insights which led to his book *Cybernetics* was that such deficient feedback may be involved in certain types of human illness.

For example, his analysis of feedback systems led Wiener to predict two types of human malfunction. Clinician friends confirmed that two varieties of disease corresponding to these malfunctions did indeed exist. In one, a patient cannot stand upright without his eyes open, and walks in a very uncertain manner, having to continually watch his feet, which he kicks forward in succession. Such a patient has *tabes dorsalis*, which has destroyed part of his spinal cord, so that his brain cannot obtain feedback from his joints, tendons, muscles, or the soles of his feet. In the other, a patient seems normal when still, but if he tries to pick up a glass of water, his hand swings back and forth, spilling all the water before he can bring his hand to his mouth. His spinal feedback system is not damaged, but he has a damaged cerebellum and—in view of our foregoing discussion—it appears that the damage yields insufficient inhibition of muscular activity with the resultant exhibition of unstable oscillations in the form of a purpose tremor during voluntary movement. We thus see that not only is feedback necessary, but also that it must not be overapportioned or underapportioned in the computations of the controller if smooth coordinated activity is to ensue.

After having gained some appreciation for the importance of feedback in control systems, it is important to stress that when we turn to brain theory we shall be interested in feedback systems in which the signals comprise whole patterns of activity rather than single numbers. To make this clear we should briefly discuss the control of eye movements (a more detailed discussion will occur in Chapter 7) as a basis for the discussion of a more general scheme of feedback control based on the work of Pitts and McCulloch [1947].

Many authors, in applying control theory to modeling the fixing of gaze upon a stationary or slowly moving object, would note that two crucial parameters were involved—the present angle of gaze θ, and the desired angle of gaze, θ_d. They would then analyze the problem in terms of such a control system as shown in Figure 12, asking what function of the desired and actual gaze is computed to determine the rotational acceleration $\ddot{\theta}$ of the eye.

Such an approach has proved fruitful in analyzing behavior of biological systems, but it may be dangerously misleading in unravelling the details of neural circuitry, for it suggests that we view the brain in terms of a central executive which manipulates a few variables such as θ and θ_d to issue such directives as the current value of $\ddot{\theta}$.

However, θ_d is not immediately available to the brain but is instead encoded in terms of peaks of activity in a whole layer of neurons, the rods and cones of the eye. Again, in the case of eye dynamics, $\ddot{\theta}$ cannot be effective as a single control signal for a rotary actuator but must rather control the opposed activities of at least one agonist-antagonist pair of muscles—and even here, two signals are not enough, for

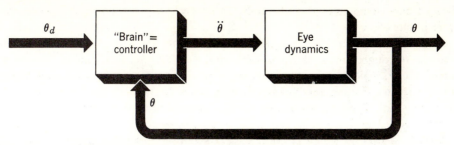

FIGURE 12 A gross approximation to the feedback system for control of eye movements. θ_d = angle of visual target; θ = angle of gaze; $\ddot{\theta}$ = angular acceleration of eye.

the contraction of each muscle, itself a population of muscle fibers, must result from the overall activity of a whole population of motoneurons.

Thus, although it would be possible to design a robot with a "brain" structured like the centralized $(\theta_d, \theta) \mapsto \ddot{\theta}$ converter of Figure 12, it would require special preprocessors to "funnel down" the whole input array of retinal activity to provide the single number θ_d. Indeed, this scheme might make sense in a robot whose task was to track single targets rather than interact with complex environments, and whose effector was a single rotary actuator for which $\ddot{\theta}$ was an appropriate control signal. But if the output must be played out upon a whole array of motoneurons, as in the biological case, so that $\ddot{\theta}$ would have to be fed into an elaborate processor to be "parcelled out", then one begins to doubt the utility of the centralized processor.

To "go parallel" we must have the idea of a transformation which can act upon a whole array of information. In fact, familiar examples abound as we may see by recognizing all the patterns in Figure 13 as being squares, though they appear in different sizes, orientations, and positions. As we shall now explain, the changes required to transform one of these squares into another form part of a *group of transformations* (we shall thus require some mathematics here). Even the nonmathematical reader should gain something from reading between the formulas, even though a

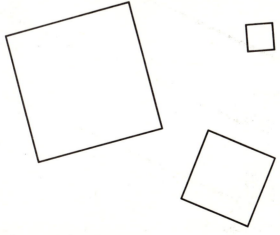

FIGURE 13 A square is a square is a square.

detailed understanding of those formulas is not necessary to follow the later development of our ideas.

Let us first consider ways in which we move figures about in the plane of the page without rotating them or changing their size. In this case, each point is moved the same amount, which can be described by giving the length and direction of the *vector* which joins the old and new position of each point. Let us then use T_a to denote the *translation* in which the motion of each point is described by the vector α as in Figure 14.

Clearly, if α is the vector 0 whose length is zero, the corresponding translation T_0 will leave every figure in the position identical to that in which it started. We thus speak of T_0 as the *identity* translation.

Given any pair of translations T_a and T_β we may carry out T_a first and then T_β to get the overall translation $T_\beta \cdot T_a$. [The order is "backward" because we write $T\phi$ for the result of acting with T upon the pattern ϕ. It thus seems natural to write $T_\beta \cdot T_a$ for the transformation which turns ϕ into $T_\beta(T_a\phi)$.] As we see from Figure 15a, $T_\beta \cdot T_a$ is equal to the translation $T_{a+\beta}$ defined by the sum of vectors of the original translations. Again, as we see from Figure 15b, it does not matter if we complete the overall translation $T_\beta \cdot T_a$ and follow it by T_γ, or complete T_a and then follow it with $T_\gamma \cdot T_\beta$; the effect is the same:

$$(T_\gamma \cdot T_\beta) \cdot T_a = T_\gamma \cdot (T_\beta \cdot T_a) = T_{a+\beta+\gamma}$$

Again, as Figure 15c illustrates, if we follow or precede T_a by T_{-a}, which is the translation of the same length but inverted direction, it "undoes" the effect of T_a:

$$T_a \cdot T_{-a} = T_{-a} \cdot T_a = T_0$$

We call T_{-a} the *inverse* of T_a and often denote it $(T_a)^{-1}$ where the superscript indicates the forming of an inverse.

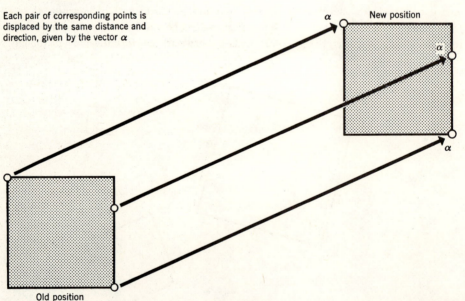

Each pair of corresponding points is displaced by the same distance and direction, given by the vector α

New position

Old position

FIGURE 14 The translation T_a of a square determined by the vector α. (Note that the diagram also affords an example of an optical illusion—the three vectors are parallel, but do not appear to be.)

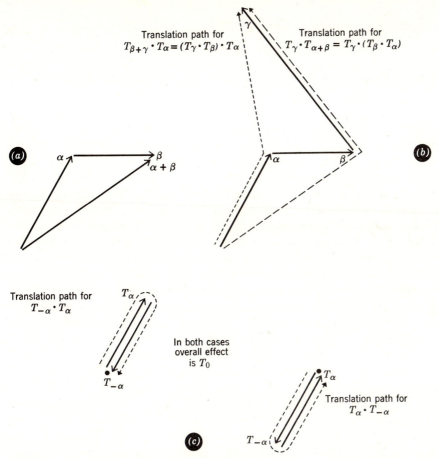

FIGURE 15 (a) Following translation T_α by translation T_β yields translation $T_{\alpha+\beta}$. (b) *Associativity:* translation T_α followed by translation T_β followed by translation T_γ gives the same overall translation, however we break down the overall journey. (c) Every translation T_α has an *inverse* translation $T_{-\alpha}$, such that each undoes the effect of the other to yield the *identity* or zero translation (no move at all) T_0.

Thus the set of all plane translations together with the operation of composition which combines each pair of two translations T_α and T_β into $T_{\alpha+\beta}$ has an identity T_0, each translation T_α has an inverse $T_{-\alpha}$, and any three translations satisfy what is called the *associative law*

$$T_\gamma \cdot (T_\beta \cdot T_\alpha) = (T_\gamma \cdot T_\beta) \cdot T_\alpha$$

They then form an example of what a mathematician calls a *group*, which she defines as follows:

DEFINITION. A *group* is a set G together with an operation which assigns to each pair g_1 and g_2 of elements of G a third element $g_1 \cdot g_2$ of G for which the following conditions hold:

1. The operation is *associative*: For any three elements g_1, g_2, g_3 of G we have

$$(g_1 \cdot g_2) \cdot g_3 = g_1 \cdot (g_2 \cdot g_3)$$

2. G contains an *identity* element e with the property that for all g in G we have

$$g \cdot e = e \cdot g = g$$

3. To each element g in G there corresponds an *inverse* g^{-1} in G such that

$$g^{-1} \cdot g = g \cdot g^{-1} = e$$

For example, ordinary nonnegative numbers combined by addition do not form a group unless we append negative integers to enable the formation of inverses, while the integers cannot form a group when combined by subtraction since associativity fails: $(a - b) - c \neq a - (b - c)$ unless $c = 0$.

Returning to transformations which preserve such properties as "squareness" we see that not only do the translations form a group, but so also do the dilations—changes of scale characterized by a magnification factor $k > 0$. The identity is given by a magnification $k = 1$ which leaves size unchanged, and the inverse of a magnification by k is a magnification by $1/k$. Similarly the rotations form a group. [What are the identity and inverse?] The reader may recall from her study of Euclidean geometry that two figures are said to *congruent* if they can be obtained from one another by a "congruence transformation" made up from rotations and translations, whereas they are *similar* if the group of transformation allowed includes all combinations of rotations, translations, and dilations. In fact, the great nineteenth-century mathematician Klein suggested that all geometry (Euclidean or non-Euclidean, even topological) could be regarded as the study of properties which remained invariant under some given group of transformations.

Against this background, it is natural to ask for a network whose output would depend only upon properties of its input which are invariant under transformation of elements by operations of some given group G. In discussing one of the schemes which might be suggested to underlie our ability to recognize patterns despite such transformations, there is a crucial point about Figure 13 to bear in mind: There is no way of viewing the figures—even one at a time—which does not make the differences in *retinal* stimulation far outweigh the similarities. Thus further processing beyond the receptors is required to detect their commonality.

Pitts and McCulloch [1947] designed a scheme to find a transformation T from G which will transform a pattern ϕ in such a way that $\phi_0 = T\phi$ is in standard form. (In Section 7.3 we shall consider the case in which we also use transformations of output activity, to assure that the relation between input and output is in standard form.)

They generate the transformation in two steps:

1. Associate with each pattern ϕ an "error vector" $E(\phi)$ such that $E(\phi) = 0$ if and only if ϕ is in standard form.

2. Provide a scheme W which will associate with each error vector a transformation which is error-reducing; that is, for all patterns ϕ we demand that $E(\phi)$ be reduced after $W(E(\phi))$ is applied to ϕ:

$$\| E[W(E(\phi)) \cdot \phi] \| \leqslant E(\phi) \tag{1}$$

with equality only in case $E(\phi) = 0$. Henceforth, let us use W_ϕ to abbreviate $W(E(\phi))$.

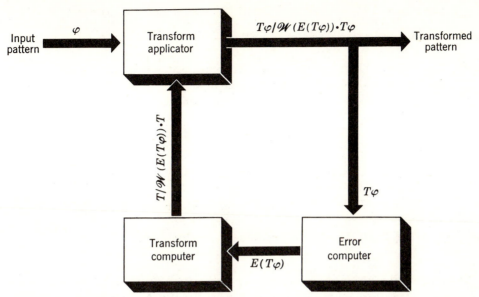

FIGURE 16 A generalization of the Pitts-McCulloch scheme for transforming a pattern to standard form. (The notation A/B on a line means that the signal on the line is A at time t, and B at time $t + 1$.)

The hard work in establishing such a scheme is actually defining an appropriate error measure E and then finding a mapping W, which can make use of error feedback to properly control the system so that it will eventually transform the input to standard form.

There are two main implementations of such a feedback scheme, only the second of which was explicitly considered by Pitts and McCulloch [1947].

In a *ballistic scheme*, W is so structured as to virtually reduce the error to zero in one step:

$$E(W_\phi \cdot \phi) \doteq 0 \text{ for all patterns } \phi$$

A controller would then proceed as follows:

1. Given ϕ, compute $E(\phi)$ and thus W_ϕ.
2. Form $W_\phi \cdot \phi = \hat{\phi}$.
3. Proceed on the assumption that $\hat{\phi}$ is in standard form.

Such a scheme is that used in ballistics where $E(\phi)$ is the displacement of a bullet from its target and W_ϕ is determined by the initial aim when the shot is fired—there is no possibility of making midcourse corrections. This is in distinction to a guided missile in which repeated corrections can be made.

In a *tracking scheme*, then, the error $E(W_\phi \cdot \phi)$ may be little less than the previous error $E(\phi)$—all we demand is that under a feedback scheme employing *repeated* application of the error-correction the error eventually goes to zero. A controller implementing tracking would then proceed according to one of two schemes. The first corresponds to continually modifying the pattern until one is found which is in standard form; the second corresponds to continually modifying the transform until one is found which will bring the given pattern to standard form:

I. Here ϕ will be the latest transformed version of the input pattern.

    1. Replace ϕ by the new input pattern.
    2. Use $E(\phi)$ to obtain W_ϕ.
    3. Form $W[E(T\phi)] \cdot \phi$ to obtain the new pattern ϕ.
    4. Is the new $E(\phi)$ close enough to zero?
        YES: Exit, ϕ may be treated as in standard form.
        NO: Go to 2.

II. Here ϕ will be the *fixed* input pattern, and T will be the updated transform to be applied to ϕ.

    1. Initialize T to be the identity transformation: $I \cdot \phi = \phi$.
    2. Use $E(T\phi)$ to obtain $W[E(T\phi)]$.
    3. Form $W[E(T\phi)] \cdot T$ to obtain the new transform T.
    4. Is the new $E(T\phi)$ close enough to zero?
        YES: Exit, $T\phi$ may be treated as in standard form.
        NO: Go to 2.

To guarantee that the schemes converge we need a stronger condition than (1). One condition is that there exists some number δ such that $0 < \delta < 1$ and

$$\| E(W_\phi \cdot \phi) \| \leqslant (1 - \delta) \| E(\phi) \| \text{ for all patterns } \phi$$

Convergence then follows from the fact that $(1 - \delta)^n \to 0$ as $n \to \infty$.

Figure 16 shows a discrete-time system which will implement Scheme II to generate, for any ϕ, a transformation T_ϕ which will transform it to standard form.

The transform application box is memoryless—input pattern ϕ and transform T at its input yield transformed pattern T_ϕ at its output. The error computer box is memoryless—an input pattern at its input yields the corresponding error at its output. The transform computer box is a deterministic system: if its state at time t is the transform T, and its input at time t is the error vector e, then its new state and output at time $t + 1$ will both be the transform $W(e) \cdot T$.

There will be applications in which a controller may wish to use a mixed ballistic-tracking strategy—using a transform generator W_1 to compute a first "giant leap" to bring the pattern fairly close to standard form, then a second transform generator W_2 to be used in a tracking strategy to iteratively "fine tune" the pattern ever closer to standard form. In Chapter 5 we shall suggest that the use of such a "mixed strategy" is a basic "organizational principle" in the CNS.

3.4 ADAPTATION

At the heart of control theory is *the control problem*: "Given reasonably accurate descriptions of a system and some performance required of it, to find inputs which, when applied to the system, will elicit (a reasonable approximation to) the desired performance."

A common situation which complicates the control problem is that the controlled system may not be known accurately—it may even change its character somewhat with time. For example, one of the most intriguing properties of the brain of a growing animal is that it must control a body which is not only increasing in size, but is also changing in relative size of different portions as time progresses. Further, external objects of fixed properties have differing properties relative to the organism, and these too must be repeatedly adjusted for. Thus, whether in adjusting for the growth of the body or in learning to interact with new objects in the environment, the brain must continually solve what control theorists call *the identification problem*: "To use repeated experiments upon the input-output behavior of a system to build up a state-variable description for a system which yields similar behavior."

Identification procedures are of real importance to the control theorist. For instance, suppose one wished to control a system, but did not know the dynamic equations of that system. Then, rather than build a controller specifically designed to control one actual system, we would instead build a general purpose control which could accommodate to any reasonable set of parameters to control the system given by that set of parameters. Then, rather than hook up the controller directly to the system to be controlled, we would interpose an identification procedure. (Possible use of such a scheme in cerebellar control of movement is discussed in Boylls and Arbib [1972].) The controller would thus work at any time upon the system of parameters which the identification procedure (Figure 17) provides as the best estimate of the real system's parameters at that time.

If the controlled system is sufficiently slowly time-varying that the identification procedure can make accurate estimates of system parameters more quickly than they actually change, the controller will be able to act efficiently, despite the fluctuations in controlled system dynamics. The controller, when coupled to an identification

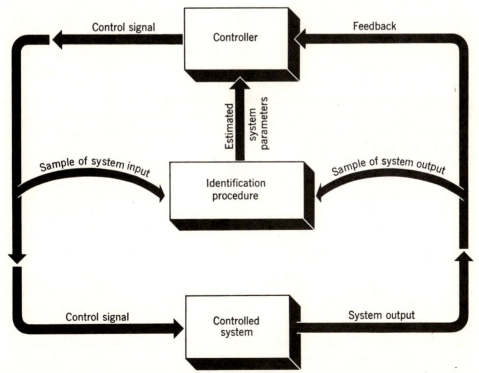

FIGURE 17   A controller using system parameters estimated by an identification procedure to better control the controlled system (cf. Figure 8).

procedure, is precisely what is often referred to as an "adaptive controller": it adapts its control strategy to changing estimates of the dynamics of the controlled system.

We note, without elaboration here, that it might also be necessary to have the identification procedure generate some of the input to the controlled system—in other words, apply test signals to try out various hypotheses about the parameters of the controlled system. One would then have to design a strategy to trade off the loss of optimality we get by not having a very accurate estimate of the state parameters against the loss of optimality we get by having the controller relinquish control to the identification procedure from time to time.

In other words, the "brain" (controller + identification procedure) interacts with "environment" (which includes the body as well as external objects) on the basis of an internal model (the latest set of adaptation parameters), and *its interactions must be designed to update its internal model as well as to change its relationship with the external world in some desired way.*

System theory has provided algorithms for the identification problem of how to go from the external behavior of systems of limited complexity to a compact description of its internal behavior. We must emphasize, however, that the algorithms are only efficient if the "dimensionality" is rather small. We have a great deal of theory ahead of us in finding gross states of the organism to which such a theory can be applied, as well as approximation methods which will help us in handling systems without involving ourselves in their full complexity. The experimenter, on the other hand, has the task of finding significant subsystems to which existing theory can be meaningfully if not completely rigorously applied.

To make it more credible that identification procedures can help a system—for example, the brain—obtain amazingly sophisticated interaction with its world, let us briefly outline the identification procedure used by Samuel [1959] in his early studies of programing a computer to play checkers. No one knows an explicit set of rules which will ensure winning at checkers so, instead, Samuel programed the computer to look several moves ahead to try and determine its best next move. (He supplied the computer with several rules to cut down the number of possible moves it had to look at, because even a machine carrying out a million operations per second can suffer limitations of time. These rules are related to the techniques of heuristic search that we shall discuss in Section 4.2.)

Samuel's problem was then to give the computer a way to determine the value of various board positions in checkers. If asked to give a numerical rating of six different checker-board positions, one might be able to point to one board as best, one board as worst, and have difficulty in articulating anything more about the remaining four. Such an evaluation is not precise enough for the computer program. We do not, at a conscious level, come up with such numerical weightings, and so no amount of interrogating master checker players is going to give us these numbers (unless multidimensional scaling will yield some insights). Instead, we adopt an adaptive system theory approach. Not knowing how we evaluate a board, we can at least be sure that its value depends on such things as the number of pieces each player has, the number of kings, balance, mobility, control of the center. To these we can assign precise numbers. Let us pick, by talking to checker players, some 16 such parameters which contribute to our evaluation of the board.

In Figure 18, we see a geometric representation of the two-parameter case. Here we represent each pair of parameter values by a point labeled (x_1, x_2) in the base

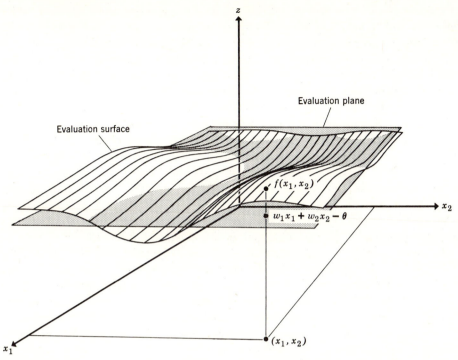

FIGURE 18 Here we see a plane (linear surface) approximating a curved surface. For each parameter pair (x_1, x_2), its real evaluation $f(x_1, x_2)$ is approximated by its linear evaluation $w_1x_1 + w_2x_2 - \theta$.

plane, and indicate the board value by a point at height $z = f(x_1, x_2)$ above this. As (x_1, x_2) varies, so do the points $z = f(x_1, x_2)$, and they trace out a surface which we have labeled the evaluation surface. There are quite a few bumps in the surface, but we see that it is nonetheless always fairly close to a flat surface, which we have called the evaluation plane. It is a basic mathematical fact that such a plane can be described by the equation $z = w_1x_1 + w_2x_2 - \theta$ for suitable choice of the numbers w_1, w_2, and θ. Similarly, no matter how "bumpy" the 16-dimensional evaluation "surface" of board value against parameter values might be, we *might* still hope that a "plane" would be a good enough approximation to the actual evaluation to play a good game. In other words, we might hope to get by with an evaluation function of the form $z = w_1x_1 + w_2x_2 + \ldots + w_{16}x_{16} - \theta$ (called a *linear approximation*) for some choices of the 16 weights $w_1, \ldots, w_{16}$ and θ. In fact, in deciding which is better of two boards, the constant θ is irrelevant—adding the same amount to all the different evaluations does not change their relative values—and so there are only 16 numbers to find in getting the best linear approximation.

In the context of system theory, then, the strategy that Samuel adopted in his first paper [1959], in addition to cutting down the "look-ahead", was to *guess* that the evaluation function was approximately linear. That was a guess, and might have been completely useless, but he went ahead on that assumption and "bet" that a good enough description of the evaluation surface over the 16 parameters was a flat one, and that all he had to do was to find the 16 coefficients to describe how that flat surface is oriented in the 17-dimensional space.

On the basis of the current weight-setting, the computer chooses a move which appears to lead to boards of high value to the computer. If after a while it finds that the game seems to be going badly, in that it overvalued the board it chose, then it will reduce those parameters which yielded a positive contribution while increasing those which did not. Of course, the actual scheme is more sophisticated than that, but the point is that Samuel could set up a routine whereby the computer could compare its prediction of what the board would be worth in a few moves, and what it turned out to be worth, to keep adjusting those parameters. Samuel's first checker-playing program could in fact only play a moderate game, thus indicating that a linear evaluation function is only a moderately good fit. In a more recent version, Samuel's program [1967] uses a more complicated evaluation, called the "signature table" method, and generous use of look up in a library of master's games to play at state championship level.

This, then, is an example of a problem where we can improve the performance of a computer significantly by starting it off in a class of solutions, and then using an identification procedure to update a few parameters to get the program that really is adapted to the situation at hand. Human learning seems to involve an analogous adaptive scheme, after finding the appropriate "mental structure" within which the adjustment is to take place. For instance, in driving a car, the words we hear in early instruction resemble the sort of program that Samuel could put into a computer to play checkers. (In other situations there is no such ready-made scheme with parameters to be lined up, and that's where we begin to talk about creativity.) Having got that "program," you don't drive very well—there are many parameters to adjust, for it is not enough to turn to the left when you see an object coming from the right, unless one has adjusted one's steering so that the actual angle of incidence determines the appropriate angle of escape.

With this as background, we see that much of the brain's interactions with the world are of a kind which may well be described as an identification process. To see some of the subtleties of such a process, let us consider the following example.

Suppose you wish to lift a cube 6 inches above the table on which it is lying. If it looks like a hollow steel cube (Figure 19), you may expect it to be sufficiently light for you to lift it with one hand. However, if the bottom half of the cube—obscured from your view by the nearer edges—is filled with lead, the cube will be too heavy, and you will be unable to lift it with one hand. This failure will cause you to increase your estimate of the weight drastically, and you may then change strategy, using two

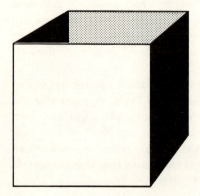

FIGURE 19   A hollow steel cube?

hands to lift the cube successfully. Alternatively, despite its deceptive texture, the cube might be made with a wire frame across which are stretched thin sheets of aluminum—and now, the force you applied will be far too great and the cube will be jerked up further than you intended, so that you will have to then lower it somewhat to reach the intended height of 6 inches. Thus, in addition to various feedback mechanisms (Section 5.2) which can smoothly compensate for small misjudgments, it is necessary to have higher level mechanisms to "get into the right ballpark" if we are to interact successfully with objects in our environment. The slide-box metaphor which we shall introduce in Section 4.1 gives us some idea of how this may be done (see also the discussion of Section 5.5). The box-lifting example of Figure 19 serves to bring a number of important points to our attention:

1. The object has to be recognized as a box and, out of the many possible interactions with a box, a decision made to lift it.
2. The organism has to decide what effector behavior will provide the right "input" to the box to move it as intended.
3. The brain must compute the appropriate signals which must play upon the spinal cord if the motoneurons are to elicit the pattern of muscle fiber contractions which will yield the appropriate movement of the effectors.

This threefold decomposition must be handled with some delicacy, as we shall try to now indicate by the following observations:

(i) The three stages may be commingled. As we shall see in Section 7.2, the brain of the frog seems to be so "wired up" that stages (a) and (b) are not necessary: it does not appear that the frog recognizes a fly, decides to snap at it, then decides on an appropriate tongue trajectory and finally computes neural commands to effect it; but rather, at least as far as we can currently tell, the frog has no way of recognizing a fly (or "wiggle") other than by executing an appropriate orienting or snapping action. [Two caveats are in order: (a) Forebrain mechanisms can modify the frog's behavior —it will *not* repeatedly snap at bumblebees; and (b) we would concede that a paralyzed frog could be said to recognize a fly in that it still reaches a neural state appropriate to snapping. In general, our thesis is that perception of an object (at least at the preverbal level) involves gaining access to routines for interaction with it, but does *not* necessarily involve execution of even one of these subroutines. We shall take this point up at some length in Section 6.1.]

(ii) Note that even when a human does consciously decide what an object is and what she is to do with it, an *explicit* estimation (e.g., one that is verbally reportable) of a parameter such as weight may not occur; it is enough that the recognition and decision so bias the pathways from receptors to effectors that the action of the effectors be appropriate to the parameters that actually pertain. We can stress this point by asking what would happen if we gave Samuel the sixteen numbers $w_1, \ldots, w_{16}$ used by his computer. Samuel, we presume, would not play a better game with this information. People normally deduce that this implies that the numbers have nothing to do with the way Samuel plays, arguing that the computer uses numerical evaluations, searching of trees, adapting of weights, and that humans don't play in that way, which is why the numbers do not help Samuel. However, let's consider an unusual argument, which, even though I *don't* think it's true in this particular case, gives us a bit more insight as to what we are up against in modeling the brain. Think of your brain as a network which, when you are shown a board position, does not go through instruction by instruction looking at one move, then go instruction by instruction looking at an alternative move, and so on, to eventually come upon the solution; but rather computes in parallel, "zapping" the whole pattern into the neural circuitry where patterns "ripple" and interact and "ripple" and interact, until the result emerges without going through any central executive. Now suppose (I stress that this is to make a philosophical point—I am sure no such simple correspondence exists in the brain) that the 16 adjustable weights in Samuel's program corresponded to the weights of 16 adjustable synapses in Samuel's brain! Then, even if Samuel were told the optimal weights of these synapses, he could not use his explicit knowledge of their values to adjust them, and so he still might have no better way of adjusting them than continually playing checkers. (Irrespective of its value as a debating point, the discussion reminds us that today's man-made computers are usually highly serial, whereas the brain functions in a highly parallel fashion.)

(iii) However, humans can sometimes use "higher-level processing" to inhibit activity while a strange object to be lifted is analyzed consciously as "well, it looks like two chairs stuck together and that weighs about the same as a table" and then releasing upon the output circuitry a moderate simulacrum of the neural firing patterns that might be elicited by viewing an appropriately located table that one wished to pick up. This ability to employ linguistic "decomposition" or "analogy construction" to obtain the measure of a system without having to perform physical experiments upon it is a most important human attribute. This ability has important precursors in nonhuman animals, and these—we argue—provide the basis for language.

(iv) The "action-oriented" viewpoint is very important here. If one has decided to lift a chair, then details of its construction or surface texture are unimportant, but its weight is a crucial parameter, whereas if we have to paint the chair, essentially the opposite is true. We tend to attend to those features of an object most relevant to our current or anticipated interactions with it. In fact, we often do not recognize an object per se, but rather simply note that it has certain features—so that in stage (1) above we may not recognize the box as such, but only decide that it must be lifted, for example to place a tablecloth underneath it.

In summary, then, a system needs a broad "data base" or "internal model of the world" if it is to successfully interact with a complex environment, but the utility of a relatively simple model of the world can be improved immensely if the system can adjust parameters in it to adapt to new or changing circumstances.

4 | Artificial Intelligence and Robotics

Artificial intelligence (AI) may be defined as the area concerned with programing computers to behave in a way that one would call intelligent—if one did not know that a computer could do it! Unfortunately, once one has explained how a machine can be programed to perform some process, it is hard for a human to regard the process as requiring intelligence. Perhaps the structure of that last phrase—"as requiring intelligence"—reveals the problem: we tend to think of intelligence as a single "thing," possession of which by a human allows her to behave in subtle and adaptive ways. But may it not rather be the case that there is no single "thing", but rather a plexus of properties which, taken one at a time, may be little cause for admiration, but any sizable portion of which will yield behavior that we would label as intelligent?

Turing [1950] noted that we would certainly regard a machine as intelligent if it could pass a test of which we present the following variant: An experimenter sits in a room with two teletypes by which she conducts a "conversation" with two systems, which she knows only as A and B. One is a human, the other is a machine. If the experimenter —after asking many questions—is likely to have much doubt about which is human and which is machine, we would concede intelligence to the machine. But—unless one dogmatically insists that being intelligent entails behaving in a human way—it should be realized that it is "harder" for a machine to pass Turing's test than to be intelligent. For instance, whereas any computer can answer problems in arithmetic quickly and correctly, a much more complex program would be required to ensure that it answered as slowly and erratically as a human. Again if asked to describe its naked body, it would be simpler to print out a copy of its blueprint than to simulate the embarrassed and evasive reply of a shy human! In other words, to be intelligent, a system must share many functional abilities with a human problem-solver, but it seems unreasonable to demand ability to pass as human. Of course, Turing realized this; his aim was not to find a necessary set of conditions to ensure intelligence, but rather to devise a test which, if passed by a machine, would convince even the most hardened skeptic that the machine had intelligence so that he could use a discussion of this test to focus a discussion of machine intelligence. (However, if a machine did pass the test, a real doubter might never be convinced that one of the teletypes was operated by a machine.)

In Section 4.1, then, we shall look at a few properties which may contribute to intelligence, and relate them to the idea of an internal model of the environment. In Sections 4.2 and 4.3 we shall discuss two lines of work, heuristic search and scene analysis, so that we may see, in Section 4.4, how they come together to form the "artificial intelligence" of a robot.

4.1 INTERNAL MODELS AND INTELLIGENCE

We have already argued, in Section 2.1, that perception is (in a suitably subtle sense) action-oriented. In this section we further suggest that—for complex systems in changing environments—perception is in fact inseparable from memory. Perception can then be seen as the construction of a partially predictive internal (short-term) model, using long-term memory to incorporate past experience. To be intelligent is then to perceive elements of a situation beyond "raw sensation."

If I come into a room and my eyes receive light reflected from a surface (which happens to be the top of a table), I perceive that were I to strike my fist down toward it, the fist would not go through, that a certain thumping sound would be emitted, and that I would feel a measure of pain. However, if we consider building a perceiving robot, we suddenly discover that such perception is not as simple as might first appear. Just by monitoring the reflection of light from a surface, the robot is to predict whether or not the surface will support weight, something about its texture, what its relative position is with respect to the effectors of the robot, and to predict other ways in which the system would react on making contact with the surface.

We might build in a range finder to enable our machine to *locate* (find the *where* of) a surface, but it must also "know" what different interactions with it are appropriate. A human can look at a white surface and know that it is of a plate of ice cream and that an appropriate action is to pick up a spoon and delve into it; or look at a white surface in a different context to know that it is a writing pad, and that an appropriate action is to lift up one corner with the thumb while pressing down on a nearby portion of the paper with the forefinger, then pulling up with the thumb and pressing in with the forefinger to grasp the corner of the paper, finally pulling upward and so tearing the paper off. The very tedium of this last example—and such examples can be multiplied *ad nauseam*—suggests that a machine exhibiting anything like the complexities of human behavior would require a huge "library" of "programs" concerning what to do in different situations.

However, there is more complexity here than mere number of situations, for even a fairly detailed sequence of actions such as presented above has to be effected (in animals, at least) via the patterned contractions of millions of individual muscle fibers in the muscles controlling the shoulder, elbow, wrist, fingers, and so on. We shall suggest, in Section 5.5, that the nervous system has in some sense evolved hierarchically in a way that makes complex movements and interactions more tractable for the organism. Grasping with thumb and forefinger, or moving the arm in a certain direction, would seem to be used in many different combinations without the actual implementation of these basic movements in terms of muscle fiber activity having to be learned separately for each combination (though study of the cerebellum suggests that much fine tuning of combinations of movements may still remain to be learned separately for each combination, albeit at a subconscious level). We shall discuss another hierarchy of control when we look at the integrated design of a robot in Section 4.4.

Irrespective of these fine details of implementation, it is clear that as a human interacts with her world, she builds up a broad knowledge of such aspects as the use of language, the meaning of various facial expressions, the purpose of tools and buildings which are not "built in" genetically (though—as we shall see in Section 8.1—the *means* to their understanding may be). We might say that she generates *a model of the world*, which allows her to take partial information from her world—such as receiving light reflected from a table top—to predict (with varying accuracy, (Figure 1) for there is no claim of infallibility here) the result of interacting with the current environment in various ways, such as predicting other sensory information she could obtain from the current source of stimulation, for example, the texture of the table top were she to touch it. Obviously, for such a "model" to be of any use the universe must be highly "redundant". It would be useless to "know" that seen tables were hard to the touch if this were only occasionally (and unpredictably) so.

We further suggest that internal activity—save perhaps at such abstract levels as involved in human linguistic activity—must be continually referred to what we shall call the ACTION FRAME, namely, the frame of reference induced by the posture and activity of the system, the former serving to stabilize the frame offered by the latter for the system's active exploration of its environment by means of its receptors. The repertoire of possible actions of a system, and of possible questions it may have to "answer", helps to determine the most appropriate internal representation of information. We shall survey our current (primitive) ideas about these representations in Chapter 6.

This is consonant with the point established in Section 2.1 that perception involves not so much "What" as "How to relate" and "Where". Distinguishing spatial from other relationships is not an arbitrary decomposition of the perceptual process—in fact the "What to do" of perception and the "Where" of perception seem to be basically different functions mediated by different regions of the brain, as we shall see in Section 6.3, although they are integrated in the (short-term) model.

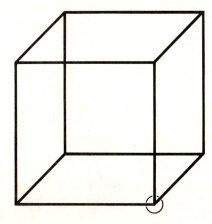

FIGURE 1 The Necker cube: is the circled vertex near us or far from us? Stare for a while.

Since learning which are the salient features in the environment is so crucial to the acquisition of skills, one may suggest that in some learning situations, what we learn is not what a sensory input pattern is, but rather what is the appropriate question to ask about it or, in other words, the most appropriate feature, or, stimulus, to attend to. For example, a rat in a maze is not simply pairing a response with a stimulus—it is executing complex muscular activity while being bombarded with a mass of sensory input. A rat might perfectly well remember how it got to the food on a certain trial and still fail at the next, because it does not know whether it was a subtle smell, the texture of the floor, a direction, a patterning of its muscular activity, or a mark on the door that was significant. Thus, even with "perfect" recall on what happened at each trial, it might take many, many trials until the rat learned to disregard irrelevant stimuli and consistently use the type of cue used by the experimenter to locate the reward. An animal's behavior in a learning experiment shows periods of little progress followed by a sudden jump in performance, as if the animal had hit on a new strategy or learned to pay attention to some relevant feature of the experimental situation. One may, then, imagine learning progressing by a cumulative procedure in which the learner saves time by learning to apply the current strategy to fewer of the irrelevant features, to construct new features within the current strategy, and to change strategy. Anything which could tell the rat which aspect of its stimulation mattered would lead to almost instant learning—by directing attention, rather than conveying a specific message as to the location of food. Perhaps such "focusing of attention" is responsible for the "one-shot learning" some researchers have claimed to obtain by injecting brain extracts from trained animals into untrained animals. Less fancifully, much of the most basic usefulness of language resides in its ability to direct (or misdirect!) the attention of the listener.

Clearly, to the extent that a system can stimulate the environment and get the desired response (e.g., the stimulus might be closing your teeth about a region of space where you had sensed a reddish-green object, and the response might be the insertion of a piece of apple in your mouth) it has "modeled" some aspect of its environment (in this case, the fact that an apple is appropriately positioned). Such a model may be layed down genetically in the brain of an organism, or programed in by the designer of a robot. We are stressing that, in *addition,* systems interacting with complex environments will need to modify this "model" to accommodate aspects of the environment that were not initially provided for, perhaps because they have changed relatively recently. For this reason, we shall find it worthwhile to distinguish two main types of model. The first encompasses relations of the organism with its immediate environment —we speak of a "short-term memory" or "short-term model" (STM), and—in the case of the reader—it might encompass your knowledge of the fact that you are in the early part of this book, knowledge of the details of the room behind you, and awareness of your commitment to meet someone at a designated time and place in the next 24 hours. This may be contrasted with your "long-term memory" or "long-term model" (LTM), which corresponds to standing properties of your world such as your ability to recognize an apple or ride a bicycle or recall the details of your sixth birthday party.

Incidentally, it is important to distinguish the learning of *skills,* which is what our discussion of long-term memory here has really emphasized, from the memorizing of *events.* A skill may result from evolutionary shaping—or may result from much experience in "tuning" sensorimotor coordination as in driving a car. We stress that in acquiring a skill the memory of events plays at most a subsidiary role, as in Samuel's Checker Player (Section 3.4) where memory of events (access to a library of master games) played a role subsidiary to the adjustment of the key parameters, whose values reflected the cumulative effect of play rather than bearing the marks of any single move.

The value of a short-term memory—which, it must be stressed, we do not conceptualize as a "tape-recording" of recent input—is as a synthesis (using long-term memory heavily to "fill-in details") of the whole spatiotemporal frame in which it moves. Thus the system (human, animal, or robot) is not tied to immediate sensory cues in establishing its course of action but can make a decision such as that suggested by the following human verbalization: "I've got to be at work in 15 minutes (short-term memory). That bus is too crowded (immediate input as processed with the aid of long-term memory to recognize people, etc.). I can't stand standing in a crowd (long-term memory). I'd better walk (looks at watch). Oh, if I run I can make the trolley (runs, catches trolley, rides to work)." The reader can easily supply more parenthetical elaboration to this excerpt. The point is that our commuter was using her model of the world to plan ahead; for example, implicit in the above excerpt was her realization that she was more likely to get to work on time if she rode the trolley than if she walked.

We must not be too literal in our interpretation of the word "model." None of us would be so naive as to imagine that if we were to peer through the layers of cerebral cortex of the young child, we would see a global replica of the world, which under great magnification would reveal cardboard replicas of her family and friends. Rather, we should simply imagine a neural network so changed as a result of experience, that if the pattern of spike trains entering it can in some sense encode a question about the world, then the pattern of spike trains leaving it can represent an answer about the world, without any actual inspection of the real world at that time being necessary to gain that answer. As time goes by, then, the computer in our head is so adjusted that our actions are better adapted to a whole range of properties of the world, in addition to those that confront our senses at the very moment. The word "model" in the phrase "internal model of the world" is thus to be used in this rather abstract sense, rather than some more pictorial sense. We have then distinguished LTM as *the* internal model of the world—the collection of properties which reflect past experience in a way which will help us compute our present behavior and improve the model itself—from STM as *an* internal model that represents our current "ambience." We do not perceive what we sense in front of our eyes. If we are in a room, we perceive our presence in that room with what is in it so that we may, for example, reach for an object previously seen behind us, without searching for it anew. Our perception does not involve independently processing a succession of "snapshots" of the room, but rather involves an initial comprehension of the room and the more salient of its contents, after which we need merely note discrepancies between our model and what we need to know of what is out there to "fill in gaps" and update this momentary model—as when we reach for that object behind us only to find that someone has moved it. We repeat that this modeling and updating is all encoded in terms of the properties and activities of neurons and has little resemblance to a photographic record.

As a further justification for our separating spatial from other relationships with other objects, we should add that it must not be thought that we have a different model for every different object of every different size or position in space. Rather the models must be flexible, in a way which may be suggested by what I call *the slide-box metaphor:* Drawing each frame of a movie cartoon individually is too inefficient. Instead, use is made of the observation that, since the cartoon might run one whole minute without the background changing, it makes sense to draw it just once. In the middle ground, there might be a tree about which nothing changes during a certain period of time except its position relative to the background. It could thus be drawn on a separate slide from the background and could then be displaced for succeeding frames. Finally, in the foreground, it may well be that one could draw most portions of the actors for repeated use, and then position the arms, facial expressions, and so on, individually for each frame. The slides can then be photographed appropriately positioned in a slide-box for each frame, with only a few parameter changes and minimal redrawing required between each frame.

A similar strategy for obtaining a very economical description of what happens over a long period of time might be used in the brain, with a long-term memory (LTM) corresponding to a "slide file" and short-term memory (STM) corresponding to a "slide-box". The act of perception might then be compared to using sensory information to reposition slides already in the slide-box and to retrieve appropriate slides from the file to replace or augment those already in the slide-box, experimenting to decide whether a newly retrieved slide fits sensory input "better" than one currently in the slide-box. Also, part of the action of the organism in changing its relationship with the environment might be viewed as designed to obtain input which will help update the STM, by deciding between "competing" slides, as well as helping update the LTM, by "redrawing" or "editing" the slides and adding "new slides."

Presumably, both evolution and development contribute to the criteria of when one slide is "better" than another. One might have a slide for "humming-bird" positioned to represent a distance of 30 feet and then the slide "insect" is popped up from LTM and when positioned to represent a distance of 10 feet fits other sensory input better and so replaces the original slide. In a case such as the Necker cube of Figure 1, two equally good "slides"—cube pointing in, and cube pointing out—are available, and these alternate since there is no contextual cue to "lock in" either one.

"Slide" is, of course, a bad name; the "slide-box" is not a box into which static slides are inserted, rather it is a mass of neural tissue lying athwart the channels which link the sensory and motor systems. "Putting in a slide" corresponds to activating this network, thus initiating transient wave forms which change autonomously. Lying athwart the lines of communication, the "slide-box" fills the whole "postural-effector frame of reference". Thus a slide does not contain information from any single modality; rather we may use cues from one or more senses, or from feedback from motor activity, to "address" the activation of a wealth of multimodal action-oriented information. Our discussion in Section 6.2 will attempt to explore the benefits of the slide-box metaphor without using terms such as "slide," which may force too rigid a view of neural activity, but will continue to emphasize that fine perceptual acts take place against a background; that we cannot recognize small details in a void; and that present "slides" strongly color the choice of each addition. In short, we always act within some context.

In our discussion of adaptive systems in Section 3.4, we saw that an identification procedure gave a controller greatly increased ability to interact with its environment, so long as the environment could be treated as having certain properties (such as treating the evaluation surface as flat in the Checker Player), that is, if the controller's "internal model" was "in the right ballpark" to start with. Let us build on this observation to note with Gregory [1969] that a system using an "internal model" to exploit the temporal and spatial redundancies of its environment will have the following advantages:

+*1.* Since objects are redundant when viewed within a limited framework of interaction, they may be identified by a few key features relative to that interaction and so a search strategy for such features can save time in determining interactions with objects. In fact, only a few of these features will be needed to recognize a particular object in any particular situation. Since different sensory modalities can be used to cue the same repertoire of actions, distortions and omissions will tend to be "harmless" so long as they do not destroy a "quorum" of basic features.

+*2.* A model is predictive in that observed features may correlate with yet to be observed features, and in particular it can continue to function in the temporary absence of input, as when sneezing while driving a car, or walking through a dark but familiar room.

+*3.* Provided a particular situation is similar to the situations for which a "model" was developed, behavior will generally be appropriate. Psychologists call this effect "positive transfer of training."

However, such systems also have disadvantages:

−*1.* When the current situation is similar to the situations for which a "model" was developed, but in fact differs in crucial respects, then the system will be misled by its model—we have "negative transfer," as when we drop the unusually dense cube because it looked lighter than it was and so we did not flex our muscles sufficiently in preparing to lift it (Figure 19 of Chapter 3).

−*2.* Internal models are essentially conservative, reflecting the past rather than the present, and can yield serious misjudgments in times of rapid environmental change.

The first disadvantage reminds us that any system which cannot afford space or time to carry out a completely exhaustive computation on its input—whether or not it employs internal models—can be fooled. A system to be successful, then, must either narrow its environmental range to reduce the risk of atypical situations, or must use feedback to determine when new features must be incorporated into the model (to meet −1), such as using texture cues to recognize the high-density material of the preceding example, or to determine that the model is no longer useful and so must be drastically revised (to meet −2). It is sad but true that if one spends too much time updating the model, one has no time to benefit from it, but if one spends too little time updating the model, one may use it long after one has exhausted its benefits.

On the basis of all this discussion of internal models, we can suggest that among the properties that contribute importantly to intelligence are the following:

Possession of a modifiable model of the world, with its attendant adaptability. A system to act intelligently must not only be able to take properties of its environment into account, but must be able to update its record of these properties to take account of new observations and changing relationships.

Flexibility and generality. An intelligent system must not only use past experience to act adaptively, but must also be able to apply its past experience to situations which are not superficially similar to those encountered before. Again, techniques which have been developed to solve one type of problem should be recognized as applicable even when a very different domain of problems is involved.

Planning. An intelligent system should use its model to plan and evaluate alternative courses of action before committing itself to one of them. For a symbol-manipulation system there may be little real distinction between planning and action, but for a robot or an animal the distinction is very real and very important—it pays to recognize a precipice in advance and plan to avoid it rather than recognizing one's mistake after going over.

The history of mathematics is studded with tales of "idiot savants"—people with a wondrous skill at mental arithmetic who, usually, were in all other ways of below average intelligence. A computer carrying out millions of operations per second is in a similar category if its programs are only set up to do simple arithmetic, as in handling a payroll. But we saw in Chapter 3 that a computer was not limited to endless repetition of low-level arithmetic, as demonstrated so dramatically by Samuel's Checker-Player, a computer so programed that its behavior depended on a number of parameters which the machine would "update with experience". Thus a program can, in some interesting sense, learn. But if checker playing seems more intellectual than mental arithmetic, it is still but a single skill and we ask to what extent one can write a program which can solve problems in many different situations. We shall study a technique—called heuristic search—which finds general applicability in such programs in Section 4.2, but this is only a partial answer. The crucial point in our quest seems to be the realization that we are learning more and more of many ingredients to understand more and more about human or artificial intelligence, rather than seeking the one magic ingredient without which intelligence cannot be claimed.

4.2 PLANNING AND HEURISTIC SEARCH

Whether we are trying to find a sequence of moves which will enable us to win a game of chess, or to find the deductive steps which will take us from the axioms to a theorem in Euclidean geometry, or to decide on the shortest route from the office to a dinner party, we may think of ourselves as operating in some vast state space. We have the set of all boards in a game of chess, the set of lists-of-already-proven-theorems in Euclidean geometry, the set of all blocks-of-streets-within-a-certain-area-of-town-and-suburb in the navigation problem. Further, we have a collection of operators which can take us from one state to another—by making a move in chess, applying a rule of inference in geometry, or turning or going straight ahead at an intersection in the navigation problem. In each case we start in some initial state and solve our problem just in case we can find a sequence of operations which will get us to an acceptable final state; moreover we will often want the sequence to be in some sense optimal, as in the navigation problem where we wish to get to the party comparatively quickly.

In the case of theorem proving, planning and action are indistinguishable. But in playing chess we must plan ahead several moves—we cannot retract an actual move when our opponent makes a devastating and unexpected reply; and there is no point in driving part way along several alternate routes to compare distances if our task is to get to the party quickly. (This last example reminds us of a trade-off which a learning system has to make: Sometimes it must explore to gather information which may prove useful later even though the "route" is by no means optimal.) Thus an intelligent system not only moves in state-space defined by (or defining) the current problems it has to solve, but also must be able to make a model which represents portions of that state-space and therein explore alternate courses of action before one is actually chosen.

To make the situation somewhat more concrete, let us suppose that a driver has at her disposal a model in the form of the map shown in Figure 2 and that—to simplify our example—distance on the map is actually proportional to the length of the corresponding portion of the road.

Now: What is the shortest path from "the office" to "party" in Figure 2? The reader is invited to find it, and then try to make explicit how she did it. It may well be that she made geometric use of being able to see the whole map, but let us now see how it might be done on a block-by-block basis.

Before we list a number of algorithms to help us *during our planning phase* find a satisfactory route through the graph which models the state-space and operations upon it, we should make a number of general observations:

1. In many cases we cannot expect to have so complete a map available to us which shows us for each left or right turn where we shall go next "all at one glance". Rather—as in the case of playing chess—we have the wherewithal to generate, from the representation of a state, the representation of the state to which any move would take us. In fact in most real-world situations the number of states would exceed the storage capacity of even the vastest computer, and so we can only have explicit storage of states which are either potentially relevant in the current problem or which seemed so significant in solving other problems that they seemed worth storing for later reference. The latter case would play a role in learning—Samuel's Checker-Player consults a library of master player's games—but will not concern us here.

2. A corollary to the comment on size of the state-space is that we can virtually never afford an exhaustive search but must somehow, and this is the whole art we will discuss, restrict our search to plausible alternatives. However, this restriction to plausible alternatives must usually rest on imperfect information. If the party is being held at the Town Hall in our example of Figure 2, it may be reasonable to expect every intersection to be posted with a sign telling us which way to turn for the City Center so that no searching of alternatives in our planning phase is required. But if the party is at a friend's house in the suburbs, then about all the information we may have available at an intersection is a vague "that street seems to lead in the right direction".

3. Playing a game like chess introduces complications that we shall not consider in our concentration on the navigation problem. In chess one is trying not only to choose a move which will yield an advantageous situation directly, but one also tries to minimize the havoc a clever opponent can wreak with his reply.

4. We may be able to make use of special knowledge to "lump" the state graph and thus reduce the number of alternatives we must consider. For example, if we know that the quickest way to the suburb in which the party is being held is via a

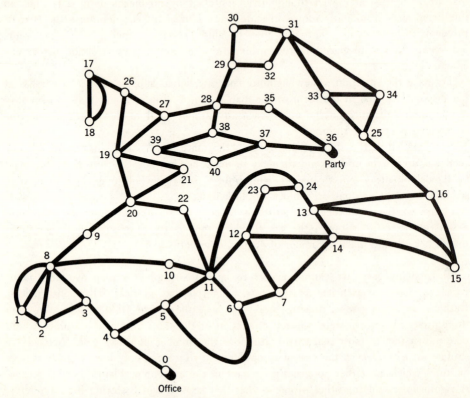

FIGURE 2 A map, distance on which is proportional to length of the corresponding portion of the road. The problem—elaborated upon in the next few figures—is to determine the shortest path from the office (node 0) to the party (node 36).

certain stretch of freeway, then we may delete from the graph all nodes corresponding to exits from the freeway other than the entrance and exit point we intend to use, and only retain in our map nodes corresponding to intersections in the actual suburb for which we are heading.

5. A useful technique in looking for an optimal path is "bidirectional search". Some readers will have found the optimal path in Figure 2 by "growing" paths both forward from the office and backward from the party. Others will recall the virtue of working backward as well as forward in solving exam problems in mathematics where the form of the answer sometimes provides valuable clues to aid in solving the problem. The methods we discuss here are only for "unidirectional searches" moving out from the initial state, but their bidirectional refinements do exist.

Let us now discuss various techniques which help us avoid considering all possible paths within the model during a planning phase. We can represent the set of alternative paths through the graph of Figure 2, by a tree whose root is the initial node 0

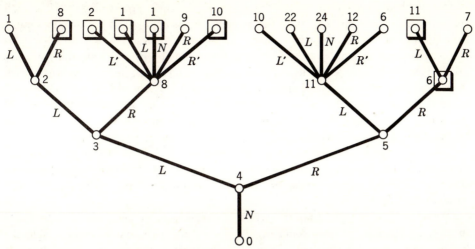

FIGURE 3 The first five layers of the "decision tree" for Figure 2. From each node we grow "branches" to the nodes which can be reached from that node in one "block" using the roads represented in Figure 2. We "prune" the tree by placing a square around a node as soon as we find a shorter path to a node with the same label. For example, we see two paths to node 8—that via nodes 4 and 3 and the longer one, whose corresponding node in the tree thus has a square about it, via nodes 4, 3, and 2. Note that we refer here to path length on the original map (Figure 2), not to the total branch length of the decision tree, as may be seen by studying the fate of node 6.

and from each node of which there issues a branch for every exit, other than the one used to enter, from the corresponding node of the graph. We depict the first few layers of the tree corresponding to Figure 2 in Figure 3. In the following discussion the reader is urged to repeatedly refer back to Figure 2 to see that she agrees with the distance estimates that we use to choose and delete vertices for our decision tree. They may not always be right, so this is a real test of comprehension.

Even with only five layers, it is already apparent that we can begin to "prune" the tree. For example, the tree has three vertices corresponding to node 1 in the graph and it is clear that if the shortest route to the party lies through node 1, then the segment from the office to node 1 in that route must itself be the shortest segment from the office to node 1. Thus we need not grow the tree from any vertex corresponding to node 1 for which there exists another vertex representing node 1 as reached by a shorter route. Thus in Figure 3 we may "prune off" the 1-vertices corresponding to the paths NLRL and NLRN, for they are both longer than the path NLLL to a 1-vertex. Similarly we would "prune off" the 6-vertex corresponding to the path NRR and in fact all the nodes marked with a square.

A point particularly worth noting is that the path to 6 that we eliminated was the first—rather than the second—path we encountered. This is because, as is clear from Figure 2, the two-intersection path via nodes 4 and 5 is longer than the path through 4, 5, and 11, even though the latter is looked at later in the planning phase because it has an extra intersection. In such cases we have to throw away the branches from the old node and study paths built up from the shorter path we have just found, for the shortest path anywhere via node 6 certainly cannot start with an inefficient initial segment from 0 to 6.

This method—known to control theorists as dynamic programing ("If a path from a to c via b is optimal, then the segments from a to b and from b to c must both be optimal")—certainly cuts down the number of branches we must grow in the decision tree, and must eventually yield the optimal path, for essentially we are exhaustively searching *all* paths, save those whose inefficient initial segments mark them as unqualified for the shortest path to *anywhere*. But the word "anywhere" is the key to why this type of search seems much more time consuming than the one the reader used to find the optimal path in Figure 2: the method makes no use of the specification of the intended goal.

To see how we might make use of our knowledge of the goal recall the discussion of perfect versus imperfect information in (2) above. With perfect information we saw that the decision tree "collapses" to a representation of the optimal path itself, without spurious branching.

One form of perfect information—which, we repeat, would generally be unavailable to us in our planning stage—would simply give us, for each node x of the graph, the length $h(x)$ of the shortest path from x to our goal. Then at any intersection we could always immediately determine which was the next intersection to go to, just as if we were following signposts to the Town Hall.

This observation suggests the approach used by Doran and Michie [1966] in a scheme they called the *graph traverser*: they used instead of *actual* distance $h(x)$ something they called the *heuristic*† distance $\hat{h}(x)$. Here $\hat{h}(x)$ would be some plausible measure of the actual distance which can be determined without actually chasing through the graph. For example, the obvious choice of $\hat{h}(x)$ in our navigation problem is "distance as the crow flies" in distinction from $h(x)$ which is "distance by road". Just as it is a plausible strategy when driving to take the fork of the road which seems to lead in the right direction, so Doran and Michie suggested that one could use heuristic information to "prune" the decision tree—in addition to the dynamic programing technique—by only growing at each stage the node which has minimal heuristic distance from the goal of any node adjacent to a node which is already in the tree. The reader is invited to check that this method, applied to Figure 2, yields the decision tree of Figure 4, where we have placed in brackets after each vertex the stage at which it was generated. It will help to have a pair of dividers handy to check the various values of $\hat{h}(x)$. The comments are to be read in the numbered order as encountered in "growing" the tree.

EXERCISES. 1 Double the length of the direct path from 11 to 24 and then recompute the decision tree.

2 Instead of "aerial distance" $\hat{h}(x)$ use "angular deviation" $\hat{h}_1(x)$; that is, always take the fork that is pointing as much as possible toward the goal. What decision tree does this yield?

We see that with the graph traverser method we find a path to the goal in only 26 steps, even though the height of the decision tree is 15—less than two branches on the average per level, in striking contrast to the 14 branches we encountered on the fourth level of the tree of Figure 3. Thus with a workable choice of heuristic

---

† "Heuristic" comes from the Greek "Eureka!" and can be defined as "aiding in discovery."

distance such as that used in our example, the number of paths to be searched can be reduced to manageable proportions. As the reader should already have noticed, the path we obtained was not optimal, and so the question immediately arises: Is there some way of making use of heuristic information to prune the decision tree drastically which will nonetheless yield the optimal path?

The answer is YES and was supplied by Hart, Nilsson, and Raphael [1968]. Their approach may be appreciated by looking at Figure 5 where, still using the "crow-flight" heuristic, we note that whereas the graph traverser would develop node 2 rather than node 1, there is a case to be made for developing node 1 because although it is further from the goal, it is much closer to the start.

We saw that Doran and Michie obtained their algorithm by trying to approximate the case in which we had perfect information, as given by the shortest distance $h(x)$ from any node x to the goal. Our new algorithm is obtained by using a different form of perfect information, namely $f(x)$, which is the shortest distance from the start to the goal along any path *which passes through* x. Clearly f does provide perfect information—having reached any node we always go to the adjacent node for which the value of f is smallest.

By the dynamic programing principle, we may write

$$f(x) = g(x) + h(x)$$

where $g(x)$ is the length of the shortest path from the start to x, while $h(x)$, as before, is the length of the shortest path from x to the goal.

As before we may approximate $h(x)$ by some heuristic distance $\hat{h}(x)$, but how shall we approximate $g(x)$? The method we shall adopt is that at any time t of our planning phase we shall approximate $g(x)$ by $g_t(x)$, which is the length of the shortest path to x from the start that we have encountered by time t. We then approximate $f(x)$ at time t by

$$f_t(x) = g_t(x) + \hat{h}(x)$$

Thus Hart, Nilsson, and Duda suggested that one could now use heuristic information to "prune" the decision tree (in addition to the dynamic programing technique) by growing at each stage only the node x which can at that stage be estimated to be on the path of "minimal heuristic length" $f_t(x)$ among all nodes adjacent to a node which is already in this tree. Moreover, they were able to prove that if $\hat{h}(x)$ never exceeded $h(x)$—as in our example, where aerial distance to the goal can never exceed the distance by road—this algorithm always yields the optimal path. The proof exceeds the mathematical level set for this book, but the reader may increase her confidence in the method by checking that our application, in Figure 6, of this technique to the graph of Figure 2 does indeed yield the shortest route from the office to the party. Interestingly, this search requires only 23 stages to yield the optimal path, whereas in Figure 4 we went through 26 stages to find the suboptimal path. This would seem to be the payoff for our extra work in keeping track of $g_t(x)$ for each node x we develop.

Incidentally the reader should note that the requirement $h(x) \geqslant \hat{h}(x)$ embraces both the case of no information [$\hat{h}(x) = 0$; the method then reduces to the almost exhaustive search of Figure 3] and that of perfect information [$\hat{h}(x) = h(x)$; the method then yields direct progress, without branching, from start to goal].

It is hoped that this detailed discussion of *heuristic search* as applied to the naviga-

First three stages of growing the tree

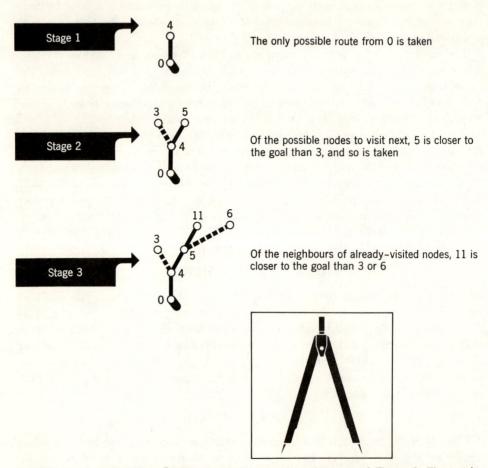

Stage 1 — The only possible route from 0 is taken

Stage 2 — Of the possible nodes to visit next, 5 is closer to the goal than 3, and so is taken

Stage 3 — Of the neighbours of already–visited nodes, 11 is closer to the goal than 3 or 6

FIGURE 4   Using the Doran-Michie heuristic to explore the map of Figure 2. The reader is invited to check to see whether we have made any mistakes; it will be useful to have a pair of dividers (provided in the insert!) to check the measurements from Figure 2. On the left-hand side we have shown the first three stages of our exploration. At each stage, the dashed lines indicate possible paths that have yet to be explored from nodes that were previously reached; while the new solid line takes us to the successor node which is closest "as the crow flies" to the goal.

tion problem has convinced the reader that many processes which to casual intro-spection seem like unitary manifestations of human consciousness—"Well, I gazed at Figure 2 and the two sort-of-lines from the start and the goal seemed to, well-you-know, join up and there was the shortest path"—can in fact be broken down into a succession of steps—"expand the node with the smallest $f_t(x)$"—which can be pro-gramed into a digital computer. As our five points preceding the example should have made abundantly clear, we do not claim that precisely such steps occur in the brain, and we are sure that other processes occur as well. As we have said before, in dis-tinguishing artificial intelligence from brain theory, our aim in this chapter is not to provide brain models, but rather to see how intelligent functions may be broken down

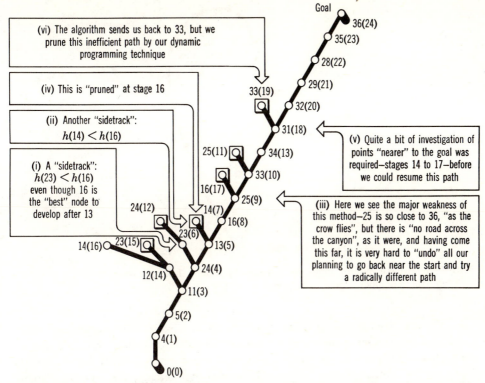

The right-hand side shows only the solid lines indicating the paths actually explored in the final search tree. *A(B)* on a node indicates that this path to node *A* of Figure 2 was opened up at stage *B* of our search. The reader should work through the 36 stages, checking the validity of the comments we have provided at stages 6, 7, 9, 7 (again—compare stage 16), 18, and 19. Why is the inclusion of stage 11 incorrect?

into elementary steps in the hope (which we do not claim has yet been realized) that this will provide clues to our understanding of how our neural activity may enable us to act intelligently.

Before closing this section, we should discuss an important program which provided one of the bases for the general study of heuristics we have just presented, the *general problem solver* (GPS) of Newell, Shaw, and Simon [1959]. Intriguingly, their general scheme has much in common with the Pitts and McCulloch scheme presented in Section 3.3, as we make clear by the comments enclosed in square brackets [. . .] below. GPS is a general framework for solving problems of the following kind:

1. We are given a set of objects. [This corresponds to the Pitts-McCulloch set of patterns.]

2. We are given a finite set of differences, and a means whereby we can determine which differences obtain between a pair of objects. [This corresponds to the Pitts-McCulloch error function *E*, but since the GPS set of differences is finite, it can only give rough indications as to "what is wrong".]

3. We are given a finite set of operators, and an operator-difference table, which tells us for each difference which operators are *likely* to reduce it. [This corresponds to the Pitts-McCulloch transform generator.]

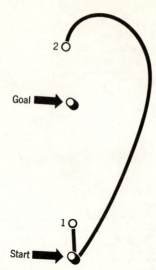

FIGURE 5   A case may be made for developing node 1, because even though it is further from the goal, it is much closer to the start.

4. We are given an initial object (say the list of axioms in a propositional logic) and a final object (say a statement we should like to prove to be a theorem) and we are to find a sequence of operators which will transform the initial object into the final object (if the operators correspond to rules of inference, then in our example, the desired chain of operators would provide the desired proof of the given statement).

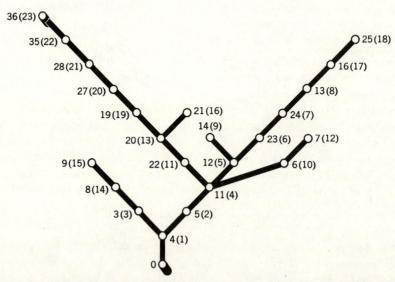

FIGURE 6   Using the Hart, Nilsson, and Raphael heuristic to explore the map of Figure 2. The method of growth is analogous to that spelled out in Figure 4, save that at each stage we develop not the node that is closest to the goal, but rather that for which the sum "distance traversed to get to the node from the start + distance 'as the crow flies' to the goal" is minimal.

The catch here is that since the difference only yields very partial information about what needs to be changed, there is no guarantee that applying a recommended operator will indeed transform the latest object into one that is genuinely closer to our goal. In fact, there is no guarantee that an operator is applicable to a given object, and one may have to find an initial transformation of the object before a "desirable" operator can be applied. Because of this one cannot proceed a step at a time as in the Pitts-McCulloch scheme. Rather, one must develop a "decision tree" in which we keep track of the application of various possible operators at various stages. The aim of the general supervisory part of the GPS program is to ensure that the most effort is put into "growing" those branches of the tree which seem to be leading toward the goal as in Figure 7.

For each node we could find the differences between it and the goal, and then determine which operators are suggested by the difference table. Some of them may not be applicable. At each stage we must decide which is the most promising node to next operate upon, and which of the possible operators we should apply.

Thus GPS involves a supervisory *control* with *memory* of various paths which may yet be found to lead to the goal; it is the design of this control program that really sets GPS off from the Pitts-McCulloch scheme.

The GPS approach was used by Miller, Galanter, and Pribram as the basis of their stored-program approach to psychology in their book *Plans and the Structure of Behavior*. They set forth the notion of a *plan* as "a hierarchical process that can control the order in which a sequence of operations is to be performed" and suggested that it provided the mechanism for converting comprehension into action hitherto

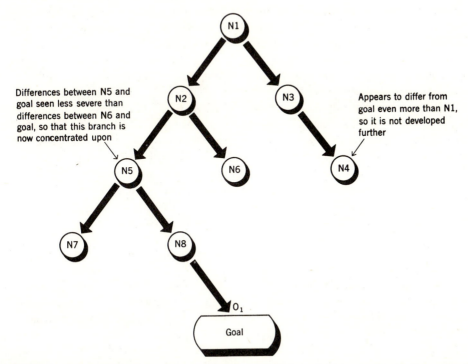

FIGURE 7   An example of the sort of "decision tree" that might be grown by the general supervisory part of a GPS program.

lacking in theories of cognition. They assume that an organism probably has access to many plans other than the one currently being executed.

The basic functional part of their theory is akin to a GPS operator-difference scheme or a scheme such as Figure 6 of Chapter 3. The TOTE unit (TOTE stands for Test, Operate, Test, Exit) shown in Figure 8 is a basic feedback process involving repeated testing and operating until congruity between a desired and an intended state of affairs is obtained.

They postulated that a plan is formed of a hierarchical collection of TOTE units. For instance, a nail-hammering plan could be characterized as shown in Figure 9 where the operate-box of our hammering TOTE is replaced by a combination of two other TOTE units. In this way is the hierarchical nature of plans revealed. Additional mechanisms are required to prevent endless loops when tests consistently fail (when you hit a knot) and to enable tasks to be interrupted (when you hit your finger). Note that in the hammering TOTE, the states in the feedback loops are all externally observable, whereas in more complicated hierarchies, many of the states are internal.

Where in the brain are plans executed? The authors cite physiological evidence which they took to indicate that a plan is selected or substituted for another by the frontal cortex (which we must think of as involved in tactics), and the limbic system initiates its execution. People with frontal lobotomies act as if their "now" is shortened. It's not that they don't care—they just don't seem to be able to plan ahead as well as "normals". There is also some lack of motivation, another symptom of living for the moment. One might regard the hypothalamus as similarly involved in selecting and in part handling the internal environment. Attention is directed to a considerable extent in terms of "goals" or "purposes"; so values—perhaps just "significance"— must be "given" at any time. They have been established by experience, hereditary or individual, and are related to survival. Outcomes of action, rated "good" or "bad" on such criteria, can reinforce or attenuate future acts, and so establish a hierarchy of choices embedded in the central nervous system. But this is all very speculative, and they have modified a number of these identifications in the intervening years.

What may be more interesting than this attempt to correlate TOTE units and brain regions is a "discrepancy" between the GPS and TOTE formulations. The goal of the GPS program is, to take one example, to print out a correct proof of a theorem. The goal of a corresponding TOTE system is to reach a stage at which it does not have to prove theorems. This expresses a very real tension which underlies much theorizing about human behavior. "Homeostatic" theories stress the central goals of keeping bodily variables—sugar and oxygen content of the blood, temperature, and so on—within certain limits, and explain human intelligence as a rather rococco approach thrown up by evolution to solve this problem of regulating several variables. Others who would understand how Beethoven could write his symphonies may find homeostasis irrelevant. The reconciliation would seem to be that when we understand how the human brain has evolved to cope with survival problems in an unprecedented range of environments, then we shall understand its ability to create internal models so diverse that they can accommodate not only the complexities of life in a modern society but also the worlds of fantasy and imagination.

In any case, we can now return from this psychological excursion to a few comments on GPS which may serve to put our current successes in "heuristic programming" in better perspective.

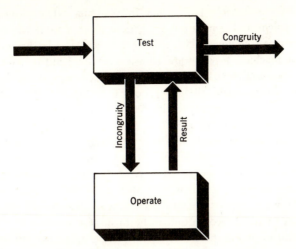

FIGURE 8 A TOTE (Test-Operate-Test-Exist) unit. The operation is repeated until the test reveals that congruity has been attained.

The claim of GPS to generality is that it can solve any problem—such as proving theorems in propositional logic—which can be solved using a tree-search of the type indicated in Figure 7 on the basis of an operator-difference table. Unfortunately, this very generality makes it difficult to incorporate special tricks developed for special problem domains. Further, not all problems are amenable to this type of solution, and even when they are, the real intelligence usually comes not so much in using a

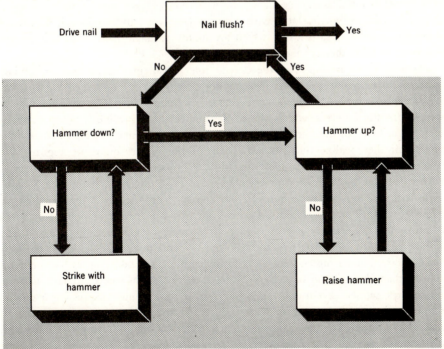

FIGURE 9 A hierarchical plan in which the operate box of a TOTE unit is decomposed into two lower-level TOTE units.

given operator-difference table but rather in realizing what differences are salient for the given problem and generating from experience a table of operators likely to reduce them. Perhaps techniques akin to those Uhr and Vossler have used (see below) in programing a machine to generate its own set of feature detectors for pattern recognition may eventually be developed to provide an operator-difference table generating routine to complement the supervisory package of GPS. However, much of the real "creativity" in solving a problem seems to be of a different kind, which we may refer to as "looking at it the right way".

To briefly summarize the work of Uhr and Vossler [1961] on a pattern recognition system that develops and evaluates its own feature detectors, we may consider patterns presented on a large square (or formal "retina") subdivided into very small squares, so that an overall pattern is presented as a configuration of small black or white squares. If we think of the retina as being 20×20, we might consider one approach to overall pattern recognition to be to inspect squares, say 5×5, to see if they include features relevant to detection. [In a more sophisticated version, one might build up on earlier preprocessing. For example, one might look for useful features in a line-segment version of the scene (cf. the discussion of cat visual preprocessing in Section 2.4).] For instance, in recognizing letters of the alphabet, it is useful to detect the small upside-down V that goes at the top of a letter A, the slanted line that corresponds to a foot of a letter A, the curve which we find in a letter B, and so forth. Uhr and Vossler program their machine to generate 5×5 masks at random, and then to try them out on a large number of different letters presented to the system. At whatever level they are generated, the technique is to save those masks that turn out to be highly correlated with some letters but not with other letters—and thus are useful in discrimination. Those masks which do not turn out to be distinctively correlated with different letters are to be rejected. The machine eventually generates feature lists which are highly valuable in distinguishing between different letters of the alphabet.

Let us give two examples of the crucial role played in human problem-solving by the ability to represent a problem in a manner in which it is more amenable to solution. For example, consider the game of taking the numbers from one through nine with two players alternately selecting one of the numbers not previously selected, the goal being to get to 15 in the sum of 3 numbers selected. For some players this is a difficult game until they realize that with the help of the magic square of Figure 10 this reduces to the game of tic-tac-toe (noughts and crosses).

Now consider the following problem (Figure 11): Given a square area 8 units on a side with a 1-unit square removed from opposite corners, cover the remaining area completely with 2×1 rectangles. It turns out that this cannot be done. But how can we prove that? Certainly not by trying all possible coverings; that would take far too long. Actually, the problem can be solved by a mathematical induction on the size of the square, but a simpler solution is to find a more tractable representation for this problem than the original one. By covering the area with a checkerboard pattern of unit squares, we see (eventually) that our 2×1 square must always cover one black and one white square, no matter what its position and orientation, but that the given area has two squares of the same color removed. Thus there are fewer squares of one color than of the other, and so no covering is possible.

This still leaves us with the unsolved question of the origin of successful representations. Here, let us simply add "ability to find successful representations" to our list

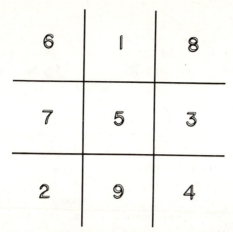

FIGURE 10   The magic square for tic-tac-toe (noughts and crosses). Each line corresponds to a sum of 15.

of "ingredients" for increasing intelligence, and turn to the next section in which we see how a computer might analyze a television picture of its environment in terms of a basic repertoire of representations of objects with which it is likely to interact.

4.3   SCENE ANALYSIS

Having seen how a computer may use a graph-with-operations model of its environment to plan a course of action, we now wish to understand how a robot might process a series of TV pictures to build up an internal model. In this paragraph we briefly discuss, by way of contrast, two types of picture processing which have been pro-

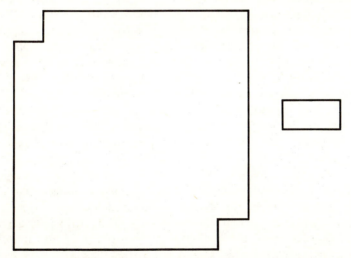

FIGURE 11   Given a square 8 units on a side with unit squares removed from opposite corners, can we cover the remaining area with a number of rectangles each 2 units long by 1 unit wide?

gramed into computers, and then devote the rest of the section to *scene analysis*, whereby a visual scene may be analyzed into a collection of objects with various locations in space. In *character recognition*, the picture is to be classified as one element of a fairly small set, say the numerals or the letters of the alphabet. In *handwriting recognition*, the picture will comprise a whole word, and characters will be modified by the way they are strung together. In trying to recognize what the word actually is, decomposition into elements then poses an extra problem beyond character recognition. On the other hand, the existence of context may invite the development of techniques unavailable for processing single characters; for example, is the character u an "a" or a "u"? If it occurs in the word *sut* where it is clearly the second letter of a three letter word "s — t", we may consult a dictionary to find that the only such words are "sat", "set", and "sot", and so decide that the character is an "a", and not a "u". Humans use wider context than this to resolve ambiguities, but at present it is impracticable to provide a computer with more than the simplest dictionary of common words or phrases, and so its use of context cannot compare with a human's use of the plot of page 43 of a detective novel to unravel a paragraph on page 217!

We now want, however, to move beyond the processing of a picture given in terms of clearly defined contours, and which is known to comprise a linear sequence of symbols and ask how we may take the ill-defined pattern of light and shade represented in a TV image (or a pattern of rod and cone potentials) and extract the information required to interact with the environment of which the pattern is a reflection. We may note that such scene analysis may proceed at two levels, at least. Contrast walking down a street where one perceives obstacles only well enough to avoid bumping into them (to one's immense embarrassment if the obstacle turns out to be a friend who complains of being snubbed)—one perceives *where* but not what—with manipulating the pieces of a jigsaw puzzle where both the what and the where of each piece play a key role in shaping behavior. However, there is no hard and fast distinction here: in navigating we note the speed of an obstacle as well as its location and (as our discussion in Section 2.1 emphasized) the *what* of an object to which we attend may vary greatly depending upon our current course of action.

Consider the specific problem of programing a hand-eye robot, comprising a TV camera, a computer, and a mechanical arm, to pick up objects from a table top (Figure 12). The computer might use different routines to control the arm depending on whether the object to be grasped is a cube, pyramid, or sphere. We may say that the robot has "recognized" an object when the computer has gained access to the appropriate routine for manipulating it. Programs currently "recognize" the cube "by name" and use the identification to call the routine. The simplicity of the environment allows action-orientation to be somewhat side-stepped. In more complex situations, routines may come to be called by a plexus of features without intervention of specific object recognition. In the limited cube-pyramid-sphere environment "recognition" may proceed swiftly—if there are no sharp corners, the object is a sphere, but if there is a face with four corners visible, the object is a cube if at least two further vertices are visible but a pyramid if only one further vertex is visible. (It is important to note that this rapid classification is only possible because the robot "knows" that it will encounter only cubes, spheres, or pyramids. This is the sort of "knowledge of context" that must be embodied in the STM of Section 4.1. We usually make decisions more quickly than we might otherwise because we can exploit known properties of our immediate

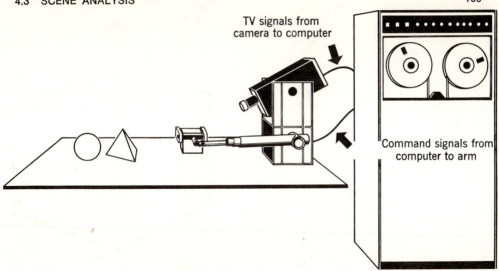

FIGURE 12 A hypothetical robot monitoring signals from a TV via a computer to control the movement of a mechanical arm.

environment. Of course, as in the case of someone who expects only a worm and picks up a rattlesnake, such "knowledge" will occasionally fail us.) Since we are dealing with a robot, the problem still remains of locating the object and its orientation in space. However, the crucial point is that, as for the cube of Figure 13, the computer need not compute all the coordinates of the cube, but it need merely compute the midpoints of the visible edge AB and the obscured edge CD to fill in the parameters in the cube-grasping routine which will ensure the correct positioning of the hand.

With this as background, let us consider a few ways of analyzing a scene as practiced by various robotics groups (see the next section) around 1970. The usual technique is first to try to replace the two-dimensional raster of light intensities by a raster approximating a line drawing of the objects in the visual field. [To simplify the problem, it is usual to have flat lighting to eliminate shadows; some research is now under way on how to stop a robot from treating a shadow as another object (as human infants do).] The first two steps are akin to the preprocessing we saw in Section 2.4

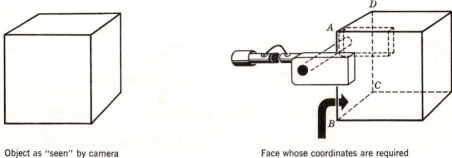

Object as "seen" by camera   Face whose coordinates are required
                                              for positioning the "hand"

FIGURE 13 Coordinates of the hidden face of a cube being used to control movements of the mechanical "hand" of the robot of Figure 12.

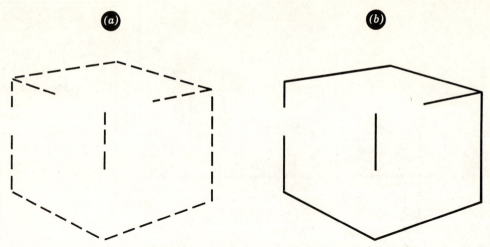

FIGURE 14   Two stages in preprocessing a picture of a cube.

to take place in the cat visual system: contrast is enhanced, and then short line segments are fitted to the points of high contrast. The result of this process as applied to a picture of a cube might look like Figure 14a. The next step fills in gaps to some extent by finding long lines, which cover as many of the short segments as possible, to get an outline such as that in Figure 14b.

We note that Figure 14b is by no means a complete line drawing of a cube: some lines are missing, especially where there meet two faces between which there is little or no change in texture, so that the contrast detectors provide no input to the line segment filters.

There seem to be two main strategies (Figure 15) for proceeding beyond an in-

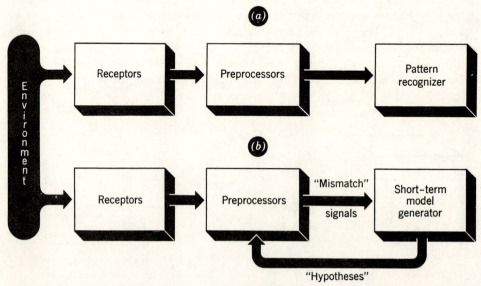

FIGURE 15   (a) *Straight-through* visual processing; (b) a form of *nested* visual processing more likely to occur in humans, in which hypothesis-based "efferent control" biases the pathway.

complete outline such as Figure 14*b*. In *straight-through analysis* one tries to complete the outline to get a "perfect line drawing", and then apply recognition techniques to the new outline. In *nested analysis* one tries to hypothesize what the object is on the basis of the rough outline, and then re-examine the original scene more closely to see if one can confirm the hypothesis. I would claim that the latter is more often the "brain way".

In straight-through analysis one might process rough outlines of a rectilinear environment by a heuristic type of search for a complete outline using the operations of adding medium length line segments with such heuristics as "lines should continue an existing line", or "start from an existing vertex and run parallel to an existing line" in an attempt to satisfy such criteria of completeness as "a line must join two vertices—it can't 'stop dead' ", or (if we can make use of stereo information) "if a vertex is at the near end of a line, then it will usually have more than two lines emanating from it". If a line is very short, it may be deleted. If two lines are aligned, the gap between them may be filled unless vertices on them indicate that they belong to distinct objects.

A nested analysis might still make use of such line completion techniques, but it would integrate them into the object recognition process. For example, a crucial idea in the approach of Duda and Hart [1970] was to find the vertical lines first, and then try to "grow out" along the spurs from the vertices of these lines, testing to see if this would yield the outline of a "known" object. In their program, analysis continues only until an object can be characterized with a level of confidence exceeding some threshold, so that "perfect" line drawings can be constructed by the computer only after object recognition, not before.

The reader might try to see if she can write a set of instructions which will program her to complete many variants of Figure 14*b* successfully. More subtle techniques could make use of cues from color and texture as well.

It would seem that humans used the nested analysis approach more than the straight-through approach: we see a contour, however ill defined, because we have recognized a cube, rather than recognize a cube because we have dutifully perceived all the contours. Much of the art of the Impressionists lay in their ability to capture the play of color on a surface, and it took an amazing amount of education before laymen and other artists could perceive that this was as "true" a representation of a scene as that obtained by using sharp contours filled in with color. As in the handwriting recognition problem, where we saw how our expectation that a word was a dictionary word enabled us to compensate for ambiguities, so does our expectation that an object is a familiar one enable us to compensate for inadequate contour information. This fact—that we seek enough cues to classify stimuli as pertaining to a known object, rather than trying to account for all the details (including omissions) of the visual input—would seem to provide a simple mechanistic underpinning for the observations of the Gestalt psychologists that we tend to perceive "wholes", as in the law of closure which implies, for example, that Figure 16 will be perceived as a square. Of course having perceived the square, we may then notice the gap in the right-hand side—but the point is that we see a square with a gap in it, rather than see "a figure made up of five line segments. You ask me if it is a square? Of course not. A square only comprises four segments".

If a human perceives a complex scene, her eyes move rapidly from point to point. The points of fixation correspond to details highly relevant to the perception of the

FIGURE 16 The law of closure exemplified: we see the figure as a punctured square.

scene. In other words, the sophisticated perceiver does not try to scan all parts of the scene equally, but rather seeks out a few features which will help her quickly make an overall judgment of the scene. Knowing where to look next is a prime example of an ingredient of intelligence. For example, Tichomirov and Poznyanskaya [1966] found that master chess players looked at boards for less time than novices and remembered positions more accurately, with the expert turning his gaze from one significant feature of the board to another, while the novice searched randomly. If the pieces are randomly arranged on the board, so that the expert has no meaningful search strategy, his performance on memorizing the board is much like that of the novice.

At this stage, the reader may object that our discussion unduly blurs the distinction between robot and human: "The robot processes a TV picture, but we perceive the real world". Although the many distinctions between humans and (extant) machines must not be minimized, the distinction expressed in the quoted sentence is based on a confusion. The human brain processing electrical potential from the optic tract is as far removed from "reality" as is the computer processing the output of a TV camera. However, what gives us a feeling of reality is that we are not conscious of the early stages of preprocessing but rather conscious [I don't claim to explain how!] of that level of brain activity corresponding to the re-presentation of this input in terms of objects located in space, a representation which has repeatedly provided a sound basis for interaction with the world. Thus it is the action-related short-term model of the environment (*cf.* Section 4.1)—and a robot may have this, even if in far simpler form than in a human—that corresponds to the perception of reality, rather than perception of the preprocessing which accompanies its elaboration.

Another implication of the nested analysis technique is that sensory processing is by no means the one-way process of Figure 15*a*, but rather has the character of Figure 15*b*, where even peripheral processing is biased by central hypothesis formation. Of course, sensory input from other modalities, as well as feedback from effectors, would complicate the picture.

Having seen that the recognition of simple objects can be programed and having gained some insight into human perception in the process, we must face the problem of analyzing a scene comprising several objects, where some occlude others. For simplicity, we shall consider only analysis of a static scene. (This simplifies the problem in that we can go back and re-explore parts of a scene, confident that they have not changed, though it deprives us of crucial cues which motion provides.) Let us further assume that we are working with a "perfect outline" in which all visible boundaries are accurately represented.

One method which works quite well when we have a scene comprising a few objects each of which is an example from a short list of "familiar" objects is *model fitting* (Roberts, 1963). This is essentially the method discussed in connection with Figure 12. For example, suppose we had "models" of cubes, wedges, and spheres. Then we might fit a cube to 9 of the lines of Figure 17a, and then remove them to leave the lines of Figure 17b to be explained. These fit a wedge better than a cube or sphere, and so we end up with the analysis of the scene as a "cube in front of a wedge".

Another approach—*again using a perfect outline,* but this time demanding that the objects have rectilinear edges, but otherwise be arbitrary—tries to decompose the scene *prior* to any attempts to classify the pieces. Guzman [1968] found a method which examines each vertex for indications as to whether or not the adjacent regions should be considered as faces of the same object. For example, consider the three types of vertex shown in Figure 18.

We may note that the "arrow" occurs in various orientations some three times in Figure 17a and in each case the two regions (1 and 2) within the angle belong to the same object, while the third (3) does not. The Y occurs only once, with all three regions belonging to the same object. The T occurs three times, and in each case regions on opposite sides of the crossbar belong to different objects.

This suggests the following scheme. Make a "score-card" with one entry for each distinct pair of distinct regions. We build up a "connection score" to decide of each pair whether or not they are faces of the same object. We use the 3 cues of Figure 17 as follows.

Starting with 0 for each entry, add 1 to the entry each time you encounter a vertex for which the pair of entries is (1, 2), (2, 3), or (3, 1) for a Y or (1, 2) for an arrow, and subtract 1 from the entry when you encounter a vertex for which the pair

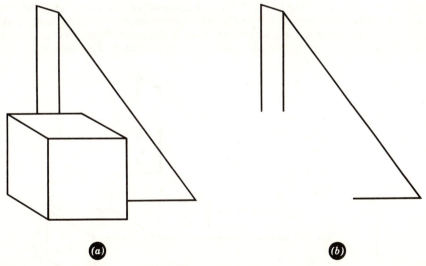

(a)   (b)

FIGURE 17   An example of model-fitting: Having fitted a cube to nine of the lines of (a) we may remove them to leave the lines in (b). These remaining lines fit a wedge better than a cube or a sphere, and so we could end up with the analysis of the scene as "a cube in front of a wedge".

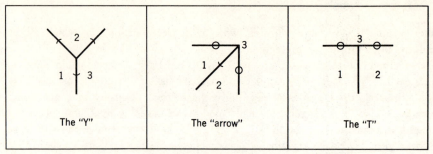

FIGURE 18 Three types of vertices that can provide cues in dissecting a figure into objects. Edges marked with a) are likely to separate faces of the same object and are scored +1; edges marked with a 0 are likely to separate faces of different objects and are scored −1.

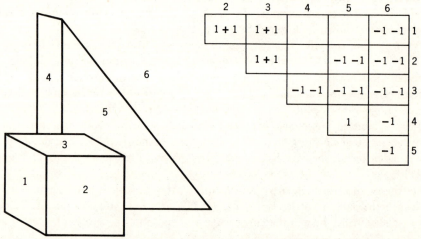

	2	3	4	5	6	
	1 + 1	1 + 1			−1 −1	1
		1 + 1		−1 −1	−1 −1	2
			−1 −1	−1 −1	−1 −1	3
				1	−1	4
					−1	5

FIGURE 19 We use the cues of Figure 18 to dissect the cube from the wedge from the background. 1 has positive links to 2 and 3, and 2 has positive links to 3; but 1 and 3 have negative links to 6, 2 has negative links to 5 and 6, and 3 has negative links to 4, 5, and 6, and so on. Thus 1, 2, and 3 are classified as faces of the same object. Similarly, 4 and 5 are positively linked, while 6 forms an "object" (the background) of its own.

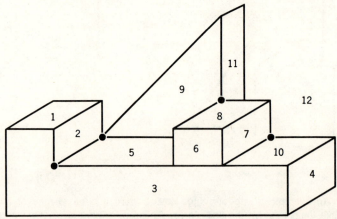

FIGURE 20 A scene that can be correctly decomposed, using the cues of Figure 18, despite a number of false indications at the vertices marked with the dots.

114

of entries is $(1, 3)$ or $(2, 3)$ for an arrow or a T. We then lump into one object all those regions which have a tie of at least $+1$ to each other.

We work out the example of Figure 17a in Figure 19. The reader is invited to apply the method of Figure 20, where she will find that some of the local indications— as at the vertex 8-9-11—are wrong, but that the combined effect of all vertices still gives a correct decomposition.

Once we have used such a decomposition algorithm, it may then be comparatively easy to apply the techniques developed for characterization of single objects to build up a usable description of the entire scene. The reader will find in Huffman [1971] an elegant extension of Guzman's work, while in two recent doctoral theses from M.I.T., Winston [1970] discusses "Learning Structural Descriptions from Examples", and Winograd [1971] discusses "Procedures as a Representation for Data in a Computer Program for Understanding Natural Language".

With these examples before us, it is now clear that a computer may be programed to analyze a scene into a number of objects with well-defined locations in space. Clearly, current methods are only practical for well-lit scenes containing a few simple objects, but a start has been made. Perhaps more importantly, we have been reminded that many processes which we take for granted—such as the ability, gained as a very young child, to perceive the objects in a crowded room—are actually very subtle indeed. In studying their implementation on the computer, we may not only gain insight into what needs to be explained, but also obtain suggestions as to which are the mechanisms we might expect (perhaps wrongly, but the mistakes should yield valuable new perspectives) to find embodied in neural circuitry. Before we turn, then, to brain theory (Part III), let us briefly see how heuristic search and scene analysis are integrated into the overall control of a robot.

4.4   THE INTEGRATED DESIGN OF A ROBOT

Scene analysis is used to build up a "model of the world"; this model then serves as the basis for planning the actions of a robot. We now analyze this integration of functions in more detail. We shall consider two types of robot. Rather then consider a robot which is "blind" and so must simply "feel" its way, bumping into obstacles and skirting them, we shall instead study a robot which can analyze input from a TV camera to "see" objects (in the manner of Section 4.3), and so may detour around objects without contacting them. In any case, it is clearly advantageous for the system to be able to remember what objects it has already bumped into, or "seen" to obstruct the path, so that it need not repeat its mistakes.

In a hand-eye robot (Figure 21a), such as those at M.I.T.'s Project MAC and Stanford's Artificial Intelligence Project, a TV camera feeds a picture to a computer which extracts from the picture the data it needs to command a mechanical arm to pick up and manipulate objects sensed by the camera. In a mobile robot (Figure 21b), such as that at S.R.I., a TV camera atop the robot feeds a picture to a computer which extracts the data it needs to build up a model of the robot's environment so that the robot can carry out tasks, such as locating an object and pushing it to a designated place efficiently without overt trial and error.

Either by use of a rangefinder, or by using pictures from two positions of the camera to supply "stereoscopic" input, the computer can gain access to distance information.

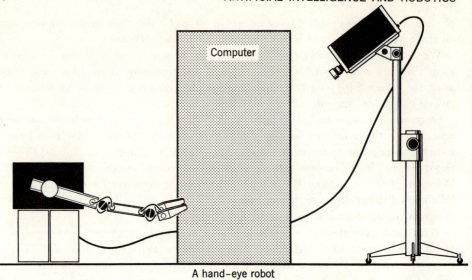

A hand–eye robot

A mobile robot

FIGURE 21   Two types of robot.

By suitable "wash-out" lighting, shadows can be eliminated to avoid the problem of having the computer try to recognize a shadow as a solid object. We have seen, in Section 4.3, some of the techniques which enable the robot to analyze these patterns of light and shade as a collection of objects located in precise places around the robot.

By 1970, perhaps the most sophisticated task undertaken by a hand-eye robot was one such as the following:

1. Analyze a scene to recognize it as a stack of three visually distinct blocks, say A atop B atop C, at a certain location on a table top.

2.   Store this analysis of the scene. Call this record M (for memory).

3.   Use M to compute the coordinates of the base of the stack. Convert the coordinates into a sequence of instructions which will cause the mechanical hand to "swipe" the base of the stack, thus scattering the three blocks around the tabletop. (The well-established branch of mechanical engineering devoted to the study of kinematic linkages provides the algorithms for this step.)

4.   Analyze the new scene and use this to reconstruct the situation stored as M. (This requires the computer to not only recognize which block in the new scene corresponds to which block in the old scene—it must also compute that, implicit in the order to restack the blocks is the requirement that $C, B,$ and A be replaced in *that* order and that a space must be cleared for block C before it is put in place. Further, since the program we are sketching does not make use of visual feedback, the computer must provide a trajectory which will not displace any blocks "by accident," and ensure that a block will move only when grasped by the mechanical hand and returned to its previous position on the stack.)

Unfortunately, there is enough play in the mechanical arm for even the most precise computation to yield defective behavior. A more refined program—involving far more computation—would make continual use of both visual feedback via the TV camera and tactile feedback via pressure sensors on the hand, to ensure that the hand would avoid obstacles and that it would not release a block till it was securely in place on the stack. (The reader may get some feel for the problem by trying to stack blocks with her eyes closed.)

Let us next describe at a similarly imprecise level a task as executed by a mobile robot:

1.   Analyze a scene to recognize a number of large obstacles and their locations on the floor of the room.

2.   Store this analysis of the scene. Call this record M.

3.   Given a command "Push the large cube to the door", use M to plan a path which will place the robot behind the large cube and then another path which the robot may pursue in pushing it to the door.

4.   Convert the plan into a sequence of instructions to the drive wheels of the robot. (Since the robot moves "with its eyes closed", it may bump into an object which was hidden behind other objects during its analysis in phase 1, and which lies on its computed path. If this happens, it must essentially "start all over".)

Let us now outline in more detail how we might program the robot control computer so that it could automatically translate "Push the large cube to the door" into an appropriate sequence of commands to the robot's stepping motors. (The following discussion is based on the work done by the group at Stanford Research Institute on their mobile robot.)

Suppose, then, that the robot has already built up in its computer "memory," an encoding of the internal model of its world that we represent by the "floor plan" shown in Figure 22. Here it has analyzed its world as a room with a doorway in one wall, and containing a large cube, two small cubes, and a sofa. In addition there are areas which may contain other objects but are labeled "unknown" because they have not been analyzed, perhaps because they have been obstructed from view by other objects.

The control computer may proceed by breaking the top-level problem "push the large cube to the door" into two second-level problems:

1. Go to large cube.
2. Go to door, while pushing cube.

The computer must then break these two down further. This phase involves *planning*—delimiting alternative paths and choosing one of them. (This is the phase where high-speed internal computation, rather than low-speed external interaction takes place. In a more complex environment the computer might have to examine thousands of alternative paths before sending commands to move its wheels. We looked briefly at algorithms for directing the planning phase in Section 4.2.) In our Figure 1 of Chapter 2 example, the robot in its planning phase might compute that it must start out on leg RC or on leg RA to avoid the nearer small cube, and that leg CD and leg AB, respectively, would then need to be traversed to bring the robot to the large cube. It might then choose the path RAB both because it is shorter and also because it does not lead through unknown territory where other obstacles might be encountered. Thus, command 1 is translated as follows:

1   i   Go from R to A.
1   ii   Go from A to B.

Similarly, step 2 might be analyzed in terms of the alternate paths $EJKGL$ and $EFGL$ (Figure 23). $EFGL$ might be chosen because it is sufficiently shorter to offset the possible risks of going through *terra incognita*. The computer would then translate command 2 *approximately* as:

2   i   Push from E to F.
2   ii   Push from F to G.
2   iii   Push from G to L.

Why "approximately"? This is to allow for the fact that the system may encounter an unexpected object when going from E to F. Thus when the system compiles "Push from E to F" it must not simply issue a sequence of move instructions, but must include a "test package" of the following kind. "Have you hit an unexpected object? If not, proceed as planned. If so, analyze the object and update your internal model. Replan your trajectory on the basis of your new model and new location. Then go to execute plan." Having mentioned the need for this refinement, we shall only spell out in greater detail the instructions needed in the obstacle-free case.

The plot thickens. To push the large cube from E to F, the robot must get behind the cube (i.e., to W' in Figure 24) and then move just far enough (namely, to Y) for the cube to get to F. Thus the computer must not only translate "Push from E to F" as "Go from W' to Y" but must precede this command by the instruction "Go from B to W" and "Go from W to W'" which will position the robot correctly to start pushing. Using "Go (R, A)" to abbreviate "Go from R to A" we see that the third level of translation will yield the program;

Go (R, A)
Go (A, B)
Go (B, W)
Go (W, W')

Go (W', Y)
Go (Y, Y')
Go (Y', Y'')
Go (Y'', Z)
Go (Z, Z')
Go (Z', Z'')
Go (Z'', L)
Stop

Next, the instruction Go (A, B) when following Go (R, A) must be broken down into an instruction-pair of the form

TURN θ
PROCEED x

telling the robot to turn through the appropriate angle θ and then go straight ahead distance x. As we have already seen in our discussion of subroutines in Section 3.2, TURN θ can finally be expressed in such terms as "Lock left wheel, advance right wheel 4 steps," while PROCEED x might compile as "Advance both wheels 12 steps synchronously."

It thus takes us through six levels of a hierarchy of increasing detail to go from the "simple" command "Push the large block to the door" to a sequence made up entirely from basic logical instructions and appropriate combinations of three wheel control instructions:

L. Locking right wheel, advance ʟeft wheel one step.
R. Locking left wheel, advance ʀight wheel one step.
B. Synchronously advance ʙoth wheels one step.

To simplify the above exposition, I have purposely left one bad flaw (and perhaps unpurposely left several) in this compilation. The reader is invited to test her comprehension of Section 4.1 by seeing if she can spot it before reading further.

To summarize, then, a robot needs the following (at least) if it is to interact effectively with a complex environment:

1. A set of receptors which can sense the world, and a set of scene analysis routines which enable it to dissect sensed data in terms of interactively meaningful relations.

2. A set of effectors, together with a set of routines well-suited to act upon the environment and to move the receptors during scene analysis.

3. An internal model which comprises an up-to-date record of the result of the system's various scene analyses and actions. It is the last point which answers the question just posed to the reader—the compiled program had no way of changing its model as the robot and the box changed position. [Exercise: Write a version of our program which does include model updating. (Hint: It may be necessary to distinguish "Go (R, A)" from "Go (W', Y) while pushing the large box".)]

4. A problem solver which can take reports from scene analysis to update the internal model can compile commands into courses of action and when necessary can interrupt other activities to update the model and replan action.

These four functions seem to be necessary for adaptive organisms, too, and we now turn, in Part III, to brain theory. In Part II, we have discussed functions required for

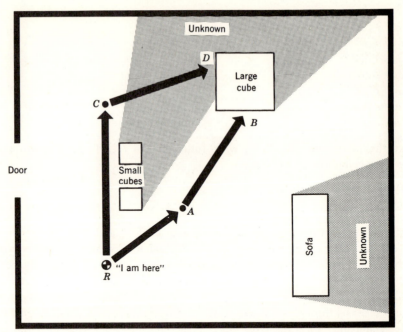

FIGURE 22 A possible "model of the world" for the robot, indicating two paths, *RAB* and *RCD,* whereby the robot might move from its present position *R* to abut the large cube.

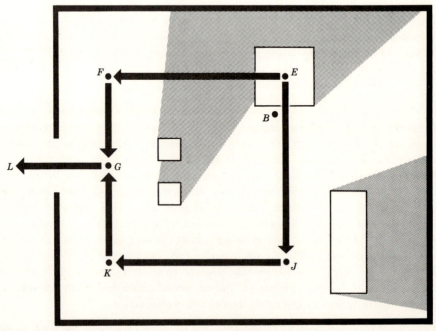

FIGURE 23 Trajectories *EFGL* and *EJKGL* through which the large cube might be pushed to the door.

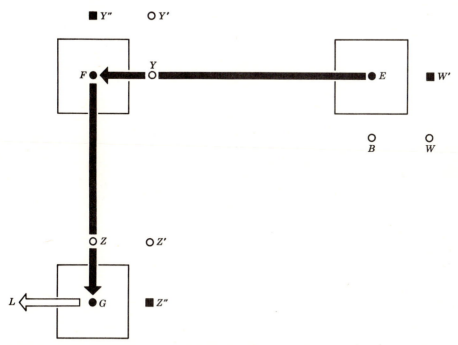

FIGURE 24 The detailed trajectory *BWW'YY'Y"ZZ'Z"L'* through which the robot must move from position *B* if it is indeed to push the large cube along the trajectory *EFGL*.

intelligence, and ways in which some of these functions may be implemented on a computer. Our challenge now is to benefit from the understanding of function so gained without falling into the trap of believing that the brain operates as a serial computer. As we have already stressed in Section 1.1, whereas most of the artificial intelligence approach is based upon carrying out series of simple operations upon data passively stored, our brain theory will emphasize parallel activity of a multitude of operations within an array of interacting data and control schemes relevant to action.

Brain Theory

5 | Neural Control of Movement

In Part III we turn from general functional considerations to a study of the structural substrate the brain provides for the mediation of perception, memory, and decision-making. Given our emphasis on an action-oriented approach to these functions, it is appropriate that we devote the present chapter to a study of the neural basis for some of the movements that constitute the organism's action.

In Section 5.1 we study the operation of the musculature, and see how circuitry in the spinal cord utilizes feedback to enhance the control of movement. Section 5.2 (which may be omitted by the reader already sufficiently sated with anatomical terminology) shows the midbrain and forebrain structures that modulate and direct the computations in the spinal cord. In particular, we emphasize the great modifications in basic circuitry wrought by the evolution of neocortex in mammals. To relate these anatomical considerations to the robotic control problems of Section 4.4, we devote Section 5.3 to an all too brief analysis of taking a walk, noting the interplay of visual and vestibular input, spinal feedback, and our internal model of the world in directing purposeful activity. The anatomical considerations of Section 5.2 and these dynamic considerations of Section 5.3 naturally coalesce to turn our attention, in Section 5.4, to hierarchies of motor control. In particular we see the interplay of high-level and reflexive "fine-tuning" in refining the effects of gross motor "commands" issued by older regions of the forebrain. An important principle here seems to be that large movements involve both a ballistic command and the resetting of a feedback mechanism to "fine-tune" the last portion of the trajectory.

Finally, in Section 5.5, we relate the preceding four sections to the dominant theme of our brain theory—that computation in the brain proceeds in a highly distributed fashion, rather than under the centralized control of any single executive organ.

5.1   FEEDBACK AND THE SPINAL CORD

One important task in studying the neural basis for motor behavior will be to understand the crucial role played by spinal cord circuitry in patterning limb movements,
coordinating the limbs, compensating for vagaries in environmental conditions, and
providing the postural adjustments which let the animal keep its balance during complex motor activity. In this section we shall consider some of the feedback loops in the
spinal cord, while the next section will give a gross outline of "higher-level" circuitry
related to the behavior of the organism.

The spinal cord (Figure 1) runs almost the whole length of the spine. Any cross
section separates into *gray matter* (neural tissue rich in cell bodies and dendrites) and
white matter (neural tissue mainly containing axons). The input and output are
neatly separated with *primary sensory cells* (cells whose "dendritic" processes are
specialized as sensory receptors) having their cell bodies in the *dorsal root ganglions*
("dorsal" means "on the back side," i.e., posterior), with their axons traveling the
dorsal root to enter the *dorsal* or *posterior horn* of grey matter in the spinal cord;
while the motoneurons have their cell bodies in the *ventral* or *anterior horn* of gray

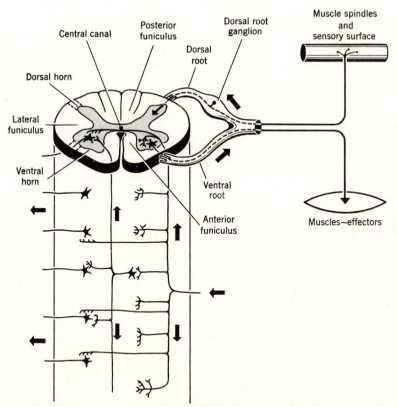

FIGURE 1   A cross section of the spinal cord, showing that sensory input (including feedback signals) enters dorsally (from the rear), while control signals to the effectors exit
ventrally (from the front). The network schematized below the cross section reminds us
of the wealth of transactions passing up and down the spinal cord.

matter, and send their axons out along the *ventral root* ("ventral" means "on the front side"). The ventral and dorsal roots coalesce in a nerve trunk. The body is naturally divided into "segments," each segment being innervated from the nerve trunks at the same level of the spinal cord.

As is clear from Figure 1, much of the spinal cord is white matter. In the regions of white matter, axons course up and down the spine, linking segments of the spinal cord, as well as communicating with the brain stem and forebrain. The gray matter partitions the white matter into four tracts, called *funiculi* (think of the funicular railway as a cable railway to remember that a funiculus is a cable of axons), the *lateral funiculi* to each side, the dorsal or *posterior funiculus* to the rear, and the ventral or *anterior funiculus* to the front.

The role of tracts from outside the spinal cord can be seen from the fact that the movement of a muscle can be occasioned by a thought or a touch as much as by hearing or seeing something. Thus motoneurons can respond to inputs from any sensory modality mixed with other modalities, and in fact this "mixing" may take place far from the periphery. In this section we shall emphasize direct paths from sensory cells to motoneurons (though these are in the minority) which include the *monosynaptic* muscle-muscle reflexes (with point-for-point paths from sensor on muscle to motoneuron with only one synapse intervening) and shall allude but briefly to the intersegmental pathways which let terrestrial animals coordinate their limb movements and automatically maintain an upright position.

It is worth reminding the reader that this brief description does not do justice to the immense amount of detailed anatomical structure within the spinal cord, and that any really comprehensive theory of animal movement will have to take volumes of anatomical data into account. Our aim here is simply to provide a general framework of understanding into which so detailed an account might hopefully fit.

What we have been calling muscles are made up of thousands of individual muscle fibers. Each motoneuron, whose cell body sits in the spinal cord, synapses on and controls a number of these muscle fibers. For more delicate motions, such as those involving the fingers of primates, each motoneuron may be assigned only a few muscle fibers. In other locations, such as the shoulder, one motoneuron may control thousands of muscle fibers. The individual fibers of muscles are grouped into bundles (*fasciculi*), which are gathered to make up the complete muscle, which may comprise as many as several million fibers. The fibers of a motor unit (i.e., the fibers innervated by a single motoneuron) are widely dispersed in several bundles, so the action of a single motor unit is spread throughout the muscle. Within a muscle there are two ways of increasing the force supplied. The more important is by increasing the number of fibers that are actually being instructed to contract by synaptic activation; a much lesser increase is obtained by increasing the activation of the individual muscle fibers. As we contract a muscle more and more, we get subpopulations coming in at different sizes. First we get fairly small fibers being brought in, and then as we go on, we get larger and larger fibers, so that at any stage the increment of activation involves about the same percentage of extra force being applied, aiding smoothness of movement.

We saw in Section 2.2 that since we can stop ordering a muscle to contract, but cannot directly order it to expand actively, pairs (at least) of opposing muscles are necessary. For convenience we often label one set of muscles as the "prime mover" or *agonist,* and the opposing set as the *antagonist* (Figure 2). However, in such joints as the shoulder which are not limited to one degree of freedom, many muscles participate,

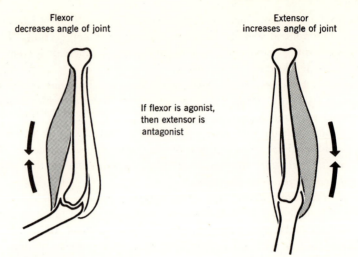

Flexor
decreases angle of joint

Extensor
increases angle of joint

If flexor is agonist,
then extensor is
antagonist

FIGURE 2   Agonist-antagonist pairs: active contraction of the agonist yields passive expansion of the antagonist, and vice versa.

so here it is not very useful to try to identify an agonist-antagonist pair (see Figure 5, Chapter 3).

Most real movements involve many joints. For example, the wrist must be fixed in a position bent backward with respect to the forearm for the hand to grip with its maximum power. Muscles known as *fixers* are concerned with this. *Synergists* are muscles which act together with the main muscles involved. A large group of muscles works together when one raises something with one's finger. If more force is required, wrist muscles may also be called in; if still more force is required, arm muscles may be used, and by this time, muscles all over the body are involved in maintaining posture.

The spinal cord exhibits many useful reflexes. For example, the spinal animal (i.e., the animal in which no part of the CNS above the spinal cord can control the body), possesses the scratch reflex—it can move its leg to scratch an irritated part of the body. The joints tend to move together (synergy). In the intact animal, the same general reactions occur, but here the individual joint rotations may be modulated. Thus in addition to the low-level spinal feedback which we shall see allows reflexes to act in a load-independent way without intervention of higher centers, we also have that gross actions may be shaped by higher centers to yield finely patterned actions. (It should be mentioned that even if the spine has been transected, *some* information can be passed from the head to the body. If the head turns, the skin on the neck will transmit the effects to the body, perhaps triggering natural postural reflexes. Also, moving the head will alter the center of gravity. It is safe to say, however, that the information transmitted to the body is very seriously diminished by spinal transection and certainly insufficient to mediate the reflexes mentioned.)

We would then take the task of the brain above the spinal cord to be to select and modify synergies in an orderly fashion, sequencing them appropriately and suppressing unwanted components. Such an arrangement may be efficient for most tasks, but, of course, it restricts the possible motions. (Rubbing the stomach while patting the head becomes difficult. That it is nonetheless possible for humans is an example of the

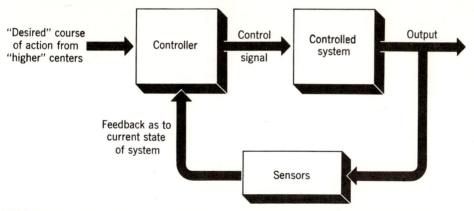

FIGURE 3   A feedback system in which the controller compares actual performance with some "desired" performance to compute its control signal.

adaptability that results from neocortical expansion.) A major problem is thus to understand how the animal selects, alters, and coordinates these synergies in a goal-directed way.

We saw in Section 3.3 that *feedback* (Figure 3)—comparison of actual performance with some "desired" performance—must play an essential role in the control of an organism or a robot. As in driving a car we must press the brake pedal when going downhill and press the accelerator when going uphill to maintain a constant speed, so in the nervous system we must not expect any constant command from higher centers to be related to constant response—rather we must expect an intricate varying of control activity to yield smooth coordinated action. In particular, let us now see how local feedback within the spinal cord yields desired behavior despite varying loads upon the organism.

For example, the nervous system uses feedback to keep the length of a muscle relatively constant despite small variations in load. To understand how the CNS gets feedback information for this type of compensation, consider a piece of elastic, which is of a particular length l_0 when unstretched. Suppose we fixed the two ends of the elastic to two anchors which we could move to be various distances l apart, as shown in Figure 4. If we choose two points on the elastic, say A and B, whose distance apart is d_0, for the unstretched elastic, then if the distance between the two anchors is no more than l_0, so that the elastic is unstretched, the distance between A and B remains d_0. But if the anchors move further than l_0 apart, the elastic stretches, and the distance between A and B increases proportionately to the increase in the length of the elastic; mathematically, the distance d between A and B is then given by the equation $d = (l/l_0) d_0$ so long as the elastic is stretched. Thus we can measure l indirectly by measuring the distance d between A and B, and then recapturing l as $l_0(d/d_0)$ *so long as l exceeds l_0.*

In fact, this is essentially the scheme the nervous system uses to tell how long a muscle is. If we look at any muscle, we see not only the big "workhorse" muscle fibers called *extrafusal fibers* whose contraction changes the relative position of the bones to which they are anchored, but also little muscle fibers called *intrafusal fibers* which have the endings of receptors called *muscle spindles* inserted into them, the intensity of whose firing signals how much the region they attach to is stretched, just as in the

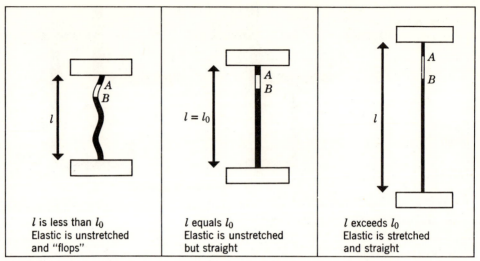

FIGURE 4   The length of the segment *AB* is proportional to the distance *l* between the two supports so long as that distance is no less than the unstretched length l_0 of the elastic.

case of the elastic, where sampling of "the *AB* region" gives a good measure of the overall length of the muscle, so long as the muscle is longer than some standard length.

The feedback scheme used by the CNS to control muscle length is then essentially that shown in Figure 5, although for simplicity we only show one motoneuron, one extrafusal fiber, and one intrafusal fiber, whereas in the real CNS whole populations of these are involved in each gross muscle. We think of the top anchor as fixed, while the bottom anchor may move up and down under different conditions of loading and

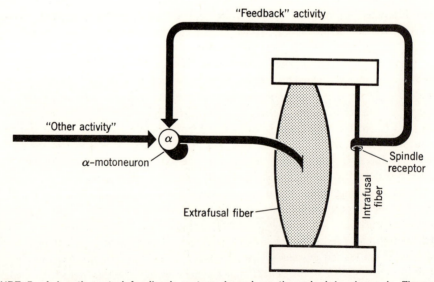

FIGURE 5   A length-control feedback system, based on the principle shown in Figure 4, in which the spindle receptor monitors the extent to which the length of the intrafusal fiber exceeds its resting length and uses this signal to increase α-motoneuron activity, thus causing the extrafusal fiber to contract to reduce this excess.

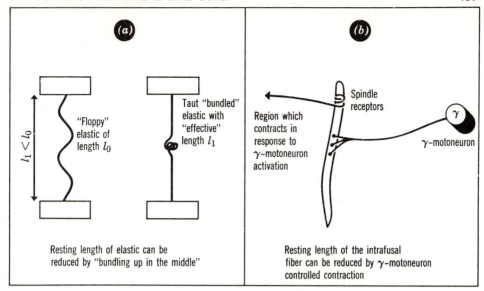

FIGURE 6 Just as (a) the resting length of the elastic of Figure 4 can be reduced by "bundling up in the middle", so can (b) the resting length of the intrafusal fiber of Figure 5 be reduced by γ-motoneuron controlled contraction.

of muscle contraction. Here the α-motoneurons (the motoneurons that control the "workhorse" extrafusal fibers) receive two kinds of input—"other" activation (the combined effects of "higher control", interlimb interaction, etc.) and "feedback" signals from the spindle receptors. So long as "other" activation is intense enough for the "workhorse" fibers to keep the overall muscle sufficiently contracted for the spindle to be unstretched, the spindle receptor will add little to this "other" activity. Suppose, however, that the "other" activity is such as to maintain the muscle at precisely the full unstretched length of the intrafusal fiber. If we now add a weight to the bottom anchor the following will happen:

1. The muscle will be stretched beyond its previous length because of the extra weight.
2. As a result, the spindle receptor will be stretched and start to signal back.
3. This will increase the total excitation to, and then the total output of, the α-motoneuron.
4. Thus the muscle will further contract and so in time will be restored at least part way to its original length.

This scheme, then, has two features:

i We can get the muscle to any length shorter than the resting length of the intrafusal fiber by "blasting" the α-neuron with enough intensity—but unfortunately the required "blasting" intensity varies with the loading of the muscle.
ii We can get the muscle to maintain its length with only minor sensitivity to the loading—but unfortunately this only holds when that length is the resting length of the intrafusal fiber.

The perceptive reader may have already guessed the way out of our misfortune: *change* the resting length of the intrafusal fiber. Going back to our elastic of Figure

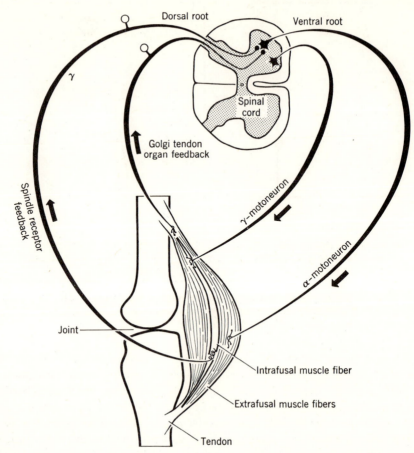

FIGURE 7 Here we place the mechanisms of Figures 5 and 6 in a less schematic frame-work, indicating the relationship of the muscle relative to the joint and showing that the control loops pass through the spinal cord.

4, it is as if, as shown in Figure 6a, we were to bundle up the middle portion of the elastic. The nervous system accomplishes the same effect by having, in addition to the α-motoneurons which control the contraction of the "workhorse" extrafusal fibers, a set of γ-motoneurons (Figure 6b). Such a neuron synapses upon the central region of the intrafusal fibers, causing it to contract and thus reducing its effective resting length. (Note that motoneurons are located in the spinal cord, and that their axons may have to traverse vast distances to reach the muscle fibers.)

Thus, if we wish to change the length of a muscle, we can supply the α-motoneurons with the activation which would yield appropriate muscle contraction under minimal loading, while giving the γ-motoneurons the activation which will cause the intrafusal fibers to set to provide feedback for the new length. In this way, α-activation quickly brings the length "into the right ballpark", whereafter γ-activation "fine tunes" the length by tailoring the α-activity to the vagaries of the current loading.

Actually, the picture is more complicated than this. For example, in Figure 7 we see that there is a second source of feedback: the Golgi tendon organs, which provide feedback on the force registered at the tendon joining muscle to bone. Again, beside the length-monitoring spindle receptors we have studied, others provide feedback on

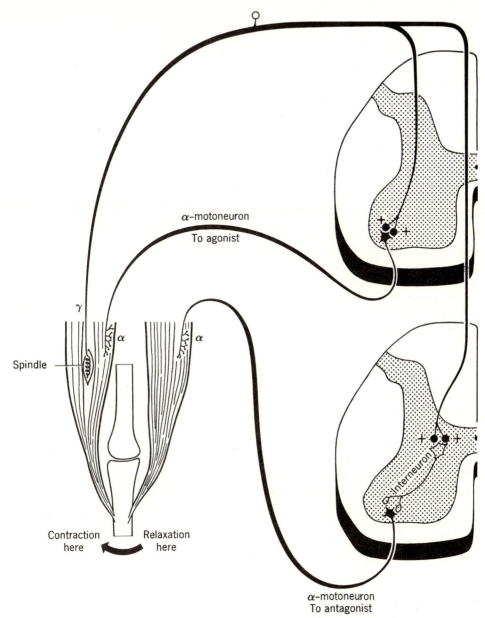

FIGURE 8 Here we complement Figure 7 by noting that feedback from the spindle in an agonist will not only serve to raise the level of α-motoneuron control of contraction of the agonist, but will also serve, via an inhibitory interneuron, to lower the level of α-motoneuron control of contraction of the antagonist.

velocity and so can play a role in smoothing ongoing movements as distinct from steadying given postures. Complementing this proliferation of feedbacks is an unsettled controversy as to how the nervous system apportions the control of any movement between the α- and γ-systems. Despite all these exciting open questions, we have at least gained a basic understanding in seeing how the α-system can quickly elicit approximately correct response, with feedback "follow-up" freeing the rest of the nervous system from having to involve slight variations in peripheral conditions in their computations. Returning to our discussion of Section 3.3, it is tempting to regard the α-system as providing the ballistic component, and the γ-system as super-posing a tracking component, in a mixed ballistic-tracking strategy, which gets the system into new states quickly without losing the benefits of feedback compensation.

Having gained a reasonable feel for the role of feedback in simplifying "higher-level" control of a single muscle, we must now note the implications of the fact that each joint is controlled by at least one *pair* of muscles. Consider then a flexor-extensor pair, as shown in Figure 8. Clearly the angle of the joint will depend on how much contraction of the flexor exceeds contraction of the extensor. Just as clearly, it would be very inefficient to have both muscles contract strongly to get that difference; thus when, for example, the nervous system is to reduce the joint angle, it should not only *increase* flexor contraction, but should also *decrease* extensor contraction. In Figure 8, we see the feedback circuits which automatically ensure this joint action. Here we have shown a spindle receptor not only activating an α-motoneuron of its own muscle (as in Figure 6) but also decreasing the activity, usually (but perhaps not always; see Scheibel and Scheibel [1969]) via an inhibitory interneuron, of the α-motoneurons of the antagonist muscle. Thus the spindle output not only contributes to agonist contraction, but also to antagonist relaxation, to yield economy of muscular effort for a given movement.

With these considerations, we see the joint virtue of hierarchical organization and of local feedback to "reduce the burden of computation on higher levels". Our exami-nation of circuitry could continue, showing how the neurons controlling the various joints of a single limb are interrelated; how the two limbs of a single pair are related by what are called *intrasegmental reflexes* because they occur within a single segment of the spinal cord; and how these are built upon in the *intersegmental reflexes* which unite various segments of the spinal cord in smoothly controlling automatic postural adjustments and the sequence of stepping in locomotion. However, rather than detail such circuits here (and it must be stressed that even were we to provide them, many would perforce be somewhat speculative, the spinal cord being so rich a system that it still holds many mysteries for the neurophysiologist), we instead give the reader some feel for the complexity of interconnected subsystems involved by presenting a discussion of walking in Section 5.3. Some readers may first wish to peruse Section 5.2 to see the gross anatomy of a number of brain structures involved in the control of movement.

5.2 ANOTHER ASIDE: NEUROANATOMY OF THE MOTOR SYSTEM†

The task of this section (a knowledge of which is *not* necessary for reading the rest of this book) is to build upon our discussion in the previous section of the spinal cord's various reflex mediating pathways for which sensory signals enter the cord dorsally and motoneuron "commands" leave ventrally. The reader may find it helpful to review the terminology introduced in Section 2.3.

---

† This section may be omitted at a first reading.

We first explore the schematic of neural circuitry presented in Figure 9. It is based on drawings made by Nauta at the 1966 presentation referred to in Section 2.3. We first concentrate on the unshaded boxes and the solid lines of Figure 9. Besides the "local channels" which are both intrasegmental and intersegmental, there are two other important channels in submammalian vertebrates. A fourth channel, the "new" spinothalamic tract, is found only in mammals, and will be dealt with in our later discussion of shaded portions of the Figure. The second channel is the cerebellar, ascending from secondary sensory cells to the cerebellum, which sits dorsal to the brainstem. The third channel is the *primordial lemniscus* (lemniscus = band; primordial indicates that it arises in submammalian forms). It is not explicitly shown, for reasons that will appear in the next paragraph. This lemniscus is the "old" portion of the *spinothalamic tract* which has two phylogenetic components, with different functions and different central terminations, passing from the sensory nuclei to the forebrain via cells in the thalamus. [Transection of the spinothalamic tract causes, at least temporarily, disappearance of pain, and so it has been dubbed the pain pathway. The virtue of pain is that it biases the reticular formation (more of which below) in the direction of arousal, but if this effect is too great it can cause fatigue even to the point of death.]

Actually, only a tenth or so of the fibers in the spinothalamic tract go directly to the thalamus even in humans—the rest "drop out" and go to the *reticular formation* (RF), which may be thought of as comprising that class of neurons in the brainstem and cord, but not in the forebrain, which are not monopolized by any sensory modality. (The reticular formation is a classic case of a region with demarcation disputes; the present definition is perhaps the most inclusive.)

The RF cells have been dubbed "jungle" cells because they are entangled in information from many modalities. The brainstem RF is often called the "nonspecific" organization of the brainstem because it is not specific to any sensory modality. However, do not be misled by the name into thinking that RF neurons do not have specific *functions*—what looks like chaos to us is not always chaos. There seems to be a temporal migration of functions within the RF in that the same cell may seemingly be attuned to entirely different stimuli at different times. We should not think of this as odd—unless we are overly anxious to apply data from peripheral projections to the richly interconnected central cells. Nor should we feel that the seeming migration of function means an unlimited capability for each neuron. We must look for the degrees of freedom in such changes, just as in postural reflexes where we may be amazed until we realize that what is happening is quite strictly defined. It should be clear that as soon as the job of a region is to control something, and the nature of that control can depend upon many modalities, such lack of monopoly is inevitable—we can lift a foot because we have trod on a pin, seen a step, heard a command, and so on.

The RF exerts a remarkable range of control over the entire organism. In our remote ancestors, it may have been the highest control level of the nervous system. RF still governs much of "posture" and "stability." It shares with the local channels of the cord the maintenance of antigravity posture, that is, of stability in space. RF merges into the *hypothalamus* and shares with it a role in homeostasis, the maintenance of a moderate stability or constancy in the interior milieu (CO_2 level in the blood, blood sugar level, etc.), keeping respiratory mechanisms going and regulating blood pressure. It also has a role unto itself, establishing various "modes" of the organism's behavior,

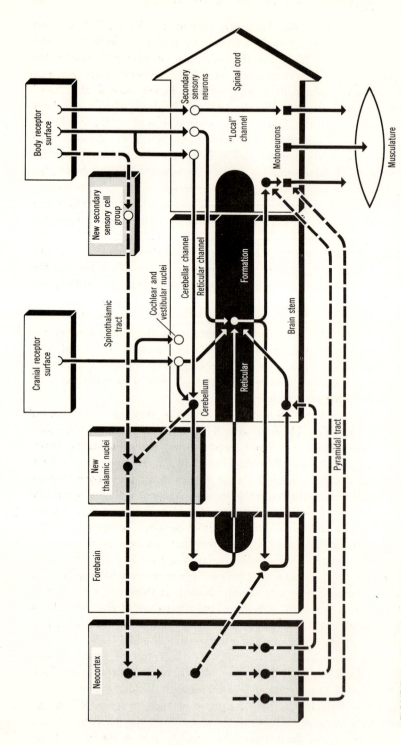

FIGURE 9 To make sense of this complex figure, we should study it in two stages. In the first stage, we ignore the three shaded boxes and the dashed lines, to obtain a schematic view of the basic neural circuitry of a submammalian vertebrate. We may follow the solid lines to see how signals from the receptors are processed in spinal cord, brainstem, and forebrain to yield the moto-neuron signals that control the effectors. To gain an understanding of the additions to and modifications of this basic neural circuitry that occurred in mammalian evolution, we may then focus on the shaded boxes and the dashed lines. The dominant addi-tion is the neocortex, which receives its sensory input from the new thalamic nuclei, which both samples old signal channels and receives more finely discriminated signals from the new secondary sensory cell groups via the spinothalamic tract. Neocortex not only modulates older structures in forebrain, but—via the pyramidal tract—can exercise new controls on motor activity at all levels from the brainstem down to the motoneurons.

136

especially sleep and wakefulness, and switching the organism from one to another. Of all the properties of RF, "mode control" is the one we shall select for scrutiny and modeling in Section 7.1.

We now turn to the shaded boxes and broken lines of Figure 9: The neocortex, a new outgrowth of the cerebral hemispheres, was a "sudden" occurrence in evolution, and is as much a characteristic of mammals as their unique system for live birth and suckling of their young. The more neocortex an animal has, the longer-term its activity can be—the more "plans" it makes. From the mesencephalon down is the "here-and-now" department. Even the chimpanzee does not have man's ability to anticipate future occurrences in planning his actions. Long-range planning is also facilitated by the complex social interactions made possible because parts of man's cortex are well adapted for speech.

With the new cortex come new channels. New thalamic nuclei (cell groupings) are formed, and the *spinothalamic tract* synapses there, carrying information to the neocortex free of the pooling effects of the old RF pathways. Similarly, there is a new direct motor pathway, the *pyramidal tract,* which carries instructions directly from neocortex to spinal cord. The pyramidal tract is so called because it grossly resembles a pyramid at the decussation† of these axons, not because of the preponderance of pyramidal cells in the cortex which gives rise to these axons. Primates, with their ability to perform delicate manipulations (is it a pedipulation if you use your feet?) even have some direct paths from neocortex to individual motoneurons.

These new regions do not exist apart from the older structures; rather, they tend to augment and modify the functions of these. We shall consider a related scheme of neocortical modification in Section 6.3 when we suggest natural ways in which the visual cortex may be somatotopically interconnected with superior colliculus to yield visual behavior in mammals more subtle than that of submammalian forms. The pyramidal tract, again, tends to bypass the older motor pathways, but only 10% of its fibers pass directly to the motoneurons. Perhaps this is both because much motor control is hierarchical in the sense that *groups* of motor neurons are patterned rather than individuals and also because much of the outflow consists of predictions of what groups of effectors will do, and so goes to relatively high spinal centers for checking against feedback from lower regions and the periphery. These "correlation centers" can then "report" to the cerebrum on the extent to which movements are "progressing as planned". (This is much the same as the idea of *internal* feedback in Evarts et al. [1971].) Each central pattern for the initiation of movement has its neuronal repercussions upon central sensory patterns, and each performed movement introduces alterations in sensory input patterns. In this way, sensory and motor systems are bound together both internally and externally.

Ironically, the "new" pyramidal pathways are called classical pathways in the literature, since physicians, with their clinical studies of human neurology, understood them much earlier than they disentangled the evolutionarily older pathways from the RF. In addition to these totally new pathways—the *neospinothalamic* (*classical leminiscal ascending*) *sensory pathway,* and the *pyramidal* (*classical descending*) *motor pathway*—there are new pathways building on the old—the *parallel extralemniscal*

---

† A *decussation* is where the fibers of a contralateral projection (page 32) pass from one side of the brain to the other.

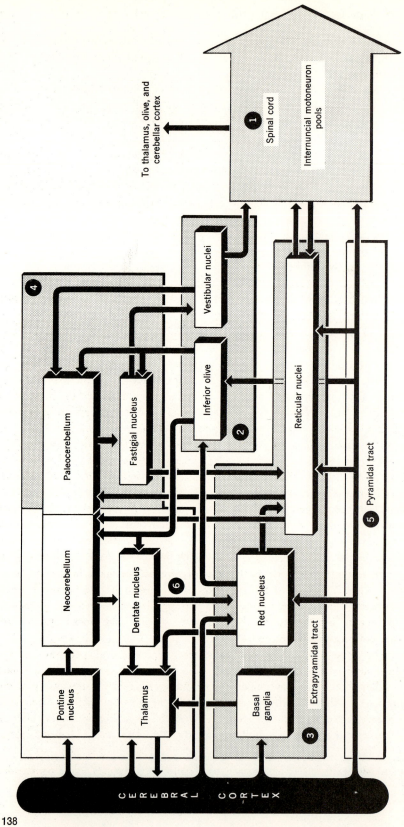

FIGURE 10 A schematic view of the cerebellum in relationship to the pyramidal and extrapyramidal pathways. The evolutionarily "older" system (1), (2), (3), and (4) (shown shaded) is augmented in mammals by the pyramidal tract (5), and the thalamus, neocerebellum, and related systems of (6).

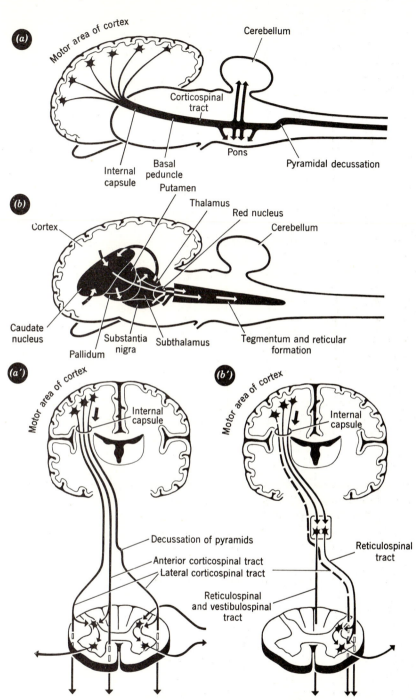

FIGURE 11   In these four views we re-present the information schematized in Figure 10, by artificially separating the pyramidal and extrapyramidal systems. We see views of the pyramidal system in (a) a side view of a "generalized" mammalian brain and (a') a front view of a human forebrain and cross section of spinal cord. (b) and (b') give the corresponding views of the extrapyramidal system. It may help to compare the siting of the structures in Figure 12a.

ascending sensory pathway, building on the phylogenetically older lemniscal system, which it joins in the midbrain, and which reaches widespread cortical regions via the brainstem RF, and the parallel *extrapyramidal motor pathways,* which descend to the motor nuclei indirectly by way of the basal ganglia and the brainstem RF. It should be added that brainstem RF exerts modifying influences both "upstream" on the cerebral and cerebellar hemispheres, and "downstream" on both motor and *sensory* nuclei; there seem to be centrifugal sensory control mechanisms where fibers run *outward* in the classical ascending sensory pathways. These pathways are not really partitioned, as the diagram might suggest, but are, in fact, mutually interacting. Paralleling the classical succession of ascending neurons appears a descending system which links the same nuclear processing stations from above downward.

To provide an alternative view to that of Figure 9 we present a modification of Brookhart's [1967] schematic of how this basic circuitry is built upon, by showing in Figure 10, the cerebellum and its environs, to see how the evolution of neocere-bellum matched the evolution of neocortex and neothalamic structures. The inter-nuncial neuron pools of the spinal cord (1) have already been discussed in Section 5.1. Areas (1) and (2) provide the basic postural system (sometimes the visual system as well can aid posture). A substrate of postural stability is necessary for more complex behavior because goal-seeking movements are based on a posturally stable initial point. The extrapyramidal system (3) is (evolutionarily) an old, richly interconnected part of the nervous system and can act by itself or be modulated by the cerebral cortex. It is probably the locus of stored (innate) programs for such motor activity as running, mating, fleeing, fighting. The pyramidal tract (5) is a "young" system appearing only in mammals, whereas in birds other systems which are less significant in mammals become highly elaborated.

We need some sort of feedback from the controlled system to the controller to correlate posture (1), (2), and the control of movement (3), (5), as well as to prevent conflicting commands from being sent to the internuncial pools. The old cerebellum (paleocerebellum) (4) receives inputs from (1) and (2) and the reticular nuclei, and provides a feedback path via its "backporch" the fastigial nucleus. It has a restricted output through the roof of the cerebellum toward the postural control centers as well as to the reticular nuclei and the internuncial pools. The "newer" parts of the nervous system seem to use new parts of old analogous parts for communication and feedback. For example, the neocerebellum (6), the two cerebellar hemispheres of the cerebellum, must coordinate the more finely graded positional changes now possible. Inputs to the neocerebellum include pathways from cerebral cortex (by way of the pontine nuclei) which seem to be part of the pyramidal tract, suggesting that the neocerebellum is receiving information about the actual motor commands being issued. However, many of these fibers also come from the so-called motor association areas rather than from primary motor cortex. Its output is through (and mediated by) the dentate nuclei. Note that each nucleus receives the same input as its corresponding region of cerebellar cortex, and provides the output of the cerebellum from its own computations as modified by cortical tuning. To contrast the regions (4) and (6) the paleocerebellum seems involved with levels at or below the reticular nuclei, whereas the neocerebellum has available refined information from the basal ganglia, the sub-thalamus, and the red nuclei.

Our next three figures are designed to complement our schematics by showing roughly how some of these pathways are positioned. In Figure 11a we see a side view of a generalized vertebrate which suggests how the axons from cells all over *motor-sensory cortex* come together in the *internal capsule* from which the fibers of the *corticospinal tract* course down, sending collaterals to the cerebellum as they pass through the *pons* then (further down) the *pyramidal decussation* where the bulk of the fibers cross from one side of the body to the other, as is made clear in the "front" view of Figure 11a'. In Figures 11b and 11b' we see some of the structures involved in the extrapyramidal system where we note that a crucial role is played by subcortical forebrain structures of the *basal ganglia*. The geography of the basal ganglia is depicted in Figure 12, where we see the relative positions of *thalamus* (sensory pre-processing en route to cortex), *internal capsule* (communication tracts), *basal ganglia* (motor systems), and *limbic system* (the four F's) as we move outward to the *neocortex*. In the left half of Figure 12a we see a horizontal section through one-half of the brain, with a corresponding side view on the right-hand side. In the center is the thalamus, on either side of which lie the two subsystems of the basal ganglia—the *lenticular nuclei* and, curving around these structures, the *caudate nucleus*. The arrows indicate the plane of section, which is high enough that we do not see the abutment of the lenticular nucleus upon the head of the caudate nucleus. The *internal capsule* on each side is then revealed as the "V" of white matter formed by the axons of various sensory pathways, as well as various motor pathways coursing down from motor cortex between thalamus and the lenticular nucleus. Further details of the limbic system are shown in Figures 12b and 12c.

In Figure 13 we complement our sketch of the motor systems by schematizing the tactile pathways of somatosensory and motor-sensory cortex. In Figure 13b we again see the role of *thalamus* as "way station" and note that the paths from thalamus to cortex also lead through the *internal capsule*. The thalamus receives somatic input from the head via the *trigeminal nucleus*, while input from the body comes from the spinal cord directly via the *lateral spinothalamic tract* and, for proprioception, via synapses in the *gracile and cuneate nuclei* receiving from the *posterior funiculus*. The lateral view in Figure 13a reminds us of the brainstem collaterals to *cerebellum* and *superior colliculus*, while we see that in cortex signals go not only to *somatosensory cortex* but also to *motor cortex* and to various "association areas" in *parietal* and *temporal* cortex. Note that all sensory input to cortex, except for smell, passes via the thalamus, presumably for preprocessing, but that motor cortex can "talk" directly to the spinal cord. However, cortex does send signals to thalamus, and these may serve in part to "tune" sensory pathways by actually changing the transfer characteristics of the thalamic preprocessors. Similarly, there exist return projections to thalamic motor nuclei. In Figure 14 we present a purely hypothetical example in the form of a schematic neuron for which cortical tuning can change a cell from detecting *coincidence* of signals to simply detecting the *presence* of any signal.

With this, we complete our brief introduction to the geography of the brain. We cannot close without reminding the reader that, as in a one-day tour of a great city, many landmarks remain unvisited, and for those we have visited much that is important remains untold. However, just as the one-day tour may help structure one's appreciation of the city's many delights on later, more extended, visits, so should our two sections on neuroanatomy serve to give the reader some reference points to help tackle the research literature with some small degree of confidence.

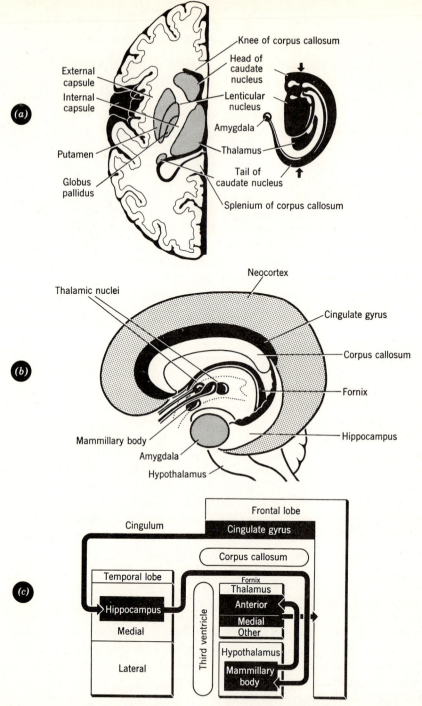

FIGURE 12   In the right-hand half of (a) we give a three-dimensional side view showing the basal ganglia surrounding the thalamus. [The basal ganglia comprise corpus striatum and amygdala, while the corpus striatum comprises the caudate nucleus and the lenticular nucleus (= putamen + globus pallidus)]. The left-hand half of (a) indicates a horizontal section through the left-hand half of a human brain at the level indicated by the arrows in the side view. The internal capsule is the white matter (axonal cable system) running between the thalamus and basal ganglia; the external capsule is the white matter passing around the basal ganglia. These views are complemented by the side view of part (b) which indicates the limbic system of the monkey. View (c) presents a schematization of the relation between the structures portrayed more realistically in (a) and (b).

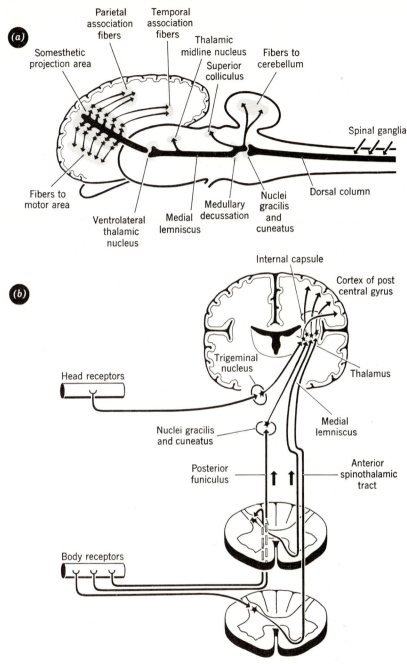

(a)

Parietal association fibers

Temporal association fibers

Thalamic midline nucleus

Superior colliculus

Somesthetic projection area

Fibers to cerebellum

Spinal ganglia

Fibers to motor area

Ventrolateral thalamic nucleus

Medial lemniscus

Medullary decussation

Nuclei gracilis and cuneatus

Dorsal column

(b)

Internal capsule

Cortex of post central gyrus

Trigeminal nucleus

Thalamus

Head receptors

Medial lemniscus

Nuclei gracilis and cuneatus

Posterior funiculus

Anterior spinothalamic tract

Body receptors

FIGURE 13 These two views of the somesthetic pathways to cortex complement the corresponding views of the pyramidal and extrapyramidal systems shown in Figure 11.

143

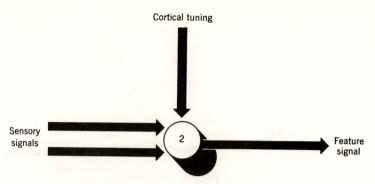

FIGURE 14   A hypothetical neuron which can be turned from an AND gate into an OR gate (compare Figure 1 of Chapter 1) by a tuning signal.

5.3   TAKING A WALK

It is a tribute to how well our motor systems are "designed" that most of us have never since infancy had to concentrate on the purely physical parts of walking. The following "experiment" is intended to get us to notice what is going on. (Even if you cannot conveniently carry out the "experiment" now, I do urge you to try it later, and compare your experience with the observations reported in the text.)

TAKE A WALK, AND WATCH SOMEONE ELSE TAKING A WALK

I   on smooth ground
II   on rough ground
   (a)   with eyes closed
   (b)   with eyes open
      (i)   normally
      (ii)   when dizzy
      (iii)   after sitting cross-legged long enough to induce "pins and needles."

Try to describe the motion of the center of gravity of your body, and of your four limbs in each case. On the basis of this, try to say something about the relative importance of visual, somesthestic, kinesthetic, and vestibular information. How do you take into account objects located in the room? It may take too long to try all the combinations, but try at least a few.

This was the first assignment for a course (EE 304) that I gave at Stanford University in the winter of 1969, and the following paragraph is taken from the class responses:

I am walking on smooth ground. My eyes scan for obstacles. I can feel (or, more likely, sense the effects of) muscle movements, but I am not aware of commanding those muscles to move. I am aware only of wanting to walk. My arms swing, somewhat in phase with the contralateral leg. I seem to be swaying a bit from side to side as my weight shifts from one foot to the other. It is a smooth feeling of motion accompanied by automatic muscle movements supporting me as I flow from one point to the next.

The overall response of the students is tabulated in Table 1; note that the combination of "pins and needles" and "dizziness" was not only hard to induce, but almost completely incapacitating in the rare cases that it was achieved.

The reader may come to appreciate that there are not only many ways of describing walking, there are many ways of walking. To simplify things, let us assume a basic set of reflexes which may be elicited and altered to provide for the needs of a particular situation. The most important such reflex is the *stepping* reflex. This exists even in very young babies and is depicted in Figure 15. It seems to be initiated without conscious effort when the center of gravity is sufficiently in front of the original point of support. We might then view normal walking on smooth ground as a process of cyclically casting our center of gravity forward, performing the stepping reflex with one foot, then carrying out the mirror image process. Describing walking this way should not lessen our appreciation of its complexity, however; the point is that *even though the muscle activity is quite complex, the high-level computation required need not be.*

In normal walking there is a succession of unstable states, though in a dynamic sense the system is stable. The way to view this, perhaps, is to take a control system point of view (Section 3.3). Let the mass and skeletal configuration of the body be considered as the controlled system, and the action of skeletal muscles and the nerve cells and reflexes which drive these muscles be considered as the controller. Anybody who has had a bad attack of vertigo knows that the body can at best be at an unstable equilibrium when standing unaided, in that it will fall over without proper muscular control. It is thus the job of the controller to either redress motions away from equilibrium (i.e., postural adjustments, should we wish to stand still) or exploit swings from equilibrium so as to cause the body to pass through another equilibrium situation after a translation (i.e., build up motion in terms of a smooth sequence of postural transitions).

That, very briefly, covers the "normal" mode of walking such as one might use in broad daylight on smooth ground. There are other modes, one of which is the "seeking" mode such as one might use in the dark on obstacle-strewn ground, in which walking takes place as a series of statically balanced configurations. Here the stepping foot is lifted and swung forward but the center of gravity remains over the supporting foot. This way the walker is not committed to transfer her weight to the stepping

FIGURE 15 The stepping reflex: When the girl is pulled forward so that her center of gravity moves in front of her feet, she steps forward to regain her balance by getting her center of gravity within the area above and between her feet.

TABLE 1

	NORMAL FEELING (NOT DIZZY, EYES)	"PINS AND NEEDLES" OR NUMBNESS (NOT DIZZY)	"PINS AND NEEDLES" OR NUMBNESS (DIZZY)	NORMAL FEELING (DIZZY)
ROUGH GROUND — EYES OPEN	Vision used to choose next place for support. Might use seeking mode.	Trouble using seeking mode—not enough information about footing.		Can't seem to place front foot where we want. Much effort to keep balance. Ground seems to be in motion.
ROUGH GROUND — EYES CLOSED	Seeking mode, exaggerated balancing motions.	Very slow progress.	Almost incapacitated. Doesn't even look like goal-directed behavior. Knees bent, arms spread and flailing.	Real trouble. Some real and some spurious feelings of being off balance. Amodal gait if we move at all. Severe disorientation.
SMOOTH GROUND — EYES CLOSED	No balance problem, normal except we don't go in a straight line.	Lower center of gravity (bent knees, etc.) wobbling, overcorrections, tense sensation.		Constantly correcting for perceived imbalance. Can't walk straight ahead. Disorientation.
SMOOTH GROUND — EYES OPEN	Normal. Need little conscious attention. Arms swing rhythmically; comfortable gait.	Movement jerky, but no real problem. Use eyes, perhaps hands, for information about leg position.		Staggering gait, balance difficult. Tend to move to one side. Ground seems to be in motion.

foot. Instead, she can "test" the ground by rotating the foot about the ankle, thus applying force with the ball of the foot. If the ground is found worthy, weight is transferred to the exploring foot and the process may begin on the other side.

A useful distinction here is that, in the normal mode of walking, we rely extensively upon our model of the immediate world to provide a feedforward type of control of walking (i.e., we confidently predict where our foot will hit the ground without explicitly testing it), whereas in the stepping or seeking mode each step is dependent on fed-back information about the spot on which the foot will land. The reader may appreciate the reality of this distinction by recalling the discomfort when she is in "feedforward mode" and her prediction fails, as when one misjudges the number of steps on a staircase. (Medieval psychologists exploited this effect in the design of castles: by making the top step of a flight different in height from all the others, they increased the chances that an invading knight would lose his footing and fall helplessly in his armor!)

If we try to schematize all these observations by drawing a block diagram, we immediately gain some feeling for how sparse a bunch of boxes connected by lines really is. Even the most hardened control theorist must feel a little bad about having a box labeled "VISION" with a single line coming out of it, and it is this feeling we shall try to assuage in the next section. Vision and the vestibular sense seem involved in keeping us going straight. The visual input yields much more accurate control, but when we are dizzy even vision can't keep us going straight. In Figure 16, we try to represent the logic involved when we are in the seeking or stepping mode. The reader may wish to compare this with the discussion of TOTE units in Section 4.2.

We might also try to indicate that there can be an internal model of the environment so that (for a short time after we close our eyes) we can walk confidently around obstacles. Also, we get some feeling that the amount of computation we must do and the amount that must be under conscious control increases drastically as various parts of the system are "knocked out". If we could somehow quantify this notion, we might better understand the functions of the various receptive systems.

Although we have been discussing only walking here, there are other gaits possible for humans. To gain a feeling for how little conscious control is required to direct quite complex body movements, the reader might wish to try "skipping", or "galloping". These gaits may be a bit hard to initiate, but once they are started they feel quite natural. We also are "wired" for four-legged gaits as the reader can see by crawling at different speeds—the relative phase of leg and arm movements changes as we crawl at different rates.

This discussion of walking has been in no way intended as a rigorous analysis of bipedal locomotion (see for example Chapter III of Bernstein [1967]) but rather as an aid to the reader in placing our discussion of feedback and hierarchies in vivid perspective, for it should make clear that we do not consciously command individual muscle fibers to fire in particular patterns, and that if one form of feedback is lacking, others may be used (if you can't feel the surface, look at it; if you can't see, you can listen for echos from large objects, etc.). Finally, high-level control seems to be kept free for settling broad questions of strategy, or fine details of manipulation, while intervening systems ensure that our motor activities issue in smooth, well-connected movements. The reconciliation of such general considerations with the detailed anatomy of the previous section is very much an open question that is beginning to receive more attention from researchers.

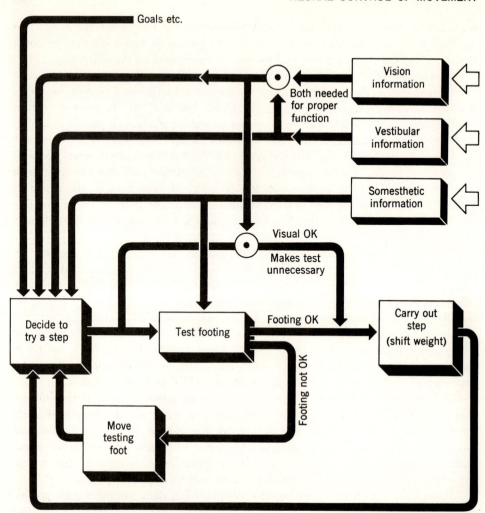

FIGURE 16 Schematization of the logic involved in the seeking or stepping mode—we stride ahead or tread cautiously depending on whether or not we have visual assurance of the possibility of safe positioning of our feet.

5.4 HIERARCHIES OF MOTOR CONTROL

In the preceding sections of this chapter, we have seen the crucial role played by spinal cord circuitry in patterning limb movements and we have indicated the problems involved in coordinating the limbs, compensating for vagaries in environmental conditions, and providing the postural adjustments which let the animal keep its balance during complex motor activity. However, in this section, rather than stressing details of actual circuitry, we wish to note that for certain tasks, sufficiently high-level choice of strategy need not involve specification of the details of execution at the muscular level.

If we decide to write a word, we use a completely different set of muscles if the instrument available is a pencil for use on a piece of paper or a paintbrush on the end of a long pole which must be held in two hands if one is to write upon a wall. How is it that we can still obtain our characteristic mode of writing with these two different systems, even if we have never written the desired message on a wall in this fashion before? Perhaps we would do well to recall the notion of an interpreter for a computer (Section 3.2). Finding it expedient to program a computer not in the machine language which directly controls the basic operations of its machinery but rather in terms of some high-level language, we may provide the computer with a supervisory program called an interpreter which will enable the computer to translate each instruction from the high-level program and then execute it. Using our "humans are machines" metaphor, we may imagine that in learning to write as children, we not only learn the sequence of appropriate movements to control a pencil held in our hands but also learn a higher level description of the writing in terms of a temporal and spatial sequence of strokes. We may thus suppose (and the reader should note how hypothetical this discussion is) that the brain accumulates high-level routines in terms of sequences of variously directed motions in terms of relative position without any specific reference to the absolute position in which, or the part of the body with which, those motions are to be effected. However, it might be hypothesized that our learning has also built up an interpreter for these high-level routines, one such interpreter for each of many different body systems. Thus, so long as the high-level program is available, any such system may execute fairly skilled movements even though it has never executed them before. This explanation seems to accord well with our example of the handwriting on the wall. Of course, it still leaves open a huge number of questions as to what mechanisms may actually exist in the brain for abstracting high-level routines from skills learned solely with one system, for constructing interpreters for different systems, as well as the question of to what extent it is really tenable to make so sharp a distinction between high-level language, the interpreter, and the machine language of the effector systems themselves.

In any case, the foregoing discussion suggests that we view complex motor activity as being performed by piecing together substructures, each of which deals with limited aspects of the problem. An important task in building up brain theory, then, is to isolate the substructures of motor behavior and to investigate ways in which they are combined to produce coordinated actions—a problem which has been treated with considerable thought by Greene [1964-1970]. To gain some feel for this composition problem, we may follow Greene [1968] in looking at a visual display system designed by Dertouzos [1966, 1967] to generate patterns by directing a beam of electrons in a cathode ray tube. Clearly, the most general approach is to describe a pattern by its brightness at every point on the screen. This way, all possible patterns can be displayed. A second method, which is much more efficient for most "interesting" patterns, is to piece together standard, parameterized curves. We saw something of this "synthesis" approach when we presented the "slide-box metaphor" in our discussion of short-term memory in Section 4.1.

Dertouzos' display uses the second method (see Figure 17). If input 2 is zero, a "draw" command on input 1 causes a diagonal beam to be traced across the tube face. By setting about four parameters to appropriate values by means of input 2, "almost all" smooth curves can be traced when the "draw" command is issued (compare the utility of a "French Curve" to the draftsman). The next step is to have a subsystem which generates appropriate tuning inputs for a parameterized set of about ten standard curves. Inputs to this higher level controller would be the label of the particular curve,

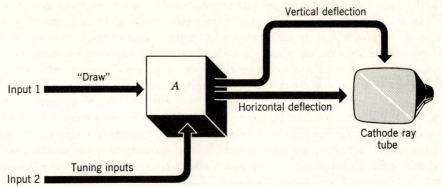

FIGURE 17   The triggering of input 1 causes a diagonal line to be traced across the screen of the cathode ray tube; but this line can be modified by "tuning" via input 2.

its orientation, time of initiation, initiation point, size, and so on. Thus we could build up a hierarchical system so that at a high level we would not be bothered with the drudgery of computing the signals to the deflection plates at every instant of time.

None of the conventional notions of control theory are discarded in this scheme. Feedback and perhaps feedforward [i.e., using a model to predict what is about to happen (cf. Section 3.4)] are used to implement each local controller. Exactly what is being gained cannot be quantified until the theory of complexity of computation is better understood, but the goal is to reduce the computation required at high levels at the expense of more local, less general, more autonomous, simpler controllers.

For the animal motor system, we would redraw the boxes of Figure 17 as in Figure 18. Here, at any stage in the hierarchy, the actions taken are dependent upon a gross command which is tuned mainly by measurements of local conditions, but perhaps also by high-level commands being sent to adjacent levels. The gross commands need only be "in the right ballpark", that is, close enough to the desired trajectory so that the tuning inputs' abilities to correct are not exceeded. A good example is the notion of a postural frame within which movements take place. Lower-level feedback via spinal reflexes can serve to keep an animal from falling over despite changing support conditions. Commands to move need not carry information about what will happen to the

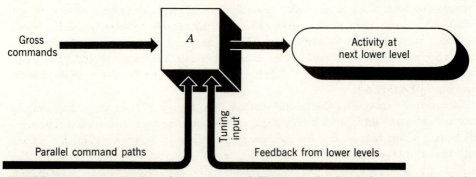

FIGURE 18   A generalization of the scheme of Figure 17. Feedback from lower levels in an animal motor system, and parallel command paths, provide tuning inputs for the movements triggered by gross commands.

center of gravity if a certain leg is lifted—the postural "tuning inputs" will cause the whole body (if necessary) to move so as to provide proper support. Parallel command paths can then impose refinements (such as the finger movements involved in playing the piano) upon the gross trajectory with feedback stabilization. (Of course, the gross commands must be directing a trajectory that is close to stable. If the high-level commands cause three legs to step off a cliff, the tuning inputs will be of little use in creating a stable, steady situation.)

It is worth noting that certain behaviors which might be complicated to simulate on a computer, may be very simple properties of the nervous system and body. Because of gravity, it requires no detailed computation to put one's arm down. Again, the relationship between the shape of the limbs and the function which they are to subserve affects requirements for neural computation. Much work is being done by anatomists, and especially those interested in evolution, to understand how change in structure of the skeleton correlates with change of function. Presumably there are many different ways one could put together joints, and get a system that could carry out certain manipulations, but for some structures these will be very easy manipulations to control, whereas for others control will be difficult. Automata theory offers theorems about how changes in input coding can drastically change the amount of time a network would take to carry out a computation. For any given function there seems to be a best way of coding the information to get a fast response from the system (cf. our discussion of preprocessing in Section 2.4). Similarly, the way in which we structure the musculature and the bones will greatly affect the amount of computation that is required to assure smooth operation of joints and easy interaction of the organism with the world. Thus an "old fashioned" part of mechanical engineering—the study of kinematic linkages—may become increasingly relevant to us, to augment our studies of pure information processing, and tell us how to put bars and rods together, and put joints between them, so that the resultant motions of the linkage describe an appropriate curve without having to be "pushed" by elaborate computation through each successive point of its orbit. Thus, although our emphasis is almost entirely upon highly parallel processing in overall active networks to combine present input with traces of past experience to control action, we must realize that the computational tasks will depend not only upon input preprocessing but also upon the output structures that actually execute the actions.

Let us close this theoretical discussion with a short catalog of advantages and disadvantages of a hierarchical type of command system arranged to make the most efficient use of the highest levels, by reducing the complexity of their computations (cf. the discussion in Section 4.1 of the advantages and disadvantages of internal models). Among the advantages are that more time is available for creative problem solving (planning) to deal with novel situations; that more space is available (more memories can be stored) if their description does not deal with all the little details; and that new tasks (or similar tasks) are more easily and rapidly learned (as long as they are not too different). Having local control also allows specific, uncomplicated actions like withdrawing from a hot stove to be performed very quickly. Another advantage is that the information flow is substantially reduced in comparison to an organization having only one level of command.

Some disadvantages are that if we were interested in the efficiency of just the motor part of a movement (i.e., ignoring central, computational complexity) we would be able to find a better pattern and sequence of muscle activation if our computation included every detail of the situation. As we have already suggested with the example that rubbing the stomach and patting the head is hard, the behavior possible to the animal is drastically reduced in degrees of freedom by the hierarchical arrangement. Thus some peculiar environmental change might result in situations that animal cannot meet. Also, learning "unusual" tasks may be quite hard (e.g., learning to walk differently as in modern dance). Nonetheless it is clear, both for animal and for robot, that most tasks will lend themselves to decomposition into familiar subtasks, and that level-by-level refinement of tasks will normally be vastly more efficient than any attempt to replace a high-level command directly with a sequence of machine-language instructions.

As we look at the evolution of neural circuitry, we might almost suggest that Figure 17 shows a system well suited to take the advantages of a hierarchical structure, with various feedback circuits in the spinal cord and above providing postural fine tuning; and that Figure 18 shows the additional machinery required to overcome the disadvantages we have noted for hierarchical systems by adding new mechanisms which can "intervene from above" to provide a new source of fine tuning based on learned refinements.

An experiment which ties such a distinction in with our discussion of feedback in the spinal cord (Section 5.1) is due to Navas and Stark [1968]. However, rather than recall the details of their experiment, let us instead suggest what they might have found if they had worked with the situation shown in Figure 19. From our study of Figure 5 we might expect that at the weight drops into the hand, spindle receptors are stretched, and their effect in increasing the firing of α-motoneurons causes the

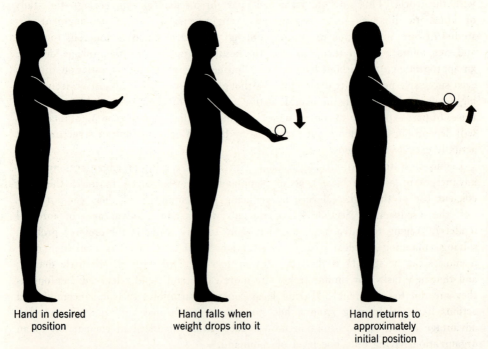

Hand in desired   Hand falls when   Hand returns to
position   weight drops into it   approximately
                                                  initial position

FIGURE 19   An indication of how the central nervous system can respond to a sudden change in load. Initially the hand is in a desired position; the hand falls when a weight is dropped into it; and then a ballistic command is computed to send the hand back toward its desired position, with a tracking control "tuning" the final location.

elbow joint to return to essentially its initial angle. In fact, the reaction time is longer than for a spindle reflex, and the spindle seems uninvolved during the early phase of compensatory movement. Rather, we appear to be dealing with a highly learned adaptive motor activity: realizing that there is a major disturbance, we determine a ballistic movement to compensate for it, with the spindles only coming in at the very end to fine tune the end of the trajectory and set up the system anew to compensate for minor disturbances.

Let us close this section with some data on the specificity of neural connections (for a superb review, see Jacobson [1970]) to remind us that "tuning" of motor behavior does indeed involve these two components of "local tuning" using spinal and brainstem level feedback paths, and "change of strategy" and "addition of fine detail" for which the evolution of new structures such as mammalian neocortex seems to be required. What experiments on neural specificity seem to show is that although learning is possible in the "higher centers" of the brain, the "lower centers" of the brainstem and spinal cord have a genetically determined structure which forms the basis for normal function; and if this structure is disarrayed during regeneration of injured nerves, normal function will not recover unless the disarrangement is *sufficiently well structured* that higher centers can actually compensate, and that *there exist appropriate higher centers.*

To appreciate the demonstration by Weiss [1941] that neuronal connections need not be learned—and in fact may not change even if they have become nonadaptive—it will help to recall from Figure 6, Chapter 3 the highly simplified control circuit for the single-joint four-muscle leg of Figure 5, Chapter 3 in which the triggering of a single ON neurons by "higher centers" could initiate a rhythmical motion described by the motor "score" (*). For our present purposes, the crucial point to note about *any* circuit that yields the "motor score" (*) is that if the Ad motoneuron is connected to the Ab muscle and the Ab motoneuron is connected to the Ad muscle, then activation of the circuitry will yield the motor score appropriate to a *backward* progression.

Consider the situation of Figure 20 in which the forelimbs of a larval salamander are interchanged so that each forelimb now "faces backward." Salamanders have sufficient regenerative capacity that the limbs heal into their new positions and are innervated by nerves from the spinal cord. One might expect the resulting connections between motoneurons and muscle fibers to be initially random, with the animal never being able to control its forelimbs, or else eventually "sorting the connections" through learning and coming to use its forelimbs functionally, even though somewhat awkwardly because of their strange placement. However, the contrary was found: the

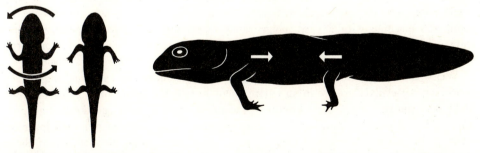

FIGURE 20 The unfortunate effect on locomotion of interchanging the right and left forelimbs of a salamander.

animal would execute forelimb movements which were inappropriate to the new position of the limbs, pushing the animal away from food or toward a noxious stimulus. (Weiss [1941] notes: "Actual regression occurs only if other means of progression, such as the tail and hind limbs, have been removed or paralyzed. If the hind limbs are present, however, the resultant effect is a constant struggle between the hind limbs and the forelimbs, the former striving to advance the body and the latter cancelling the effect by moving the body backwards by the same amount. The net result is that the animal swings back and forth without ever moving from the spot. It is almost pathetic to see how helpless the animals are about their predicament, and although some of them have been kept for more than a year, long beyond metamorphosis, their behavior has never changed.")

Given our discussion of neural circuitry for implementing the "motor score" (*), these results would suggest that the abductor and adductor have become reconnected to the adductor and abductor motoneuron pools, respectively, even though the reversal of their roles resultant from limb reversal dictates that an interchange of these connections is required for the animal's well-being. (This may be too simple-minded an analysis, but it will suffice for now.)

It is easy for the reader to respond incredulously at this point: "But couldn't the salamander see it was going the wrong way and take appropriate action?" Since the experiments clearly say "NO", it may be useful to probe the source of this incredulity. It is true, to take a simple example, that if a human were in a vehicle with the labels of the forward and reverse gears interchanged, she would eventually tire of retreating from her goal and learn to reverse her use of the gears. She would not only realize that when she wishes to go forward she should engage the reverse gear, but she would also (i) *explicitly* realize that forward and reverse gears are opposites, (ii) *perceive* that the forward gear is yielding reverse motion, (iii) *devise* and *test* the hypothesis that the reverse gear should correspondingly yield forward motion, and, finally, having confirmed the hypothesis, (iv) *remember* and (v) *use* the outcome. Granted that (i) and (iii) could be collapsed into stumbling upon the use of the reverse gear by trial-and-error (which requires that one does occasionally depart from prior procedures), it is still clear that what we regard as simple common sense action does in fact involve many stages, and that there is no prior reason to expect all animals to have brains equipped to handle all these stages. To give a final picturesque demonstration of the falsity of such an expectation, consider a computer in which we had reversed the add and subtract instructions. Even if we kicked the machine every time it gave the wrong answer, we would not expect it to rewrite its programs. In fact, we realize that we should have to equip the machine with special sensors, so that the timing of a kick could enter into its computations, and—even more significantly—we should have to equip the machine with a very sophisticated supervisory program (hopefully undisturbed by our instruction interchange!) which, when triggered by a kick, could try various schemes for modifying low-level programs until no further kicks ensued.

Weiss' experiments show that the salamander simply does not have such high-level machinery; it evolved to live in an environment in which experimental biologists were unknown, and thus could survive without the ability to make such sophisticated adaptations. The salamander is revealed to be a "wired-in" beast: if you put food in front of it, its brain sends down to the spinal cord "commands" to go forward, but if these commands make it go backward it just cannot adapt. Such an observation is a corrective to a naive stimulus-response view—closely related to the random connection view

—which holds that *all* behavior is built up by learning that an often-repeated stimulus must be paired with a certain response. We have to realize both that much is "wired-in" (it depends upon the "level" of the animal how much of its own activity is "wired-in" and how much is learned); and that, in addition to learning at a basic stimulus-response level, there are levels of increasingly sophisticated organization, so that, say, when a human writes an essay, her genetic endowment provides the substrate, and reflexes may help her keep the adjustment of pencil above paper, or finger upon type-writer key, but the actual intellectual content of the paper will come from a very high level of mental organization indeed.

5.5 DISTRIBUTED MOTOR CONTROL

To further our understanding of the brain theory approach to control of movement, we next consider how the feedback tracking scheme of Pitts and McCulloch (recalled in Figure 21), which generates, for any ϕ, a transformation T_ϕ which will transform it to standard form, may be played out over a whole array of neurons.

As we saw in Section 3.3, the transform application box is memoryless: input pattern ϕ and transform T at its input yield transformed pattern $T\phi$ at its output. The error computer box is memoryless: an input pattern at its input yields the cor-responding error at its output. The transform computer box is a sequential machine: if its state at time t is the transform T, and its input at time t is the error vector e, then its new state and output at time $t+1$ will both be the transform $W(e) \cdot T$.

The hard work in such a scheme is actually defining an appropriate error measure E and then finding a mapping W which can make use of error feedback to properly control the system so that it will eventually transform the input to standard form. Any

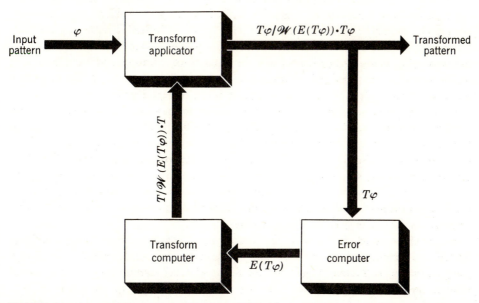

FIGURE 21   A generalization of the Pitts-McCulloch scheme for transforming a pattern to standard form.

theory of evolution and of learning must come to grips with ways in which a system may find E's and W's better suited to its task environment (we commented on this briefly in the critique of GPS in Section 4.2).

To relate all this to somatotopically structured networks, let us see how Pitts and McCulloch exemplified their general scheme in a plausible reflex arc from the eyes through the superior colliculus to the oculomotor nuclei to so control the muscles which direct the gaze as to bring the point of fixation to the center of gravity of distribution of brightness of the visual input. (With our current knowledge of retinal "preprocessing" we might now choose to substitute a term such as "general contour information" or any "feature" for "brightness" in the above prescription. But that does not affect the model which follows.)

Apter [1945, 1946] showed that each half of the visual field of the cat (seen through the nasal half of one eye and the temporal half of the other) maps topographically upon the contralateral superior colliculus. In addition to this "sensory" map, Apter studied the "motor" map by strychninizing a single point on the collicular surface and flashing a diffuse light on the retina and observing which point in the visual field was affixed by the resultant change in gaze. She found that these "sensory" and "motor" maps were almost identical (cf. insert in Figure 22).

On the basis of this data, Pitts and McCulloch erected the scheme shown in Figure 22 (their Fig. 6) for centering the gaze. They noted that excitation at a point of the left colliculus corresponds to excitation from the right half of the visual field, and so should induce movement of the eye to the right. Gaze will be centered when excitation from the left is exactly balanced by excitation from the right. Their model is then so arranged, for example, that each motoneuron controlling muscle fibers in the left medial rectus and right lateral rectus muscles, which contract to move the left and right eyeballs, respectively, to the right should receive excitation summing the level of activity in a thin transverse strip of the left colliculus. This process provides all the excitation to the right lateral and left medial rectus, muscles turning the eye to the right. Reciprocal inhibition by axonal collaterals from the nuclei of the antagonist eye muscles, which are excited similarly by the other colliculus, serve to perform subtraction. The computation of the quasi center of gravity's vertical coordinate is done similarly. [Of course, computation may be performed by commissural fibers linking similar contralateral tectal points, instead of in the oculomotor nuclei.] Eye movement ceases when and only when the fixation point is the center of gravity.

It must be emphasized that the reflex for which we have just summarized a crude, though instructive, model would be subject to "higher control" in normal function. For example, "interest" might be the criterion for determining which area of the visual field to examine, with the reflex determining the fixation point within the region (cf. the fine tuning servo on a radio receiver); gaze may then remain fixed at that point until it is "adequately" perceived. Conversely, a sudden flash may usurp the averaging operations to dominate the reflex control of gaze momentarily, forcing the organism to attend at least briefly to a novel stimulus.

It should be noted that even if the mathematical equations formalizing the Pitts-McCulloch scheme were to contain a damping term to prevent the eyeball from undergoing continual oscillations, it still has the defect of being essentially a tracking model, whereas the reflex "snapping" of gaze toward a flash of light is essentially ballistic. In fact, human eye movements can be either ballistic or tracking. Typically, a human examining a scene will fixate on one point of the visual field then make a saccadic

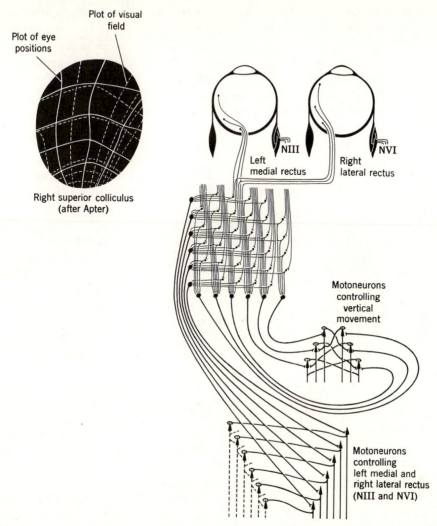

Plot of eye
positions

Plot of visual
field

Right superior colliculus
(after Apter)

NIII

NVI

Left
medial rectus

Right
lateral rectus

Motoneurons
controlling
vertical
movement

Motoneurons
controlling
left medial and
right lateral rectus
(NIII and NVI)

FIGURE 22   The Pitts-McCulloch scheme for reflex control of eye position via the superior colliculus: the eye can only be stationary when the activity in the two halves of the colliculus is balanced. The insert shows Apter's sensory map (broken lines) and motor map (solid lines) of the cat colliculus.

movement (the term for a ballistic eye movement) to fixate another point of the visual scene, until satisfied that she has scanned enough of the scene to perceive her current environment. However, in other situations, such as watching a car go by before crossing the street, she will fixate upon an object and then track it. In primates, various cortical areas can modulate activity in superior colliculus, and Bizzi has found that in one of them, the so-called frontal eye field, which is in frontal cortex, there are three types of cells: type I, which are active in ballistic eye movements; type II, which are active in tracking eye movements; and other cells more concerned with head than with eye movements. Perhaps a similar situation will be found on closer examination of superior colliculus. In any case, it does seem that the Pitts-McCulloch scheme is more suited to the tracking mode than to the ballistic mode.

To rectify this, let us then present another model, due to Braitenberg and Onesto, for a distributed computer controlling ballistic movement. (It should be mentioned that they conceived their model as a model of the cerebellum, but subsequent investigations have revealed so much new data about the cerebellum that their model cannot stand as a model of the cerebellar cortex without drastic modification. The reader may find a thorough critique of cerebellar modelling in Boylls and Arbib [1972], but it would not seem appropriate to present the details here. My aim in this book is not to say "Here is the correct model for the function of a certain subsystem of the brain", but rather to say "Here is a fruitful way to go about modelling brain function". In this spirit, I present models which give one new principles of organization, hoping to spur much further work toward discovering the biological implementation of these principles in neural circuitry; or programing their refinement in the design of control circuitry for robots.)

When a shot is fired from a gun two forces are involved—the explosion that propels the projectile toward the target, and the braking force when the projectile hits the target (if the target were to step aside, the projectile would not stop in the position at which it was originally aimed). Ballistic movements in animals also involve this "bang-bang" control. Experiments on rapid flexion and extension of *joints* have shown that muscle activation occupies only a small portion of the movement, and that the duration of this activation does not seem to be related to the extent of the movement. There is an initial burst of acceleration as the agonist contracts and the antagonist muscle relaxes, an intervening quiet period and then a final burst of deceleration as the antagonist contracts.

Experiments by Bizzi on *eye* movements, however, have revealed a system in which the "initial moment" triggers an agonist burst and antagonist silence, which continues until the "final moment" triggers a return of both muscles to the resting level appropriate to the new scheme. It's as if we simultaneously turned on an agonist burst, and a signal controlling the tracking system to its new level, but the former overrides the latter until it is turned off. In any case, in both situations described above, the duration of the movement seems to be determined mainly by the timing, relative to the "go" signal, of the "stop" signal (which has to be determined by the brain, rather than being imposed by the environment, as it was in our projectile example). Braitenberg and Onesto thus proposed a network for converting space into time (a subtle alchemy!) by providing that the position of an input (encoding the desired target position) would determine the time of the output (which would trigger the "slamming on of the brakes"). The scheme (see Figure 23) has a linear array of output cells whose output circuitry is so arranged that the firing of any one of them will yield the antagonist burst that will brake the ballistic movement. There are two systems of input fibers, each arranged in the same linear order, with position along the line corresponding to angle of flexion of the joint. The first class, the C-fibers, connect to a single output cell. The second class, the M-fibers, bifurcate into fibers which contact each cell in the array. The speed of propagation along these parallel fibers is such that the time required to go from one point in the array to another corresponds to the time the joint requires to move between the corresponding angles, assuming a fixed angular velocity about the joint.

The controller then elicits a ballistic movement by firing three signals. In the case of joint movements, one is to trigger the agonist burst which will initiate movement, one is on the C-fiber corresponding to the initial joint position, and one is on the

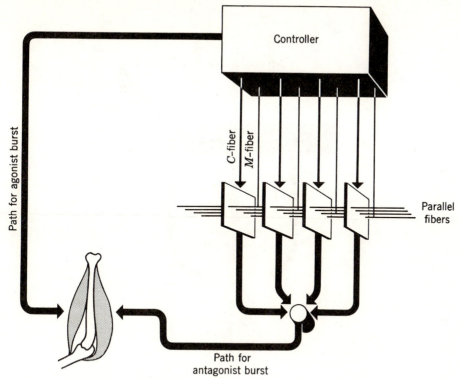

FIGURE 23 The Braitenberg-Onesto scheme for the control of ballistic movement: The *spatial* separation between the actuated C-fiber and the actuated M-fiber is transformed into the *temporal* separation between the agonist and antagonist burst.

M-fiber corresponding to the target position. (The reader may suggest the appropriate connections for a saccadic eye movement.) If we assume that an output cell can respond to parallel fiber input only if it has received C-fiber input, we see that only the output cell corresponding to the activated C-fiber will fire, and it is clear that its time of firing will correspond to its distance from the activated M-fiber. Thus it will elicit the braking effect of the antagonist burst at precisely the right time.

Note that in this scheme, we could relieve the controller of having to "know" where the joint is by having a feedback circuit continually monitor joint position and keep the appropriate C-fiber activated.

While we do not claim to have modeled *the* way the nervous system controls movement, what we have shown is that a plausible subsystem for vertebrate nervous systems may be of the type shown in Figure 24 in which position of the input on the control surface encodes the target to which the musculature will be sent. Further, we might expect that—akin to the result of merging the Pitts-McCulloch scheme with the Braitenberg-Onesto scheme—if an array of points is activated on the input surface, the system will move to the position which is the "center of gravity" of the positions encoded by that array.

It should be noted that a full elaboration of this scheme would involve hierarchical arrangements. For example, in fixating a new point in space, increasing angles of deviation might require movement of eyes alone, then of eyes and head, and then of eyes, head, and trunk. Thus the output of the motor-computer would not control a

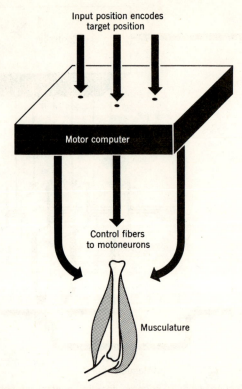

FIGURE 24 Schematic for a distributed motor control system embodying mechanisms such as those of Figures 22 and 23: a spatially encoded target position is transformed into the appropriate sequence of motoneuron commands, with an array of inputs yielding movement to the "average" of the encoded targets.

single joint but would control a whole hierarchy of subcontrollers, whose behavior would of course be modified by the low-level postural controllers alluded to in the preceding section. We should also add that the scheme must be elaborated to provide for generating particular velocities, and so on. To caricature it crudely, one may conjecture that such an option has evolved through the development of circuitry which can control tracking movements internally, rather than driving them through sensory channels.

As we shall see in more detail in Section 6.3, a crucial part of the behavior of an organism consists in being able to bring about appropriate relationships between itself and the parts of the environment with which it would interact. As we saw in Section 4.4, as the organism moves it must update its internal model if it is to provide a firm basis for guiding future interaction. To tie this in with a feedback scheme such as Figure 21 for which the "standard form" which provides the goal is "object in a position suitable for interaction", consider an animal that has an object in its visual field which is otherwise enshrouded in mist. Then the same pattern of retinal stimulation can be produced in two distinct cases:

Case 1.   The animal advances 1 meter toward the object.
Case 2.   The object advances 1 meter toward the animal.

Despite this identity of retinal stimulation, in a hostile environment such as that which shaped our own evolution, only in Case 2 does the object have such importance that the animal must orient to, and identify, the source of the retinal stimulation. Again, if the object "keeps pace" with the animal, then the animal will pay attention to it, even though the animal has no *visual* feedback signaling its own movement or that of the object. Thus we have the important notion that, although it is change in stimulation that carries information for a perceiving system, changes produced by the animal's own movements must in some sense be "subtracted out" lest they mask important changes in the environment.

Elegant experimental evidence for such "subtraction" comes from the work of von Holst and Mittelstaedt which supports the hypothesis that perception is based not on sensory input per se but rather on the difference between changes induced by the organism's own movements and changes on the organism's receptor surfaces. They carried out detailed experiments on flies, but after discussing this work, we shall mention supportive data on humans.

If a fly is constrained so that it can turn about a fixed point but cannot otherwise move, and then is placed inside a rotating drum marked with vertical stripes to make the rotation clearly visible (Figure 25), the fly will turn in the same direction as ("tracking") the movement of the drum. Now if the drum is stopped, and some smell tempting to a fly is introduced to one side of the fly, it will turn to face the source of temptation. But the fly's movement has the effect of causing the retinal displacement of stripes that would have resulted from a movement of the drum in the opposite direction. Yet the fly does not consequently reverse its rotation as we would predict if we held that it was bound to respond to sensory stimulation irrespective of its own movement. However, there are at least two satisfactory explanations for the fly's ability

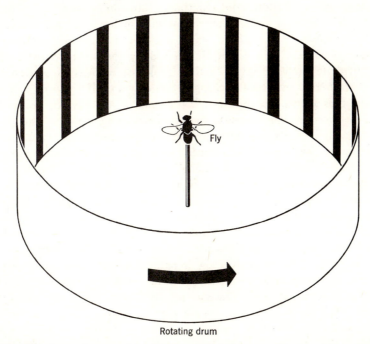

Rotating drum

FIGURE 25 Experimental setup for showing that a fly can tell the differences between changes induced by its own movements and changes induced by environmental movements.

to "ignore" the counterrotation. One is simply that the animal "blocks" all visual input while it is moving; the other is that it does indeed "subtract out" its own movement from the observed environmental movement. Von Holst and Mittelstaedt elegantly ruled out the first hypothesis by rotating the fly's head relative to its body through 180°; this can be done without breaking the neural connections between eye and body. They found that such a fly, once it started moving, would continue rotating until it dropped from exhaustion, suggesting that, rather than "blocking" input it indeed subtracted the projected movement from the observed movement (which, because of the rotation of its head, was completely opposite to the projected movement) and responded to the resultant discrepancy as if it represented the true movement of the environment.

Humans report corroborative experiences. When a human first dons inverting prisms, she finds that the world "jumps" every time she moves her head. Here again the inversion results in a direction of change of retinal excitation opposite to that usually associated with the movement. Intriguingly, though, humans can eventually adapt to the inversion, whereas flies cannot. The reader should try to predict what is perceived by a human with newly paralyzed eye muscles when she "wills" an eye movement.

Having thus seen experimental confirmation of the animal's ability to compensate for the effect of its own movement on its perception of a single parameter, we must note the even more subtle problems for a system such as a mammal which has delicately controllable receptors which bear many-dimensional relationships to similarly complex effectors. We suggest that this requires mechanisms which operate conceptually like those shown in Figure 26.

Figure 26 shows the input array about to enter a "storage surface" where it will soon replace the last such input. The input array also enters a mechanism which compares, in parallel, features of the input array with features of the "anticipated new scene". This anticipated scene is one computed by altering the last input scene (held on the "storage surface") in a way determined by the self-produced motions the system is currently carrying out as well as projected motions of perceived objects. Regions in which the new scene is changed due only to self-produced and projected motions will thus match the corresponding regions of the "anticipated new scene" and inhibit the corresponding regions of the pathway leading from the "storage surface" to the first "analysis surface". (Actually, a mixed ballistic-tracking strategy seems to be involved here. The "ballistic" movement induced by the transformer may not be completely accurate, and so some "fine tuning" may be required to try to match patterns before inhibition can either take place or be ruled out. This refinement seems to have been noted first by MacKay; for a recent overview of his work, see MacKay [1966]). Regions in which the new scene does *not* match the anticipated scene are not inhibited as they lead to the "analysis surface" and are exactly those regions to which the system must attend. We emphasize that Figure 26 is a tentative formulation—the "transformer" and "shifter" are themselves highly parallel devices, and may transform different parts of the array in different ways. Further, it is very much an open question in my mind as to what extent the processes involve direct efferent control of the early stages of the input pathways and to what extent the output clusters of the "analysis surface" themselves feed back to control much of the activity of the "transformers" and "shifter".

Although, for Pitts and McCulloch, the point of their model of colliculus was that

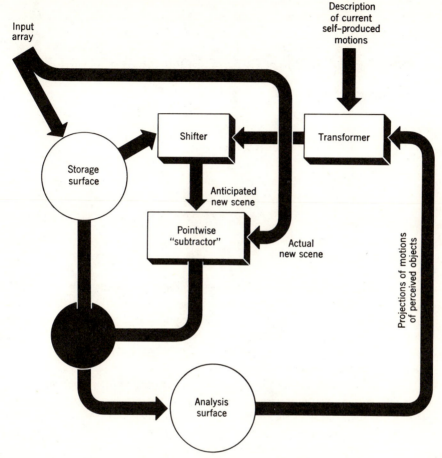

FIGURE 26 Schematic for ignoring inessential changes in sensory input. The analysis surface only receives as its input those aspects of the input array to the whole system that have not been anticipated by its analysis of its own movements and those of objects in the environment that it has already perceived.

it gave an implementation of their scheme that did justice to neurophysiological data, our essential point is that it demonstrates the feasibility of *a somatotopically organized network in which there is no "executive neuron" that decrees which way the overall system behaves; rather, the dynamics of the effectors, with assistance from neuronal interactions, extracts the output trajectory from a population of neurons, none of which has more than local information as to which way the system should behave.* It is a thesis of this book that the study of such networks must become a central element of our brain theory, and we shall elaborate this thesis in the next section.

6 | Memory and Perception in a Layered Computer

In this chapter we elaborate the theme established in Section 5.5—that computation in the brain proceeds in a highly distributed fashion, rather than under the centralized control of any single executive organ. We start by bringing this principle together with the other principles we have developed, relating them to Warren McCulloch's unpublished Introduction to a *Tractatus Neurologico-Philosophicus*. Then in Section 6.2 we introduce the notion of an output feature cluster as the appropriate action-oriented complement to the sensory features discussed in Section 2.4, tying them in with our discussion of Short Term Memory in Chapter 4. In Section 6.3 we then discuss how the array of output feature clusters in memory may be continually transformed to appropriately relate the organism to its world, stressing the role of forebrain and midbrain in subserving the "what" and "where" of visual perception, respectively. Finally, we assess the extent to which the hologram may furnish an appropriate metaphor for thinking about memory structures appropriate to the highly distributed computer that we posit the brain to be.

6.1 ORGANIZATIONAL PRINCIPLES

To understand how nervous systems "work," we need plausible inferences as to how nervous systems are organized. We can make recordings from single cells, but to measure the activity of most cells in a brain would be both too much and too little. Too much, since we would be swamped by the sheer volume of the data. Too little, because relevant patterns would not be displayed. In this section, then, we try to enunciate organizational "principles" which may help us to avoid this impasse, and may make the experimentalist's data collection task more manageable.

In the early 1960s, Warren McCulloch planned to write a *Tractatus*

Neurologico-Philosophicus. He wrote the introduction, and we reproduce it here (by kind permission of Rook McCulloch) for it makes clear the extent to which his view of neurology has influenced our brain theory. Unfortunately, the rest of his book was not written. However, the reader will find many of the ideas in *Embodiments of Mind,* a collection of McCulloch's papers.

Warren McCulloch: Introduction to the Tractatus Neurologico-Philosophicus

0.0. Man's knowledge of his behavior, his psychology, had existed two millennia before he ceased to think his brains only cooled his blood, and four millennia before he knew they were not jelly in which fibers precipitated. To understand brains may help us to explain man's behavior by explaining him, but it cannot take into account the things to which he behaves. Thus neurology falls short of psychology wherein the relations involve three things; for example: A acts as if B were C to him. We are not proposing a calculus of triadic relations, nor any logic for psychology.

0.10. We exhibit only a logic adequate for neurology, which is the science of nervous systems. They are to be found only in animals with many cells and they are composed only of cells called neurons. Histologically neurons are identified by their affinity for certain dye stuffs. Anatomically our neurons constitute one system, one net, for within it there is a path from any neuron to every other. Electrically, neurons are identified by the impulses they transmit. Physiologically, neurons constitute one system, for the occurrence of impulses in any neuron affects the occurrence of impulses in some adjacent neurons and is affected by the occurrence of impulses in other adjacent neurons. The net is such that every efferent peripheral neuron (i.e., every neuron that controls an effector, be it muscle or gland) can be indirectly affected along several paths through the net by each afferent peripheral neuron (i.e., each neuron that is directly affected by a receptor be it sensory cell or other transducer). Every neuron is traversed by at least one such path.

0.11. Each adjunction of neurons at which one affects another, called a synapse, operates predominantly in one direction only. Thus transmission of effects along any path goes in that direction only. However, circuits, i.e., circular paths, are numerous and, even in afferent peripheral neurons the generation or propagation of their impulses is usually affected by other neurons. Moreover receptors themselves are affected by effectors controlled by efferent peripheral neurons. Circuits regenerative over our receptors keep us alive: By these we breathe. Circuits regenerative within the net keep us lively: By these we attend. Those circuits whose output decreases their input, our reflexes, and similar inverse feedbacks within the brain, establish a state of the system by returning it toward that state when it is disturbed. To return it to that state is the function of each such circuit, its purpose. The state so established is the end in, and of, the operation of the system, its entelechy.

0.12. Our receptors are ordinarily exquisitely sensitive to minimal changes in the intensity of specific forms of energy or in the concentration of certain substances. These changes are thus normally the causes of the sequences of impulses in adjacent afferent peripheral neurons in that state which has been then and there determined by the nervous system. So the sequences in each and every afferent peripheral neuron signify to the nervous system the events surrounding it. The sequences are thus signals provided that the stimuli are adequate and the recipient neurons in the determined state. Sequences that arise from any other causes are what the engineer now calls noise. Signals and noise, necessarily distinguished by the engineer and by the neurologist are explained, but not distinguished, by the physicist in terms of matter and energy. They differ functionally; that is as they serve or fail to serve the ends of that nervous system.

0.131. Due both to the homogeneity of occurrences in the world and to the vicinage of our receptors, almost every adequate stimulus affects a clump of similar transducers contemporaneously. Since one transducer may affect several afferent peripheral neurons, and it may be affected by several transducers in the clump, the signals in many of these neurons are highly correlated. By means of these redundant signals, we recognize the objects of sensation, qualities like blue, sweet, cold, hard and shrill.

0.132. Any cohesive source of adequate stimulation that moves over a surface like the retina or the skin affects neighboring transducers successively. These affect neighboring, overlapping, afferent peripheral neurons in which the resultant changes in the sequences of impulses outlast their causes. By means of concurrent signals so correlated we recognize the coherent objects characterized by having a trajectory, like a flying spark, a scratching twig or the whistle of a passing train. Any afferent peripheral neuron of the somatic sensory system or a bipolar cell of the retina is affected by more than one kind of transducer in its clump, although the effect on the sequence of its impulses may vary with the kind of transducer. Thus changes in the qualities of a moving object, if they be not too great or too sudden, need not prevent us from identifying it by its historic route or trajectory.

0.133. But for these uses of redundancy it is difficult to imagine how any animal could spot its parent, capture its food, avoid obstacles, defend itself from its enemies, find its mate or care for its young. They enable us to identify and qualify objects despite irrelevant adequate stimuli from the world and despite noise engendered by malfunction of transducers. We are not concerned with these questions, but nature's solution of these problems has given us nervous inputs which are correlated, and therefore we must treat the signals in afferent peripheral neurons as already encoded redundantly. This we cannot ignore.

0.141. Moreover the central terminations of these neurons are such that they effectively map with overlap neighborhood of receptors into neighborhood of recipient central neurons. The central positions of our efferent peripheral neurons constitute a similar topological map of our effectors with a similar redundancy.

0.142. The simplest nervous arc of a reflex consists of a mapping of stretch receptors on the efferent peripheral neurons of the stretched muscle so as to cause it to contract. But this is not the only mapping. The second, by the same afferents, is on the neurons controlling the muscle antagonist to the stretched muscle at one or more joints so as to cause it to relax. All other sequential arcs of more neurons in series contain some interposed maps over so-called internuncial neurons.

0.143. Similarly, with the development of distance receptors at the head of the animal the same plan was followed. Thus photoreceptors map topologically on bipolar cells and these on the ganglion cells in the eye. These map on the superior colliculus and, through it, on the cerebellar cortex. They also map on the lateral geniculate and, through it, on the cerebral cortex. All of these maps are connected topologically to one another. Were it not for this multichannel mapping all the way from receptors to effectors, the location of the reception would have to be transmitted by some sequence of impulses to insure that the appropriate response be directed to that place. This, the "local sign" of Lotze,† for vision is 20 bits of selective information for each of a million ganglion cells.

0.145. By this mapping the local sign is preserved except in those parts of the brain in which signals from many or all parts of the animal must converge for purposes of decisions committing the whole organism, as in the reticular formation; or for recognition of objects mediated by any one of many sensory modalities, concepts rather than mere precepts; and for the elaboration of skilled acts and judgments depending upon these recognitions, as in the cerebral cortex.

With McCulloch's words and the experience of the first five chapters available to us, we can briefly state a number of principles which guide our quest to build a theory of the brain.

First, we have tried, especially in Sections 2.1 and 4.1, to understand the basic *functional* attributes which any system interacting adaptively with a complex environment would seem to have to satisfy, whether it be a robot or an animal. In this sense, we seem to have gone beyond the disclaimer in McCulloch's 0.10 that our logic is adequate only for neurology. In trying to understand how animals are able to move purposively and efficiently in an environment which is constantly changing, it will be important to note that the animal's environment changes in restricted ways. Thus the animal (or robot) does not need to be able to use its effectors in all of the immense number of possible combinations, but instead can deal with many problems at a

---

† See, for example, R. H. Lotze, *Medicinische Psychologie oder Physiologie der Seele,* Leipzig, 1852.

subconscious, semireflexive level in terms of a well-mastered repertoire of interactions. Perhaps in the notion of an internal model we do begin to make some sense of the relation "A acts as if B were C to him" of McCulloch's 0.0, though we by no means have any general logic for triadic relations.

Basically, our understanding of function is based on the notion that the perception of the organism is oriented toward its action; with the caveat that a system which would interact with a changing environment in new and adaptive ways must construct and modify an internal model of its relationships with its world, so that perception becomes highly dependent upon this model, and is oriented to improving the model—and thus to future action—as much as to directing current action.

In exploring implications of perception oriented to action and model, we saw that spatial relationships would play a special role among the relationships between the organism and its world; and we saw that perception by its very success in giving the system access to different courses of action would raise for it the problem of resolving redundancy of potential command—in other words, of choosing at most one of the available courses of action.

Second, we have made a number of observations which help us focus upon brains as distinct from man-made machines. One involves componentry: We ask what follows from the fact that the brain is a network of neurons. We add that brains are living systems, and that, with the rest of the body, they grew from a single egg. Many properties of the brain may be better understood in terms of the requirements of biological development than in terms of the functional requirements of the adult. Another distinction is historical: We distinguish the human brain, which has evolved from the brains of other animals in a series for which language is a late development, from robot controllers, of which even the simplest are symbol manipulators in the most formal sense of the term.

We often let our emphasis on language delude us into thinking that our interaction with the world must involve a verbal mediation of somewhat the following kind:

1. Seeing an object, name it.
2. Using the name of the object, name the appropriate action.
3. *Act* as designated.

This simple scheme, however, is elaborated by such considerations as the need to weigh alternatives. In any case, this approach yields the sort of block diagram shown in Figure 1a. Many artificial intelligence researchers have adopted this approach because they seek methods amenable to string-processing on conventional "serial" computers, rather than trying to understand the brain mechanisms underlying human intelligence.

The central (and, I submit, erroneous) point of Figure 1a is that all the input funnels down to a few well-chosen words which can be processed by some centralized executive to yield a command which can then control the musculature. Although with a few feedback loops judiciously thrown in, this may well be a useful model for analyzing much of human behavior, we would stress that there exist sophisticated strategies for sensori-motor relations which do not require an arch-controller, and that we may do well to regard verbal mediation as providing an extra level in a hierarchical structure such as that of Figure 1b. Here verbal mediation can control the output directly, but need not intervene in much of intelligent behavior which is not explicitly verbal, leaving the task to lower centers, or simply biasing the underlying

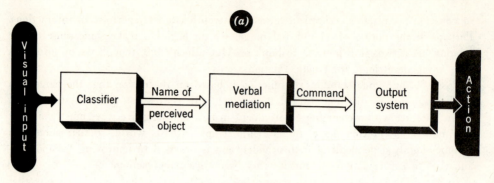

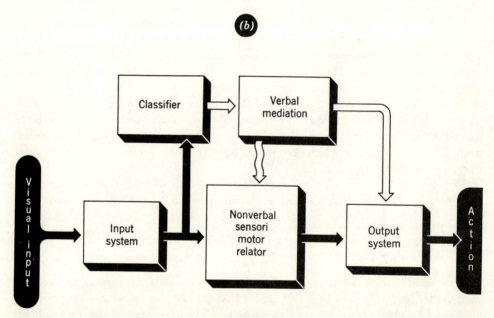

FIGURE 1   (a) The misleading verbal mediation approach to perception and action, whic. is to be contrasted with the more realistic schematization of (b) in which, although verbal mediation can control the output directly, it need not intervene in much of intelligent be- havior, leaving the task to lower centers or simply biassing the underlying sensorimotor apparatus.

sensori-motor apparatus, which does not make explicit use, generally, of verbal coding of input to compute actions.

In this book we normally ignore the "linguistic level" and instead explore the idea that the "meaning" of an input for an organism resides in the interactions that are appropriate with the object it represents, which actions depend not only on *what* an object is but also on *where* it is.

The system of Figure 1b is *anarchic,* in that there is no head or center which exclusively directs its computations. Rather, it is a distributed highly parallel computer. We thus see the need to understand how computations may take place in a highly parallel network of dynamically interacting subsystems. Such an understanding may also help us probe the effect of brain damage upon behavior. In 1929, Karl Lashley published a book, *Brain Mechanisms and Intelligence,* in which he reported that the impairment in maze-running behavior caused by removing portions of a rat's cortex did not seem to depend on what part of the cortex was removed, but only on how much was removed. He thus formulated two "laws": *the law of mass action,* stating that deficit depended on the amount removed; and *the law of equipotentiality,* stating that every part of the brain can make the same contribution to problem-solving. Such data have seemed to many irreconcilable with any view of the brain as a precise computing network, but we may effect a reconciliation if we stress the notion of a computation involving the cooperation of many subroutines that are working simul-taneously in parallel. Often, a computation can be effected by a subset of the routines. In general, removing subroutines will lower efficiency, though for some tasks the missing subroutines may be irrelevant, so that their removal saves the system from wasting time on them when other tasks are to be done. Robert White (personal communication) repeated Lashley's experiments, but rather than measure impairment by a single parameter, he judged wherein the impairment lay. One rat might perform poorly because of a tendency to turn left; another might be easily distractable; while a third might sit still most of the time, but find his way through the maze perfectly well whenever he could be "bothered" to try. Thus the law of equipotentiality is valid only if we use rather gross measurements of change in behavior—the underlying reality would seem to be the removal of subsystems which can make quite different contribu-tions to a given level of performance.

Third, then, let us explore the basic architectural features which we argue will prove useful in seeking manageable descriptions of highly distributed computation in a 10 billion-neuron brain. The basic feature is contained in McCulloch's observation in 0.143 that we see in the brain many maps, each connected topologically to one another. We shall refer to this fact by saying "the brain 'is' a layered somatotopic computer"; and we devote the rest of this section to a discussion of this principle, as well as noting, in accordance with McCulloch's 0.145, that, useful though the principle is, it is not applicable in all cases.

In Section 3.3, we suggested that, although it would be possible to design a robot with a "brain" structured like the centralized $(\theta_d, \theta) \mapsto \ddot{\theta}$ converter of Figure 12 of Chapter 3, one begins to doubt the utility of the centralized processor when the output must be played out upon a whole array of motoneurons, as in the biological case. The beauty of Pitts and McCulloch's scheme, in the last section, for the superior colliculus lay in the simplicity of its demonstration that—at least in the case under discussion— a centralized processor may be dispensed with, and all computation may be carried out in distributed fashion in the layer or layers between the input and output arrays.

As we saw in Section 2.4, Lettvin, Maturana, McCulloch, and Pitts [1959] found that most ganglion cells of the frog's retina could be classified as being one of four types, such as "moving spot detectors" and "large moving object detectors". What we want to emphasize here is the way in which the information from the four types of detectors was distributed in the tectum. The terminations formed four separate layers, one atop each other, with the properties that (*a*) different layers correspond to different types of detector; (*b*) each layer preserves the spatial relations between the original cells (i.e., there exists a direction along the layer corresponding to moving across the retina) ; (*c*) terminations stacked above one another in the four layers come from ganglion cells with overlapping receptive fields. This is another dramatic case of the neural specificity that provides the structural substrate for brain function. It should be noted that such relationships between two layers may preserve rough spatial relationships (up and down versus across), without preserving relative sizes. For example, in the layer in the human brain which receives touch information from the body, the fingers occupy a larger area than the trunk, since the brain needs detailed sensory information from the fingers if it is to control fine manipulation. Such a relationship between two layers of cells is called *somatotopic,* from the Greek *soma* (body) and *topos* (place), since it preserves information about place on the body as we move from receptors to the central nervous system. As we move further from the periphery, the relationships become less distinctive but may still guide our investigation of adjacent layers. What we are saying is that a useful way to structure the apparent chaos of many parts of the brain is to describe such parts in terms of interconnected layers, where position within the layer is a crucial indicator of the functional significance of a cell's activity, and where an analysis of one patch of such a layer may yield an understanding of the function of the layer as a whole.

In discussing somatotopy in the layers of such a distributed computer, the reader should take note that we shall use the word somatotopy in an extremely broad fashion. In the input pathways of the visual system, position encodes position in visual space relative to the eye but (and this is crucial to us) this encoding is related to body coordinates as a result of embryologically derived connections of the retina to the brain. In the auditory system it encodes frequency of stimulation near the periphery. In the tactile system it encodes position on the body. In the last case the term somatotopy is strictly appropriate; and while retinotopy and tonotopy may better connote the respective situations in the periphery in the first two cases, we hypothesize that more centrally the encoding must be in terms of body-world relationships. Again, in output pathways, position in a layer may encode the location of the target of a movement. As we move away from the periphery to layers of the brain far removed from any predominant commitment to sensory modality or particular mode of action, we can expect position in the layer to have little direct correlation with bodily position, yet we hypothesize that position in the layer will still encode a crucial parameter of the cell's function. It is in this somewhat overextended sense of a positional code that we shall speak of somatotopy even in layers far from the periphery. Further, there are structures in the brain—the reticular formation may be one—where the notion of layering is not useful.

We do not fanatically claim the universal truth of the statement "the brain is a layered somatotopic computer". Rather we use it as a convenient slogan to remind us that it is high time that somatotopy, long an important property for anatomists and physiologists, played its full role in our theories of brain function. Even in structures which are not layered, the positions of neurons will play a role that we cannot neglect in modeling their contribution to the overall function of the structure.

It was in this spirit that we closed Chapter 1 with the hope that the reader would be convinced of the viability of a long-range investigation designed to yield a model of "distributed action-oriented computation in layered somatotopically organized machines".

6.2 OUTPUT FEATURE CLUSTERS

We have stressed (especially in Chapter 5) that the spinal cord is so organized that the natural patterns of stimulation that it receives from higher levels (brainstem and motorsensory cortex, for example) do not necessarily yield twitches of individual muscles but coordinated patterns of movement which may involve a number of muscles, as attempts to wiggle the middle toe alone clearly show. Complementary to the sensory features of Section 2.4 are motor features which economically describe objects in terms of our possible interactions with them. We have also stressed (as in our discussion of the motor computer of Section 5.5) that each muscle comprises a population of muscle fibers, so that large movements of the organism (as distinct from fine finger movements in human manipulation) involve activity in a large population of motorneurons. In line with our action-oriented approach to perception we may then suggest that recognition of the current environment comprises a pattern of activation in cortex (this is still speculative), which if allowed to play upon spinal centers would yield the attempted execution of a host of interactive behaviors of the organism, each more or less appropriate to that environment. One of the central problems of nervous system "design" is thus that of resolving its redundancy of potential command: to ensure that if the competing behaviors are mutually incompatible total action patterns, at most one of them is manifested at any one time, and that the one which is manifested is among the more appropriate for the current situation of the organism. In Chapter 7 we shall study two ways in which such resolution might be brought about.

We know that at many levels the brain may be viewed as a layered computer with locus in a layer representing spatial location of the source of the stimulation which can activate cells in that locus; we suggest that in layers on the "output side", locus in the layer represents spatial location of the region in which interaction would ensue were the spinal centers to "execute" the behavior controlled by that region. Note that, since many types of sensory stimulation can occasion the same movement, single cells in "motor layers" may have immense "receptive fields" if we classify them in terms of the input that can modulate their activity. We thus distinguish (Figure 2) "sensory layers" in which the environment is encoded as a spatially tagged array of features extractable in a few layers of neural processing (Section 2.4) from the pattern of receptor responses to environmental energies; and "motor layers" in which the environment is encoded as a spatially tagged array of "output features" or "motor subroutines" which can be transformed into coordinated movements by the musculature after a layer or two of neural processing in sensorimotor cortex and the spinal cord. Between the "sensory layers" and the "motor layers," it is clear that the manifold integrations involved in planning and so forth preclude so strict a somatotopy, but the necessary diffuseness of projections does not imply chaos (a computer is neither somatotopic nor chaotic) even though our present ignorance may make it hard to discern the pattern of connections in, say, frontal cortex or the amygdala.

Now, the world is composed of objects, and it is with objects (or behavioral features or ensembles of objects) that we interact. Thus, if we are to survive in a world in which we are moving relative to objects and objects are moving relative to us (see the discussion in Section 5.5), our brain must be so structured that the features activated by stimuli from a certain object must not only remain activated while the object

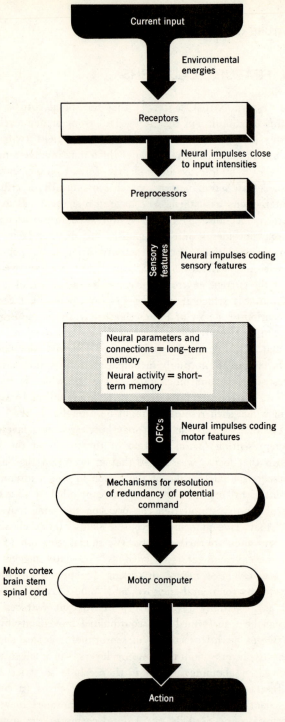

FIGURE 2   A crude block diagram reminding us of various functions involved in relating past and present input to present output. It should be compared with Figure 8 of both this chapter and chapter 7. Four immediate possibilities for refinement are: (*A*) adding feedback paths so that, for example, the mechanisms for resolution of redundancy of potential command could cause the receptors to explore for relevant data; (*B*) attempting to show how the functions separated here may indeed commingle in various brain structures; (*C*) showing how the reward system, initially activated by genetically "prewired" mechanisms, may modify the behavior and choices made; and (*D*) showing how the reticular formation might (as hypothesized in Section 7.1) influence gross choices of modes of action to provide the background for the more detailed resolution of redundancy of potential command shown in this diagram.

remains a relevant part of our environment, but must change in a way that is correlated with the movement of the object relative to the effectors whereby we will interact with it or the sensory input we intend to obtain from such interaction. Let us emphasize this point by contrasting one type of computer representation of objects with that suggested by data on the reaction of human subjects to rotated views of objects.

First we briefly consider a case of programing a computer to answer questions and contrast this with a hypothetical machine which seems to solve the problem in a more biological way. How might a computer be programed to answer the question, "Is President Nixon a man?" when it has stored in memory a data base which includes the encoding of various sentences about politics, including sentences about President Nixon. One might actually state that "President Nixon is a man", and then the computer could find it simply by scanning its data base, and then print out, "Yes, President Nixon is a man". If no such statement were stored, it would have to combine several pieces of information in memory to obtain an answer. One stored statement might be, "Nixon is President of the United States", and another might be, "All presidents of the United States have been men". Finding these strings, it would manipulate them in a purely formal way to obtain the deduction, "Therefore President Nixon is a man", and print out the answer "Yes".

In contrast to this formal approach which currently dominates artificial intelligence research, one could design a machine which uses the question, "Is President Nixon a man?" not to take sentences related to politics and President Nixon and combine them to answer, but rather uses the name "President Nixon" to retrieve a picture of him and then uses the question, "Is he a man?" to retrieve a pattern recognition routine which can determine of a picture whether or not it is of a man. The first approach is called the *syntactic* approach, the second the *semantic*. Presumably both approaches—and others besides—are used by humans in solving such problems.

To store a picture as a two-dimensional array of words, with each word giving the light intensity at a corresponding point of the picture, and then use a present-day computer which only processes a few words at a time, might be a fairly inefficient approach for computerized question-answering. However, when we turn to the brain, we find a series of approximately spatial arrays of neurons corresponding to the visual input. Since the brain has all cells continually active (as against current computers in which most storage is completely passive), it seems likely that a human brain could indeed answer such questions by recreating something of the highly parallel pattern of neural activation somewhere reasonably high up in the head between the input streams and the neurons carrying commands down to the muscles, and then compute upon this pattern of activation in just the same way as it would upon that caused by visual input. However, I would stress that such a pattern would already be highly coded, and in no way would be a simple "recreation" of the visual input. This point will be emphasized by our discussion of the hologram metaphor in Section 6.4.

A series of experiments by Shepard and Metzler gives us some insight into how we might actually distinguish between different types of internal representation. Shepard gave subjects perspective drawings of objects got by sticking together a few cubes (Figure 3). In any presentation, the subject is presented with views of two objects which are the same or mirror images of one another. If the two views are of the same object, one is obtained from the other either by rotating the object, as it were, in the plane of the page or around a line perpendicular to the page. The subject is

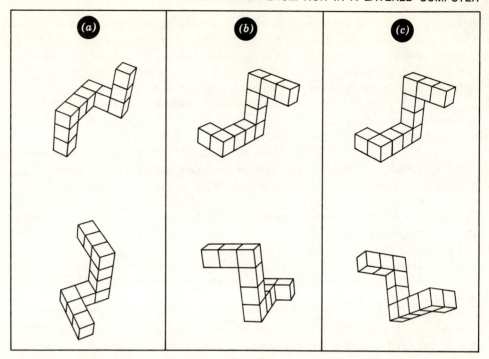

FIGURE 3   Three examples of stimuli used in Shepard's experiments. In each case we show two views of three dimensional objects—with the second view corresponding to a rotation of either the object or the mirror image of the object in the first view.

instructed to depress one of two buttons depending on whether or not he believes that the two objects are the same.

The verbal-processing approach to this problem might be to generate a verbal description of each object—" a cube here, then another going off at such and such an angle, with two right angles . . .", to which is finally added a little tag which indicates the orientation of the described object in space. If we gave such a system two of these views, it would analyze each of them to get these descriptions, throw away the orientation tag, and immediately check whether or not the descriptions were the same.

Another approach is to use the two-dimensional pattern to create within the brain the same sort of neural firing that would result from viewing the three-dimensional object. We are accustomed, when actually interacting with a three-dimensional object, to be able to turn it round, and in so doing, obtain differing two-dimensional projections. We might expect that as we look at one of the two-dimensional patterns and set up a neural representation of the three-dimensional object, it might then be possible to create the neural correspondent of turning the object. [We must not imagine (hard though it is to avoid doing so.) the process to be anything as crude as actually setting up little blocks and turning them around in the head, because we are talking of a functional relationship rather than a strict geometric relationship. We imagine that internal processes induce the transformation of the firing pattern akin to that which would be induced by directly holding the three-dimensional object and rotating it. In fact we had to assume such operations in our suggestion of a tracking component in the scheme of Figure 24 in Chapter 5]. We might then imagine that a subject answers

Shepard's test by rotating the image from one input pattern, imposing the resultant "mental image" against the input from the other pattern, and then asking whether or not they match.

Subjects claim that this is the way they solve the problem. On first trying to match views, subjects try to do it too quickly, and say that by the time they have mentally rotated an object it has "broken up": they have forgotten how it was arranged at "the far end" and have to rotate it again. But once they claim that they have learned how to go "at the right speed" so as not to forget the pattern's formation in making the mental rotation, they make no further mistakes. But introspection has been misleading in the past: How can we be sure that it is right this time? Shepard's answer was to measure the reaction time; he reasoned that if the verbal approach took place, the angular displacement between the two views should have no effect upon the time taken by a subject to respond, whereas if "mental rotation" took place, then each extra $10°$ of rotation should add an equal amount of time to the delay between presentation of the two projections and the subject's response. In fact, there *is* a complete linear relationship between the number of degrees that the objects would have to turn to get congruence and the number of seconds the subject takes to give his response. This seems to prove that there really is a "mental rotation". Shepard found that he rotated his mental image at $62.6°$ per second!

Such experiments form interesting attempts to probe the ways we represent the world, inside our brains. We did not evolve simply to interact with static two-dimensional patterns. We move about in the world, we manipulate and rotate objects and we move around objects—and so if we are to function in a useful way, we must be able not simply to classify objects but also to relate them to ourselves, to know where they are, knowing how we must move them or move ourselves to bring them into a desired relationship with the frame of reference induced by our own bodies. Thus the idea of having within the brain not simply classifications or verbal descriptions, but also the wherewithal to move relative to objects, and to move objects relative to us, is very important. When we add to this the specification that the brain is tied to a whole musculature which in some sense imposes natural coordinates, we see, further, that it is not enough to specify a rotation simply by having somewhere in the brain a number; we want to have that number poised, so to speak, to be actually played down upon the muscles to assure appropriate action. The crucial thing about Shepard's experiment is that by looking at the rate at which people responded he got information one could not get by just asking whether they responded correctly or not. By finding a beautiful linear relationship between the number of degrees through which objects have been rotated and the time taken to carry out the discrimination he lets us explore ways in which information is actually stored in the brain. A major goal of our brain theory must be to direct much anatomy and physiology toward the discovery of neural mechanisms consistent with this type of storage.

Let us now look at another line of evidence, that from brain stimulation of human epileptics, which suggests that the brain is organized in terms of meaningful interactions with the real world.

Before carrying out brain surgery on an epileptic patient, a surgeon may chart different parts of the brain, in the hope that she will not remove anything critical when she removes the irritant focus that is the source of the epileptic attack. She electrically stimulates little regions to see what the patient does in response. Is the region involved in hand movement or in moving the little toe, or in speech, or what have you? If the result of removing a region is an impairment of the placing action of the left foot, the patient might gladly accept the trade-off. If the result is that she is unable to speak, she might well object (though she would have to do it in writing). Some patients say that when stimulated they "relived" a vivid sequence of events from their past. Unfortunately, some scientists believe that such data show that we store in our brains a complete record of everything that ever happens, and can have access to any of it if we try subtly enough. But this is absurd, for several reasons. First, we do not know in the majority of cases that the patient is reporting actual memory; if her brain constructs something from "ingredients" based on past experience, the construct will seem similar to something that happened to her but the actual combination may not have been previously experienced. Second, we should not interpret the data as any evidence for the "Kodachrome hypothesis" that the patient sees an exact view of the original scene, for what is constructed as a result of stimulation may well be at a very abstract level of neural activity, far removed from the actual visual input. Also, it is only in epileptic patients that such phenomena have been observed. However, it is noteworthy that they report that such "reliving" feels quite different from "normal recall". Rather, the data do indicate that the brain is so structured that when you get fairly high up into the brain and "kick something", what you get is not the raw data of visual input, but something akin to the conscious perception of objects rather than, for example, random spots and flashes of light. Sticking an electrode into the brain at random and driving current into the brain sets up transient activity in a neural network. It is not surprising that the transients often yield aspects of what the network is used for, namely, conscious perception, rather than an experience of little dots of light coming in at various places in the visual field. (Would this occur in nonepileptics too?) We would suggest that it is the ability of the brain to resolve redundancy of potential command that transforms random assortments of output features into clusters of activity associated with vivid and more or less real subjective experience.

Thus a crucial notion in our model is that of the *output feature cluster* (OFC) as the encoding of an object in the action frame, that is, as a cluster of features that might be appropriate for interaction of the organism with the object. (The OFC represents our attempt to capture the notion of "slide" from Section 4.1 in a somewhat less metaphorical form.) Whereas in lower animals the relationship between sensory features and motor features may be essentially direct and innate (cf. the discussion of the frog tectum in Section 7.2), in many forms there is a great additional mechanism which allows development of relationships which have their bases in the past experience of the animal. We thus do not distinguish at this stage *genetically* specified mechanisms from those which are *learned,* for since in general both are active in a perceptual situation, *together* they define the animal's long-term model of the world.

We are thus stressing that we regard a perceiving system as representing its environment in terms of possible motor options, rather than creating a "little copy of the world" in any photographic sense.

We thus model LTM (*long-term memory*) as *residing in the intervening network between sensory layers and motor layers.* It is represented in the parameters of the network which enable the array of sensory feature activation to be segmented and transformed into a spatially tagged array of OFC's, each of which in indeed appropriate for interaction with the objects yielding the sensory features from which they were obtained.

We reiterate that the array of OFC's activated at any time will most often contain far more subroutines than the organism would be able to execute at that time, and so much neural machinery must serve to commit the organism to only one set of compatible actions at any one time.

We further suggest that STM (*short-term memory*) *comprises the totality of current activity of OFC's*. It is LTM that allows the organism to generate an OFC from partial (probably ambiguous) sensory information about an object; it is STM that keeps appropriate OFC's activated (even though they may supply only a weak context for currently sensed objects) rather than providing OFC's simply for current input. As we have already suggested in Section 4.4, and reinforced with our discussion of Shepard's data, the brain must be able to continually *relocate* or *modify* an OFC so that its location remains appropriate to the corresponding object, though such relocations are relative and may involve remappings of input (sensory) and output (motor) pathways. Hence, as we move around a table, the arm movements required to pick up a pencil change continuously, whereas if we move away from the table, the pencil output features acquire such "background features" as the need to walk up to it if we are to successfully reach for it. "Of course" (two words which beg a thousand questions!) in a human adult these action-oriented features enter consciousness only in such verbalizations as "It's 6 feet away". (Note, before we go metric, how our units remind us of the active basis of our measures: "pace out three lengths of your foot to equal the distance—the yard—of extending your arm".) The neural circuitry should be such that it is in general easier to detect that an activated OFC matches sensory features despite a discrepancy in locus ("Oh—you've moved") and relocate the OFC appropriately, than to use LTM to generate a whole OFC ("Who are you?"), little of which bears any direct relationship to current sensory features. Thus STM and attention are "interwoven": we attend only to that which is changing (or that in which we have judged a change to be imminent and important), and affect all layers or processing.

We emphasize again, then, that an OFC is a pattern of neural activation representing an object in terms of one or some of the organism's possible interactions with it. (The same object may elicit different OFC's on different occasions: a cat may activate the output feature "stroking" on one occasion, and the output feature "pushing off" on another. We may say that the transformation from object via sensory features to OFC's yields a polythetic classification.) STM's status as a collection of data on what to do with the environment may be considered equivalent to having an internal model of the environment which is nearby in space, time, and relevance. This is clearly far more useful to the organism than a simple tallying of current sensory stimulation. An OFC is thus not a simple recoding of (in the case of visual sensation) two-dimensional patterns. For example, Figure 4 shows two perspectives of a cube which give rise to distinct collections of sensory features but which may nonetheless elicit the same OFC, appropriate to (probably among many other things) grasping a cube, save, for example, for differences in a parameter reflecting the different angle at which the thumb-finger opposition would have to approach a real cube were it responsible for one of those two-dimensional projections.

With this as background, we can now turn to a scheme in which we see how transformations may act upon both sensory input and post-OFC motor output to enable an organism to smoothly interact with its world.

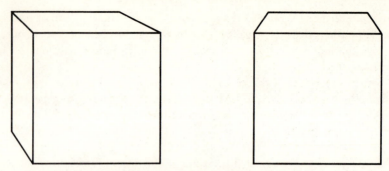

FIGURE 4   Two diagrams not intertransformable by motions in the plane. One has seven vertices and nine lines; the other six vertices and seven lines. However, this discrepancy in sensory features is banished as soon as we recognize them both as views of a cube.

6.3   TRANSFORMATIONS AND SOMATOTOPY

Our main aim is to "insert the somatotopy" into Figure 2 by tying it in with the discussion of distributed motor control in Section 5.5 and showing where certain transformations might act upon arrays of preprocessed sensory features and arrays of OFC's to better relate the organism to its world.

To start we should emphasize the fact that a reasonable case can be made for regarding mammals as having two (highly interdependent) visual systems, a cortical system and a midbrain system. To indicate the distinction between these two systems, we recall that Schneider [1969] found that a hamster with intact superior colliculus but no visual cortex could not distinguish simple patterns, such as a cross versus a square, though it could still orient to a sound or a moving object. In other words (cf. our discussion of frog versus cat in Section 2.4), it would seem that the hamster without visual cortex can still respond to simple local features especially motion features but lacks the ability to integrate these into global determiners of OFC's. Conversely, the hamster with visual cortex but no superior colliculus can discriminate patterns but cannot use the perceived distinction to orient. In fact, this latter deficit had led other workers to believe that hamsters with visual cortex were blind if they had no superior colliculus, for a hamster placed in the apparatus of Figure 5 would seem just as likely to enter the arm behind whose door (marked with a square) waited no reward as the arm behind whose door (marked with a cross) waited a reward. However, Schneider observed that although the animal might enter the wrong arm, it learned not to go *through* the wrong door, and so would turn round when it reached the end of the wrong arm. (He ruled out shortsightedness by using a glass door with the mark on a distant surface beyond it; the animal still learned the discrimination.) This supported the contention that the animal could discriminate but could not "place" the patterns. In fact the animal could not orient to "local features" either: when exposed to a sound or moving object it would tend to "freeze", rather than turning to the source of stimulation as the animal with superior colliculus would.

With this as background, we may now turn to Figure 6 where we have drawn a crude block diagram for a system which incorporates much of the "mammalian strategy" to take account of the foregoing considerations and others that we shall explicate as we proceed. The reader will certainly appreciate that many other structures

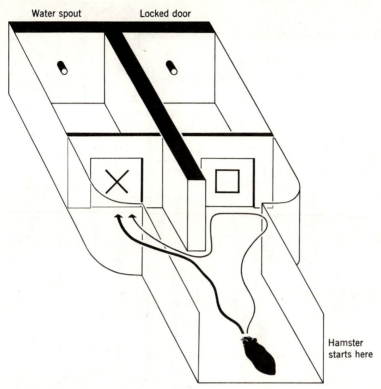

Water spout   Locked door

Hamster
starts here

FIGURE 5   A normal hamster (heavy trajectory) can orient itself with respect to visual
stimuli. A hamster without a superior colliculus seems unable to use visual patterns to
orient itself; but can still discriminate patterns, as evidenced by the light trajectory shown
in which the animal navigates by tactile cues, but only pushes against the door with the
symbol that has been paired with a reward.

could embody the same functions. Further, we shall see that despite its many boxes, it
still presents too crude a caricature of action-oriented perception. Nonetheless, we hope
that by studying it we may attain a more sophisticated level of discussion of perception
and new hypotheses to help us relate these various functions to structures in the brain.

Objects in the real world (1) may be considered to modulate environmental energy
flow. The animal's receptor arrays (2) register projections of this flux along the
different sensory "modalities" and in space. The visual receptors, tactile receptors of
the hands, and so on, may be moved with respect to the rest of the animal's body;
such changes correspond, in part, to the effect of box (4) (see below) upon the effectors.
Receptor inputs project to two major systems, one midbrain (3) and one cortical (5).
The midbrain projection suffers local (pointwise) preprocessing and enters a mechanism like that illustrated in Figure 26 of Chapter 5. Regions which contain stimulation
differing from that expected emerge to produce orientation movements through the
motor map structures (4). This route is that described by Pitts and McCulloch
[1947] as causing the eyes to bring objects to a "standard position" for the cortical
recognizers, and so acts via the effectors, to ensure that input to the cortical route is
appropriately positioned.

Turning to the cortical route, then, sensory input reach another mechanism (5) like

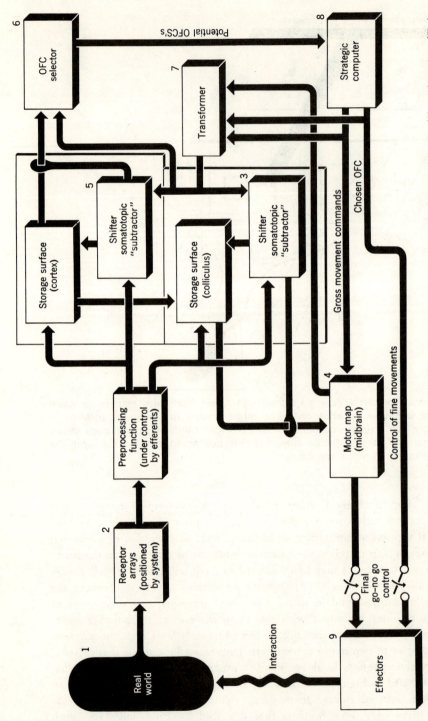

FIGURE 6 Tentative block diagram of the interaction between "the two visual systems" of the midbrain (3) and cortex (5) in maintaining the appropriate relationships between the organism and its world.

180

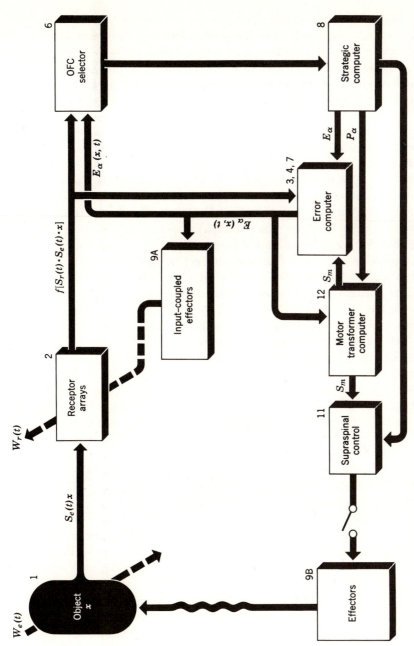

FIGURE 7 Fine detail of how the modified Pitts-McCulloch scheme of Figure 21 of Chapter 5 might be embedded as controller for the OFC selector of Figure 6.

that of Figure 26 which allows those portions of the pattern that have *temporal* changes which vary too much from that predicted by the self-motion of the organism and perceived motion of objects to pass to the OFC selector (pattern recognizer, object hypothesis generator) (6) which analyzes the firing pattern *spatially*. This works because the same unpredicted regions will [through the orienting mechanisms (3) and (4)] bring the receptor surface, as we have seen, to face these information-bearing regions, each in its turn. The OFC selector also receives a measure of what current movements are doing from (7) so that the selection of OFC's will be appropriate to the context of ongoing activity. Decisions made with respect to "goals of the organism" (the "phlogiston" of the present discussion, alas) choose one of the potential OFC's offered by (6). This strategic computer (8) then implements the chosen OFC, with control of fine movements which takes place in the context of grosser movements mediated through the midbrain-maintained body-centered reference frame.

Within this framework, we would paraphrase Schneider's results on hamsters as showing that destroying visual cortex [breaking our block diagram at (5)] yields animals capable of orientation (locating) but not recognition, whereas destroying the superior colliculus [region (3) of our diagram] results in an animal which can discriminate patterns should its eyes accidentally rest on the pattern in standard position for the OFC selector, but is incapable of appropriate orienting movements.

Imagine a person presented with a 35-millimeter slide projection of an unknown scene, which is (say) upside-down. This case requires extensive analysis of one subpart of the environment. The observer must first realize that whatever it is she is looking at is "upside-down", then must either position her receptors (2) (perhaps by standing on her head) or introduce a shift in the output motor map (4) which will be reflected by the transformer (7) in the parametric adjustment of OFC's (6). Then she will proceed to make further transformations with the aim of bringing the slide into a standard form for whatever the scene depicts. This will entail receptor positioning, altering the motor map (and perhaps effector positioning) and the preprocessing functions so that the perceptual system will be "tuned" to whatever OFC hypothesis is being tried. This means that the boxes we have so blithely labeled "OFC selector (6)" and "strategic computer (8)" must be complex and closely integrated to the other parts of the system.

Let us now concentrate on this aspect of perception which is incompletely filled in for lack of space in Figure 6. For this further discussion we turn to Figure 7, which generalizes the Pitts-McCulloch [1947] scheme of our Figure 21 in Chapter 5.

To ease the transition from Figure 6 to Figure 7, notice that for simplicity, (5) of Figure 6 has been left out of Figure 7, and that areas (3) and (4) and the transformer (7) will be considered as an error computer with its influence on OFC selection indicated by the line in Figure 7 from the "motor transform computer" (12) to the "error computer" (3, 4, 7). "Supraspinal control" (11) has been added to indicate the translation of OFC, by stages, into individual muscle fiber commands.

Thus in Figure 7 we have decomposed the OFC generating and choosing mechanisms into those parts explicitly involved in finding a correct transformation and controlling movement by OFC parameterization from the rest of the scheme, and we have hidden the anatomical distinction of the two different pathways seen in Figure 6. In reading the discussion of Figure 7, the following should be noticed: Figure 6 presumes that the system may always be said to be perceiving the scene in that the OFC's which would cause "let's walk around that thing and maybe we can see what in the world it could be" may be considered to be a percept of an object as something to walk around. Figure 7 separates out these initial exploratory parts of movement and receptor settings, making explicit how those processes could lead to "fuller" perception of an object ("oh, that's upside-down—it's a picture of the Washington Monument") essential for naming.

The orienting reaction is *not* to be considered one of the input features representing an object, though it does contribute to the spatial location of the eventual OFC's in the somatotopic action frame of STM. Orienting *allows* the fine details of OFC generation, and so precedes it, or at least its refinement. In animals with foveal vision, we might regard the cortical "pattern recognizers" as being "time-shared" (to use the computer metaphor again) with the orienting mechanism and cortical shifts of interest controlling their allocation, as if figuring out *what* is there requires more "machinery" than noting a discrepancy from what is expected. Man is thus midway between a frog —no fovea, uniform rather limited processing of visual input—and a superman—all fovea, uniform sophisticated processing of a large visual field.

The position and orientation of an object relative to the organism's surfaces determines in part what environmental energies will impinge upon the receptor surface of the organism. Let us pick a standard position x of the object. At any time t it has a position in absolute space corresponding to a displacement and rotation $S_e(t)$ so that the resultant distribution of matter in space may be described by $S_e(t) \cdot x$. The position of the receptor surface at time t then yields a projection $S_r(t)$ so that the actual neural representation will be some function

$$f[S_r(t) \cdot S_e(t) \cdot x]$$

of the two-dimensional pattern. (We are talking of visual receptors here; a slightly modified discussion would handle other modalities as well.)

Now it is true that an adult may think in terms of abstractions, or plan his movements from the outside as if imagining himself moving on a map, but we now want to consider a more fundamental "egocentric" form of perception in which the organism views objects not in terms of some absolute spatial framework but in terms of position relative to the perceiver, that is, in terms of coordinates induced by the reach of the hands, direction relative to that in which the body is facing, number of steps the object is away, and so on. Size may then be perceived to the extent that we can scale our movements for appropriate interaction; orientation to the extent that we can turn our head to center our gaze on an object, and so on. We might, for instance, say that we perceive the lines on a page of ruled paper to the extent that we can not only position a pencil on them but also adjust our handwriting size to the spacing of the lines. In other words, our theory must include a transformation $S_m(t)$ which scales muscular activity to the task at hand.

Given the important role in our theory of the generation of transformations to match motor output to sensory input, we shall find relevant here our generalization of Pitts and McCulloch's [1947] "uniform principle of design for reflex mechanisms which secure invariance under an arbitrary group G" (see Figure 21 of Chapter 5). However, where the original model considers only transformations of sensory features (e.g., rotation of a visual perspective in the plane) such as a transformation that will bring a sensory pattern to the middle of the visual field, we shall also be interested in transformations of output features which represent all possible motions of an object in space, since the organism needs data (though we shall see that they need not all be neurally encoded) on the relative position of objects if it is to successfully interact with them. (Pitts and McCulloch consider the case where the transformation is implemented as a motion of the eyes, but we argue for internal remappings as well.) On the motor side, we might want to generate a transformation that will modify the parameters of an OFC so that the hand will close about an object, and not about adjacent empty space.

In any case, recall that the original scheme was to associate with each pattern ϕ an n-dimensional "error vector" $E(\phi)$ with the property (to be relaxed in a significant fashion below) that $E(\phi) = 0$ if and only if ϕ is in standard form, and to introduce a mapping W which associates with an error some transformation which can reduce it, that is, $W:R^n \to G$ is such that

$$\| E[W(E(\phi)) \cdot \phi] \| \leqslant \| E(\phi) \|$$

for all patterns ϕ, and with equality only in case ϕ is in standard form.

We also noted the similarity of this to the difference-operator method of Newell, Shaw and Simon's [1959] GPS (general problem solver), with two crucial distinctions: (i) GPS only employs a finite set of "error-vectors" or "differences"; (ii) the operator W_D associated with a difference D does not always successfully reduce the difference; thus a procedure known as heuristic search (Section 4.2) is required to find which sequence of operators among a number of apparently likely candidates will indeed remove the initial difference. It is this less-than-ideal, but more realistic, situation that we shall have in mind when we allude to heuristic search below. The change $W_e(t)$ in object position may be occasioned both by the autonomous motion of the object (1) and by the effects of the motor apparatus (9B) upon the object. The change $W_r(t)$ in input array positioning is induced by the input-coupled effectors (9A) which act, much as in the Pitts-McCulloch scheme, on the basis of an error vector supplied by the error computer (3, 4, 7). Similarly, the motor transform computer (12) generates the appropriate setting of supraspinal control (11) on the basis of this error computer.

It is in discussing box (6) that we encounter new subtleties and something of a "chicken and egg problem". The problem is that we cannot find *the* appropriate standard form for an input pattern unless we have some idea of what object it represents—yet one of the aims of transforming the pattern to standard form is to identify the underlying object. We have suggested that an object is recognized when appropriate OFC's (as defined with respect to the organism's goals through the strategic computer box) are available to the system for interacting with it. With each such OFC we associate an error criterion: an OFC is deemed to be appropriate for interaction with an object underlying an input pattern only when that pattern has been transformed to a form in which *designated* components E^1 (here is the relaxation of the Pitts-McCulloch scheme we mentioned earlier) of the error vector are sufficiently close to zero, in which case the remaining components E^2 of the error vector serve as parameters for execution of the program. The error criterion must thus be determined both by the current goal of the system as well as the system's estimate of the class of objects to which the correctly scanned object belongs.

The OFC selector (6) conducts something akin to a heuristic search, though at the level of choice of error criterion rather than of error reduction. Having generated the hypothesis that the appropriate OFC for controlling interaction is P_a, it provides the corresponding error criterion E_a to the error computer (3, 4, 7) whose output, the error vector $E_a(x, t)$, is used by (9A) and (12) to update the receptor position $S_r(t)$ and motor transformation $S_m(t)$. Box (6) keeps track of the resultant change in error to decide whether or not the current choice P_a is adequate. We assume that it and the environment are appropriately related so that a designated component $E_a{}^1(x, t)$ becomes sufficiently close to zero to indicate that the current program P_a is applicable. As in a heuristic search, rules must be given for when to take failure to drive $E_a{}^1$ to zero indicates that a new hypothesis must be sought.

The strategic computer will allow a particular motor act to be executed only when $E_a{}^1(x, t)$ is sufficiently small; it then sets up an "interpreter level" subroutine on the basis of the current program choice P_a and the parameters provided by the remaining components $E_a{}^2(x, t)$ of the error vector. On the basis of this subroutine and error information, the motor transform computer (12) provides appropriate scaling information $S_m(t)$, appropriateness being determined by its being fed back to the error computer (3, 4, 7) and thus helping reduce $E_a{}^1(x, t)$ toward zero. Finally, supraspinal control (11) interprets the "subroutine" provided by the strategic computer (8) using the information $S_m(t)$ provided by the motor transform computer (12).

Note that this scheme does not demand that we keep a complete *neural* record of the transformation T as is suggested by the version of the Pitts-McCulloch scheme we showed in Figure 21 of Chapter 5, but allows motion of the motor apparatus to change the relative projection of the pattern, so that no *absolute* transformation is relevant. For example, a cat, in moving its head to fixate a mouse, has concomitantly adjusted its motor apparatus ready for the spring. The point is that the brain does *not* keep a record of all abstract transformations; rather it carries out operations which ensure that the relationship between organism and object is suitable for interaction.

6.4 THE HOLOGRAM METAPHOR

In trying to understand the sort of memory structure which will fit in with the schemes that we have presented in the last two sections, we may find it useful to consider the metaphor of the hologram, in which records are distributed across a structure, rather than being stored word-by-word, as in a computer. To get to this metaphor, we start by making the following claims about human memory:

1. Our memories are dynamic, and located in the "action frame" in that, for example, we recall perceiving a room about us, rather than recalling a series of isolated two-dimensional perspectives.

2. Humans may experience certain forms of gross brain damage without losing their memories (at least with respect to very rough tests, though localized damage to other sections of the brain may have gross effects, as with lesions of the hippocampal gyrus, which may destroy the ability to add new information to long-term memory).

3. Memories of many different events can be stored in the same region of the brain. (This sounds reasonable, but can it be verified experimentally?)

This has suggested to a number of workers, including Pribram [1969], that what we here insist is only a *metaphor* for the memory system may be found in the *hologram*, which is a form of photographic image with the following provocative properties:

1. The image produced is three-dimensional, and may be viewed from many aspects.

2. Each part of the hologram can reproduce much of the entire image, in distinction to the sharp localization of a conventional photograph, but resolution decreases as the area decreases.

3. Several images can be superimposed, and later recovered individually.

To understand properties (1) and (2) of real holograms, consider viewing an object through a window. The hologram may be regarded as a "freezing" of the light waves from the object as they impinge upon the window. We can thus see all aspects of the object, so long as we view it from an angle corresponding to standing in front of the window. Similarly, we can see the whole object, though we may have to move our eyes around more, as more of the window is covered.

To understand property (3), we need more technical information of the "freezing" process. A hologram takes a photograph using illumination from a laser. A "reference beam" of laser light, and another laser beam reflected from an object yield wave fronts of light which form an interference pattern on the photographic plate. The developed slide—called a hologram—can later be "read out" by shining a copy of the "reference beam" of laser light through it, which acts as if to restart the original wave fronts of light anew. The crucial point for (3) is that if we photograph several holograms on the one plate, but using a different reference beam for each hologram, then when we illuminate the plate with a single reference beam, only the corresponding wave front will be restarted, and so only the corresponding image will be reconstructed; the interference patterns for the other wave fronts will each cancel out with the wrong reference beam.

If we have two objects, referred to as 1 and 2, and record the interference pattern of the wave front reflecting off both these, the reflection from each object acts as a reference beam for the other. The reflection from one object can be used to illuminate the hologram and "read out" the other object, thus gaining a primitive *associative memory*—if two objects have been photographed together, then one can be used to recall the other. (If we use what is called a Fourier transform hologram, object 1 need not be placed in a fixed position; object 2 will always be read out in the same position relative to object 1. This can be of great use in an information-retrieval system. Suppose that object 1 is an occurrence of a key word, say "automat," that we want to retrieve, and that object 2 is just a spot of light, so that when we illuminate the hologram with the word "automat," the output will be a relatively positioned spot of light. If we now illuminate the hologram with a whole page of type, every occurrence of "automat" will yield an appropriately positioned spot of light.)

The similarity between the (1)-(2)-(3) of memory and the (1)-(2)-(3) of the hologram has suggested that thinking of the brain in this context, in terms of propagation of waves of neural activity rather than in terms of the step-by-step computations of individual neurons, we could then imagine wave fronts of sensory excitation being frozen into a "neural hologram" which may be restarted whenever the memory of that experience is called for. (Noting that the coherent beams of light used to make real holograms are generated by lasers, we should not make the mistake of the student who asked in one of Pribram's classes "But doesn't the laser process destroy brain cells?" If the hologram metaphor is to have any real utility, then the reference beams, too, must comprise waves of neural activity.) "Ghost images" elicited by almost-reference beams might then provide a sort of associative memory.

Pribram suggests that there *is* a neural hologram, and so he does not treat it as a metaphor; and that it is obtained as a result of interference on neurons between a pattern sent directly (impinging on near end of dendrites) and a slightly delayed pattern (impinging on far end of dendrites). He suggests that we test such a notion by analyzing the mathematical rules for transformation from impulse to graded potentials, and vice versa, to see if it is holographic (and, in particular, invertible). He further seems to view consciousness as a reading-out of the hologram in the head, which may be just the homunculus fallacy, for if memory reconstructs visual input we may be back to "explaining" perception in terms of a little man sitting in a control room inside the head, monitoring neural messages from the periphery, and starting an infinite regress of smaller and smaller homunculi.

However, the real interest to the brain theorist of the (1) of holography should *not* be the three-dimensionality per se, but rather the fact that we have a record of a wave front, rather than the static cross section of conventional photography. Property (2) need not excite us since we expect it in the brain as a result of the redundancy obtained by the property of mutual convergence and divergence in neural pathways: As was evident from our discussion of receptive fields in Section 2.4, as we move centrally in the input systems, each cell monitors a wider range of input. We have both convergence and divergence of information, so that each peripheral point contributes to the activity of many central cells, while, conversely, each central cell monitors many receptors. Thus the input information is both distributed and redundant. Even removal of fairly large pieces of the central pathways would still allow that at least partial information about most of the sensory periphery would be retained. Further, our ability to move our receptors, as in scanning a visual scene or running our hand over a surface, allows us to make a "mosaic" of a total scene even if our input pathways are restricted in their peripheral range. Perhaps (3), the storage of many traces in the same region, can give us the most fruitful ideas. In any case, we repeat that *to profit from the metaphor, we must avoid too literal use of it.*

We must not expect a neural hologram to share with the real hologram the exact mathematical nature of the transform from scene to record. The real hologram is essentially a spatial Fourier transform so that each point records frequencies for the whole original in such a way that the transform can be *inverted* to reconstruct the complete wave front from its transform. But it would seem to be of less value to the organism to reconstruct a visual input per se than to recall vital *features* of past experience. As we saw in Section 2.4, the early stages of an organism's input system are preprocessors designed to extract from a sensory pattern features helpful to the perceptual activity of the organism. Thus the appropriate notion for a neural hologram may not be the invertible Fourier transform, but rather the noninvertible *feature transform* in which a spatial array of intensities is replaced by a spatial array of features (we stress that this is true of all modalities, not just the visual system). Note that each point of the feature transform corresponds to a large sensory field, with much overlap. Thus portions of the feature transform may serve to encode larger portions of the original, albeit with lack of detail in certain features, even if there is a great clarity in others. In line with our discussions of Sections 4.1 and 6.1, suggesting that we consider one of the primary functions of memory to be to augment current input in determining action, it seems appropriate to consider an *action spectrum* in considering the neural model, rather than the frequency spectrum of the real hologram—so that the features considered above will be those which enable the animal to react quickly and appropriately. Rather than an invertible record from which the animal can reconstruct the original stimulus, we posit a noninvertible record from which it can construct an appropriate response.

When it comes to trying hologramlike techniques in designing neural nets to implement some of the schemes in Section 6.2, the reference beam should itself be appropriate to the memory it triggers. We saw that different images may be keyed by using different reference beams, but that in real holograms, these are chosen arbitrarily. We would suggest that in a neural analog of a hologram (if such exists) the reference beam would comprise a sampling of ongoing neural activity, both peripheral (so that the animal can recall information about what happened when it did something similar) and central (so that it may recall thoughts related to its present ones). We could then have as a special case that suggested by Pribram in which the reference beam is simply a somewhat earlier version of the present input. This sort of loop explains perfectly temporal recall of sequences, with each piece of information reading in the next at time of storage, and with each action being elicited by its predecessor at time of read-out.

We should also stress that not all information should be stored. Efferent control may operate to filter incoming information; in other words, the reference beam may act to negate input information rather than store it. (Note, too, that in acquiring a skill, "input" information for the neural hologram may be from central activity—"remember this idea"—or from proprioceptors—"remember how this feels.") Neural activity may elicit enough of a "band" of memories to force certain generalizations upon the organism: a given stimulus may activate all the experience related to certain modes of activity. Conversely, if an experience is "ordinary," it will be stored with a reference beam that can later elicit only noise so that current input will then predominate. (Why store it if it is ordinary? Perhaps it may be simpler to "store" such things irretrievably than carry out detailed computation on every item to decide whether or not it should be stored retrievably.)

One notion of a neural hologram which might serve as an apt metaphor to guide certain aspects of brain research is presented in Figure 8, which may be viewed as a research proposal rather than a polished theory, as attested to by the following sketchy discussion. Feedback plays a crucial role in this system, since retrieved memories help determine the reference beam, allowing systematic searches through memory and maintaining those portions of STM that are not consequences of the control continually exerted by the current sequence of inputs. Dreaming is then a form of activity almost completely under the control of the previously retrieved memories; it is thus free from the control of "reality", but still possesses local continuity. When awake, too great a mismatch between input and current short-term memory induces a drastic recomputation that normally remains untriggered in dreaming.

The input system extracts action-relevant features and acts under efferent control to extract data relevant to our current ideas; among other things, data can be used here to address information required to reduce mismatch between short-term memory and what is relevant in the current environment. The reference beam can be used both to retrieve information and to store further information.

The idea of focusing attention, or trying to concentrate to get something back, depends on the lower box to enhance computing certain features in the reference beam, specifically designed to get further information. We get into a loop of tighter and tighter interrogation to finally retrieve needed information. In the simplest case the reference-beam loop is just a delay, yielding recall of temporal sequences, because

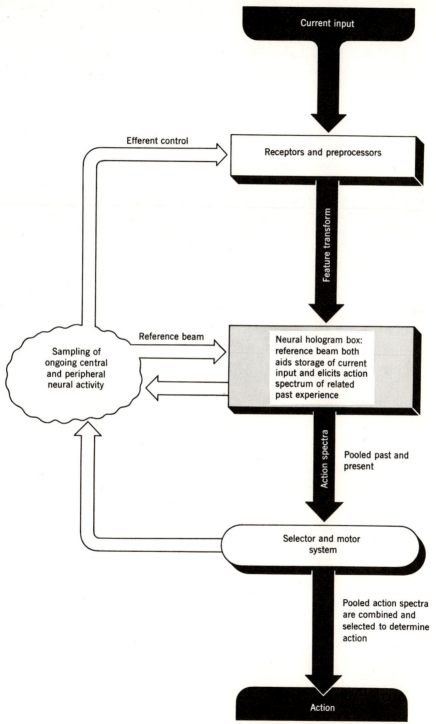

Figure 8 An adaptation of the scheme of Figure 2, using the hologram metaphor to suggest how long-term memory might be used to update the short-term model in an associative fashion.

in this case a sequence is stored by using what happens at time n to encode what happens at time $n + 1$, and so on.

In the foregoing scheme, short-term memory may correspond to current activity around the loops, whereas long-term memory may correspond to changes in the connectivity of the neural hologram box. Humans with certain types of hippocampal damage cannot transfer information from short- to long-term memory; perhaps the hippocampal gyrus corresponds to the "exposure control" for our neural hologram box. However, noting that the mathematics of complex valued waves required for optical holography differs drastically from the mathematics of neural spike trains, we see that it will be difficult enough to describe interference patterns for such wave trains, let alone model the analog of exposing photographic film.

Irrespective of the conjectures we might make about functional block diagrams for human memory, neural holography should provide a useful metaphor if we avoid the temptation to use it literally (e.g., recreating visual input) but instead exploit the idea of portions of a wave activity helping recreate the whole wave front, with different cuing waves allowing multiple storage in a region of brain tissue. This should serve as an antidote to the word-by-word view of memory we get from thinking about digital computers or the linguistic abilities of humans, and it should allow us to indeed find appropriate concepts for modeling adaptive modifications in the action-oriented, distributed computations of a layered, somatotopically organized computer.

7 | Resolving Redundancy of Potential Command

A cat is eating a mouse when a dog appears. Should the cat continue to *feed*, should it *fight* the dog, or—discretion being the better part of valor—should it *flee* to avoid an ugly confrontation? Feeding, fleeing, and fighting are three examples of *modes* of behavior, mutually exclusive types of behavior to which an animal may commit itself. As our example makes clear, the animal will often be in situations in which many modes of behavior are possible, and thus the nervous system must be so structured that the animal can quickly resolve modal conflicts to commit itself to a single mode of behavior. McCulloch has hypothesized that the brain structure with primary responsibility for modal decisions is the reticular formation (RF) of the brainstem shown in Figure 1. In Section 7.1 we shall study this hypothesis and present a computer model, due to Kilmer and McCulloch, which elaborates it.

Making a modal decision is one example of the resolution of redundancy of potential command which we saw (Section 2.1) to play an important role in the internal computations of an action-oriented perceiver. To balance our study of the RF model, then, we shall present in Section 7.2 a model of another system for resolving redundancy of potential command, the one which often enables a frog to snap at only one of two flies in its visual field. Note that in both our examples, there is a vital time constraint on the resolution of potential command. The cat must decide whether to fight or to flee before the dog is upon it; the frog must decide at which fly to zap before the fly has moved too far. With these two examples before us, we shall be able to gain some insights from a brief "comparative study" of these models in Section 7.3.

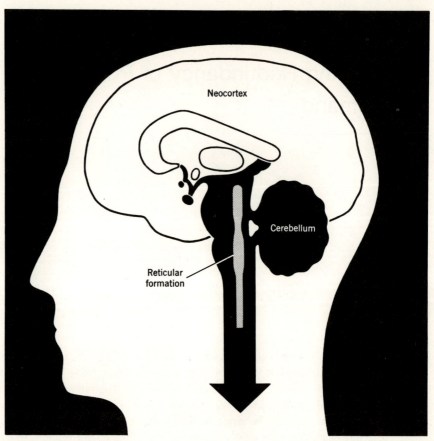

FIGURE 1   A view of the human brain, with the reticular formation (RF) indicated by the stippled area.

7.1   THE RETICULAR FORMATION MODEL

Our task in this section is to understand a model due to Kilmer and McCulloch which suggests how the RF may control the gross mode of behavior of an organism. Let us first see how neuroanatomy directed the Kilmer-McCulloch model. The Scheibels, on the basis of brainstem sections such as that shown in Figure 2 for the 10-day-old rat, observed that the collaterals both from reticular axons (at the top of the figure) and from the pyramidal tract (bottom of the figure) tend to be organized in planes approximately perpendicular to the long axis of the stem. The dendrites of RF cells also appear to lie mainly in such planes, which contrasts strikingly with cells in, for example, the hypoglossal (XII) nucleus in the top right-hand corner of the picture. They thus suggested that the reticular core might be treated as a stack of "poker chips," regions of neuropil (i.e., neural "feltwork"), as shown in the insert to Figure 2.

Thus Kilmer and McCulloch take the "module"—a formalized neuropil segment —as the basic building block in their study, as a suitable intermediate between treating RF as an indivisible unit and the ungainly task of trying to explain RF function directly at the neural level. It must be emphasized that the division of RF into these modules is somewhat arbitrary, though the differing mix of sensory modality as we move along the head-tail axis is concordant with the idea of such a partitioning.

Both the afferent ascending spinoreticular tract and the efferent descending pyramidal tract run perpendicularly through these neuropil segments (chips) and send off collaterals into the segments themselves. Within each segment there are neurons whose dendritic fields show a large degree of overlap. The input to any particular segment is nonspecific *as to modality* in that a wide variety of afferent stimuli are found to affect any given RF cell. The output axons of RF cells run up and down the brainstem for quite long distances, with large numbers of collaterals given off along their length. Thus it appears that each module in the stack has extensive communication with other modules as well as quite complex outputs to many parts of the nervous system.

So we are led to consider a structure as in Figure 3 in which we have a series in which each module is connected to a number of nearby modules and the modules receive differing input, though nearby modules may have a certain amount of input in common. We assume that each module, on the basis of its immediate input, can make a tentative decision as to the relative appropriateness of different modes. We then ask the crucial question:

THE MODE CONSENSUS QUESTION: *How can the pattern of interaction between modules be so constituted that, even though the input to different modules may initially suggest different mode preferences, an overall consensus will eventually be obtained which will commit the system to a single mode of action?*

I think it fair to say that what follows is a purely speculative, though important, attempt to answer the question. In other words, having used biological data to suggest that a crucial role (there are others that we do not attempt to model here) of RF is mode selection, and anatomical data to suggest that the configuration of Figure 3 may be the appropriate substructure for our model, we now turn our back on neural data and use any means at our disposal to fill in the boxes in Figure 3 to get a constructive answer to the mode consensus question. We shall see that Kilmer and McCulloch do provide an answer, but it will now require a new round of experimentation to see if the detailed functions they posit of a module do indeed appear to reside in a neuropil region of real RF and a subsequent round of theory will then be appropriate to explain how real neural networks might implement the agreed-upon modular functions. Thus, we repeat, the following scheme does yield mode consensus, but it is still an open question whether it bears any detailed resemblance to what goes on within the brainstem of any real animal.

Let us suppose, for simplicity of exposition, that we wish to design a mode-selector of the type of Figure 3 in which there are only four modes to be decided between. We then let the state of each module be given by a vector $\hat{p} = (p_1, p_2, p_3, p_4)$, with each $p_j \geqslant 0$ and $p_1 + p_2 + p_3 + p_4 = 1$ where p_j ($j = 1, 2, 3, 4$) is the weight (i.e., appropriateness) that the module currently assigns to the jth mode. We shall say that consensus has been reached when more than 50% of the modules attach a weight of more than $1/2$ to a single mode; this is then the new mode to which the system is committed. An unfortunate gap in the Kilmer-McCulloch scheme is that no attention has been given to the study of plausible neural circuitry which would detect that consensus has been reached, nor how the movement control circuits might be designed to respond to different mode indications. As a step toward the former, we might note

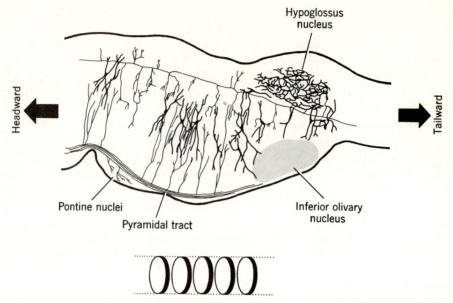

FIGURE 2   Here we see that the typical neuron of the reticular formation has axons extending both headward and tailward, while the dendrites ramify in the orthogonal plane. This suggested to the Scheibels (e.g., 1968) the caricature of RF as the stack of poker chips shown in the lower portion of the figure.

that simulation shows that whenever the model converges, it soon reaches an output level at which at least 70% of the modules assign weight of .65 or more to the dominant mode. Thus one could have a separate threshold gate for each mode, which responds only when its input reaches a total activity of at least 50% of the maximum and holds it for a few "clock times." It is then assured that only one mode-controller will fire at any one time, and thus only one mode will be triggered at a time. Such a consensus detector was used in the computer simulation, but just what form such triggering takes in the neural milieu is still an open question.

The strategy used by Kilmer and McCulloch may be compared to the cross-talk between a panel of physicians diagnosing a patient. Each physician is a specialist but does know a certain amount of general medicine. A heart specialist might base his diagnosis mainly on the electrocardiogram but still be biased by skin pallor and heavy breathing. When a new patient comes up for consideration the physicians (modules) are "globally decoupled" and each independently makes his initial diagnosis. Thereafter, the doctors talk back and forth in an effort to reach agreement, but there can also be "local decoupling" in that if one physician suddenly becomes convinced that a radically different diagnosis is required from the one that he had just been advocating, there would be a period during which the other physicians would pay special attention to his reasons for changing.

In this framework, Kilmer, McCulloch, and Blum [1968] simulated a model, called S-RETIC, of a modular system designed to compute modes according to the following scheme:

1. If the input to a module changes at all drastically, then the new $\hat{p}$ is almost

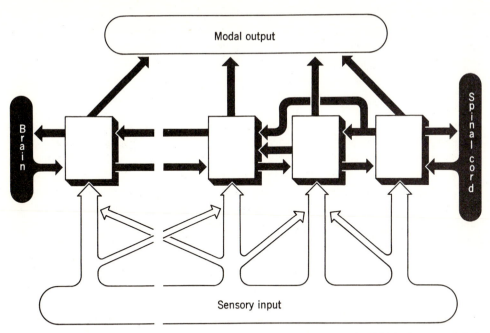

FIGURE 3   Building on the poker chip caricature of Figure 2, the RF is here modeled as a series of modules. The problem is to so design the modules that they can reach a consensus as to the appropriate mode of activity for the organism despite discrepancies in their samplings of the sensory input.

entirely determined as a function of the new sensory input. This serves to globally decouple the modules when the overall system input changes.

2. If the input to the module has not changed drastically, then the new $\hat{p}$ is obtained by normalizing a weighted average of the old $\hat{p}$ and the $\hat{p}$'s of its communicating modules. Local decoupling is obtained by giving a higher weighting to a $\hat{p}$ that has changed suddenly; potential command redundancy is obtained by giving a higher weighting to a $\hat{p}$ that contains more selection information.

As already mentioned, decision is (arbitrarily) said to be reached when a majority of the modules assign weight, or appropriateness, greater than .5 to any one mode. The overall effect of the scheme, then, is to decouple the modules initially after an input change in order to accentuate each's evaluation of what the next mode should be, and then through successive iterations couple them back together in order to reach a global consensus. Computer simulation showed that S-RETIC (at least with the coupling patterns they studied) would converge for every input in less than 25 cycles, and that once it had converged, it would stay converged for a given input. When the inputs strongly indicate one mode, then the response is fast; but when the indication is weak, initial conditions and circuit characteristics may bias the final decision strongly.

Within any mode of behavior many different acts are possible: if the cat should flee, will it take the mouse or leave it, climb a tree or skirt it, jump a creek or swim it? Kilmer and McLardy [1970] have posited that it is a part of the hippocampus (other parts of the hippocampal gyrus seem involved in the consolidation of long-term memory) that helps make act decisions with modes, at least during the behavior-formative period. It is not our task to consider this model here, for it is still controversial (cf. the alternative hippocampal model of Olds [1969]), but the reader may care to ponder why a hierarchical structure which computes modes, and then acts within modes, might in some sense be "better" (irrespective of the particular structural basis ascribed to these functions) than one which tries to determine successive acts directly.

Returning, then, to mode selection, it should not be thought that the claim "RF controls the mode" implies that in doing so it overrides all cortical influences. Rather, cortex can play a vital role in assigning the relative importance different sensory patterns will have in RF's proposed mode computations. For example, one important dimension of mode change is alertness: as the animal moves from deep sleep to light sleep to wakefulness to full alertness. A sudden sound may alert an animal, and it seems well established that this results from excitation along pathways spreading diffusely to the cerebral cortex from a region of the RF consequently labeled the reticular activating system. However, if the same sound occurs many times, the RF may no longer activate the animal, in which case we say that the animal has *habituated* to the stimulus. Such habituation can be rather complicated. A woman may sleep through a thunderstorm only to waken at the slightest cry from her baby; a deckhand may sleep amidst the clamor of the engine room but waken if the engine changes pitch. Conversely, absence of a habituated sound can serve as an alerting stimulus; Pribram [1971] recounts how New York residents, used to sleeping through the accustomed passage of the 3 A.M. train on the old el (the elevated railway) would wake at 3 A.M. after the el was demolished until they became habituated to the unexpected silence! Sokolov, of the Moscow State University, conducted experiments which showed that the brain must store an "internal model" of a stimulus to which it habituated, in that changes in any one of a large number of parameters may remove the habituation. Sokolov repeatedly presented a tone of fixed frequency and duration to a subject, and noted that the orienting reflex, as measured by the "evoked response," a gross electrical measure of the level of cortical activation, diminished with repeated presentation. A tempting explanation would be that the RF has simply learned to ignore auditory input of the given frequency. However, Sokolov ruled this out by showing that habituation disappeared to that frequency if he raised or even *lowered* the intensity of the stimulus. Further, if the tone of habituated frequency and amplitude were to be cut short, the evoked response would appear at the tone's offset. Thus frequency, amplitude, and duration were all encoded, so that habituation appears to result not from the fatigue or exclusion of a limited set of peripheral receptors or feature detectors but rather by central generation of a "template" or set of parameters which may be used in efferent control of appropriate parts of the sensory pathway, so that only a mismatch enters into the RF's computations.

The point to note, though, is that if the cortex is removed, the orienting reflex cannot be extinguished except in bizarre cases. Thus, although the orienting reflex is controlled by RF, the cortex can exert inhibitory control on the evaluation of sensory input. The Kilmer-McCulloch strategy, then, has been to study how the RF might exercise modal control irrespective of cortical influences. We hope that we may better understand human behavior in terms of evolutionary refinement of such primitive computations, rather than by trying to capture its full complexity directly. In the same way, we try to understand visual perception by seeing to what extent we can view visual cortex as a system which has evolved to refine the primitive visuomotor coordinations effected by the tectum. In both cases we see that cortex must process much information to aid subcortical structures in determining what shall occupy the focus of our attention, and that our understanding is still at a primitive stage.

7.2 FROG VISUOMOTOR ACTIVITY

To counterpoint the model of the reticular formation, and to give concreteness to the discussion of the layered computer in Chapter 6, we build upon the Pitts-McCulloch model of gaze centering (Section 5.5) to provide a somatotopically structured model of the visually guided behavior of the frog. We first sketch a few aspects of the frog's visuomotor behavior and then limit ourselves to those we shall encompass in our model.

A frog will sit immobile for hours on end, but sometimes (as we have mentioned) in response to the presence of a small wiggling object, it will either orient (turn so that it faces the object) or snap (turn to face the object and "zap" it with its tongue as well). Ingle has found that there are two distinct zones, which are defined relative to the head rather than the body, such that within the inner zone the animal, when it responds will do so with a snap, while in a larger surrounding zone the animal will only orient.

Two points, neither of which we shall attempt to model here, may be of interest about this behavior. First, the frog's motions are ballistic: it is as if it "shoots" itself at its target with no possibility of feedback once it has started, for if the experimenter jerks the stimulus away during the approximately 1/10 second during which the frog is in motion, the frog will snap at the original position of the stimulus. Second, the animal can "zap" flies even when they lie in the visual field of only one eye, so that binocular vision does not seem necessary.(Ingle hypothesizes that the accommodation of the eye required to bring the stimulus into sharp focus provides the frog with the depth information it needs, but the finding of Keating and Gaze that the frog has intertectal connections subserving binocular vision makes one wonder if more detailed studies would show "fine tuning" which is operative only when both eyes are used in concert.)

What we shall be most concerned with modeling is the behavior of the frog in the presence of more than one "fly". It becomes less likely to respond, and if it does respond it normally snaps at only one "fly". However, Ingle [1968] has found that in the case illustrated in Figure 4, in which two stimuli are moved synchronously and

FIGURE 4 A frog snapping at "the average fly".

symmetrically toward or away from the nose, the frog will usually strike right between them; we may say that it snaps at the "average fly". Our task now is to design a network which can take a position-tagged array of "foodness" intensity, either from the group II "bug detector" cells of Lettvin et al. [1959] described in Section 2.4 or from tectal neurons which modulate the Group II information with that from other layers, and ensure that usually only one region of activity will influence the motor control systems.

In view of our discussion in Section 6.1, we shall seek a distributed computation solution to this problem. Let us first, then, briefly mention the sort of strategy we are ruling out. One is the serial-scan strategy suggested in Figure 5 in which some

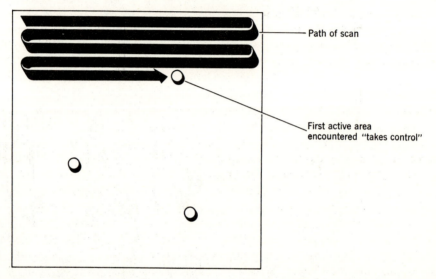

FIGURE 5   Nonbiological serial approach to resolution of redundancy of potential command.

central executive scans back and forth across the "foodness layer" until finding a region of high activity, whereupon it ceases scanning, and reads off its current "scan coordinates" to issue the appropriate command to the motor control systems to cause the frog to snap at the corresponding region. Perhaps such a scheme could even yield the average fly effect were we to posit a separate scanner for each eye so that in the case of symmetric stimuli, the two scanners would finish in a "dead heat" to take command of the animal, the opposing forces yielding the average motion as resultant. But despite such an appealing property we rule out the scanning mechanism because, in addition to our general consideration of somatotopy, it would seem to have the property that the number of items to be scanned would simply make such a scheme take too long.

For a scheme which maintains the spatial distribution of information, we turn to the work of Richard Didday in which new circuitry is introduced whereby different regions of the tectum so compete that in normal circumstances only the most active will provide an above-threshold input to the motor circuitry, which we assume has a spatially organized input surface as in the schematic for distributed motor control in

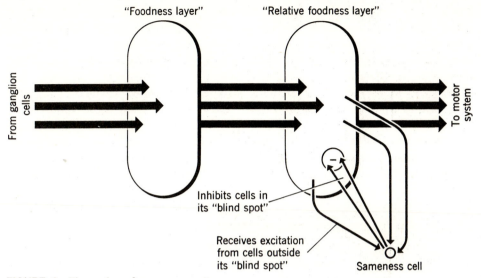

FIGURE 6   The action of sameness cells.

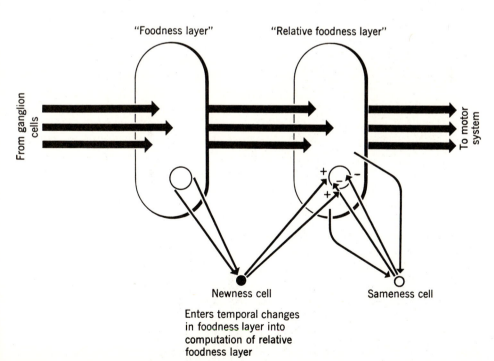

FIGURE 7   The action of newness cells.

199

Figure 24 of Section 5.5. To achieve this effect, we first introduce a new layer of cells in close correspondence to the "foodness layer," but whose activity is to yield the input to the motor circuitry. In some sense, then, it is to be "relative foodness" rather than "foodness" which describes the receptive field activity appropriate to a cell of this layer.

Didday's transformation scheme from "foodness" to "relative foodness" employs a population of what he calls *sameness* cells, each of which "sits over" a region of the "relative foodness layer", and "turns down" the activity that cells in its region receive from the corresponding cells in the "foodness" layer by an amount that increases with increasing activity *outside* its region (Figure 6). This ensures that high activity in a region of the foodness layer only "gets through" if the surrounding areas do not contain sufficiently high activity to block it.

When we examine the behavior of such a network, we find that plausible interconnection schemes yield the following properties:

1. If the activity in one region exceeds the activity in any other region, then this region will eventually "overwhelm" all other regions, and the animal will snap at the space corresponding to it.

2. If two regions have sufficiently close activity, then:

a. If both regions are very active they may both overwhelm the other regions and simultaneously "take command" with the result that the frog snaps between the regions.

b. However, in many cases these two active regions will simply "turn down" each other's activity, and that in other regions, so much that neither is sufficient to "take command" and the frog will remain immobile, ignoring the two "flies".

One trouble with the circuitry as so far described is that the buildup of inhibition on the sameness cells precludes the system's quick response to new stimuli. For example, in case (*2b*) above, if one of those two very active regions were to suddenly become more active, then the deadlock *should* be broken quickly, but in the network so far described, the new activity cannot easily break through the inhibition built up on the sameness cell in its region. Didday thus introduced a newness cell for each sameness cell. The job of a newness cell is to monitor temporal changes in the activity in its region. Should it detect a sufficiently dramatic increase in the region's activity, it then overrides the sameness cell inhibition to enter the new level of activity into the relative foodness layer (Figure 7). With this scheme, the inertia of the old model is overcome, and we now have a "frog brain" which can respond rapidly to significant new stimuli (Figure 8).

7.3 SOME POINTS OF CONNECTION

There are two fascinating aspects of the frog model that warrant elaboration here. The first is that the sameness and newness cells were introduced for purely logical reasons, to obtain a network which conformed to our principles that the network be designed to mediate frog activity rather than some abstract notion of information handling or adaptation; and that the necessary computation be implemented in a distributed fashion. By trying to conform to these principles, Didday was led to *invent* his sameness and newness neurons. But having invented them (not having yet labeled

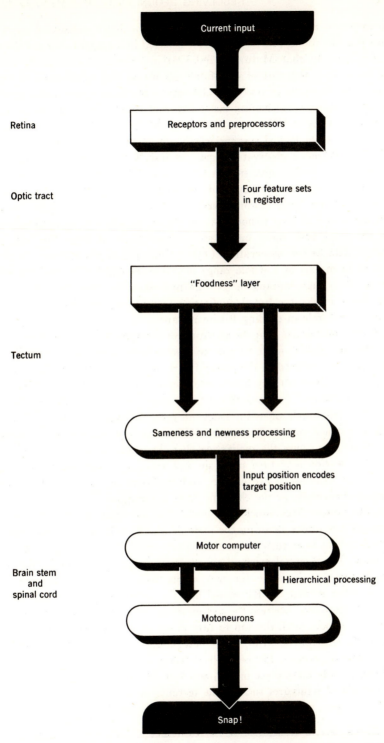

FIGURE 8   Overall scheme for frog visuomotor activity. It is similar to Figures 6.2 and 6.8, save that, in this simple model, there is no use of long-term memory to modify sensory input.

them as sameness and newness neurons, though no doubt influenced by a host of subliminal considerations), he saw that they behaved in a manner akin to† the sameness and newness neurons that Maturana and Lettvin (Section 2.4) actually observed in the frog brain. It is this sort of qualitative prediction that encourages one to pursue the use of these principles in trying to understand the brain—just as the agreement of his observations on servomechanism instability with clinical observations on ataxia (see Section 3.3) encouraged Wiener in developing the application of control and communication theories to biological systems which constituted his original version of cybernetics. Just as Wiener's observations gave us insight into relationships involving the cerebellum, so our models give insight into visual systems. However, we now know far more about cerebellar anatomy and physiology, and so we use Wiener's work as but a framework for more detailed study. In the same way, we shall change many details of our model of frog visuomotor activity as we take into account more detailed data on the frog, both more quantitative observations of frog behavior and such physiological data as the observation (Fite [1969]) that the newness and sameness cells seem to form part of a whole range of cell types which show varying degrees of habituation rather than forming the two distinct classes we have favored here. But we may confidently expect the broad qualitative features of the model to stand, and to play an important role in guiding future research.

The second aspect is one that the structure of this chapter, and the statement of our principle that the system must be able to resolve redundancy of potential command, may have already presented to the perceptive reader: The models of RF mode control and of frog visuomotor activity have a great deal in common. In fact, Didday's thesis was completed before I realized this commonality, and it was this realization that suggested that resolution of redundancy of potential command was not a topic to be briefly mentioned in relation to the RF model, but was indeed a fundamental principle. With this comes the realization that the mechanisms introduced in the two models of this section may turn up again and again in subsystems of the brain, and in robot control systems, as we explore such problems as the direction of attention, the workings of memory, or the changing faces of emotion.

Where the Kilmer-McCulloch RF model has an array of modules which must interact to get a majority favoring the same mode, the task of the second layer of our hypothetical tectum is to turn down the activity of all but one region of (or from) the first layer. The essential mechanisms are very similar; for example, the RF "local decoupling" provides the same function as the tectum model's "newness" neurons. The models differ in that the RF model has all modes evaluated in each module and tries to attain consensus, whereas the tectum model may be viewed as having a module identified with a mode with the aim to turn down all but one mode (module). In any case, the study of frog behavior sheds new insight on RF modeling, and suggests several alternate hypotheses. For example, it forces us to ask two questions: How much mode selection really takes place in RF, and how much subroutine decision takes place in more specialized structures such as the tectum? And could the RF model be more successful if it was structured along the one mode-one module line of the tectum

---

† But not "identical with." Lettvin's sameness cells were like the frog's focus of attention itself. They responded vigorously when the stimulus changed direction or speed anywhere in the whole visual field. The newness neurons adapt within a single pass to a stimulus moving in one direction. So the fit is not as good as might be desired. See the comments which follow.

model? The confrontation of the two models thus poses exciting challenges to both the theorist and the experimentalist. Our models are still crude oversimplifications of the complexities of real brains, but we believe that our partial successes show that the organizational principles of Section 6.1, all too often neglected (even implicitly, since they have not been explicated before) in the cybernetics literature, must play a crucial role in future brain theory.

Prospects

CHAPTER 8   WHERE DO WE GO FROM HERE?

8 | Where Do We Go From Here?

Having gained some understanding of the interplay between model and action in providing the basis for an animal's or a robot's perception, and having studied possible mechanisms for seeing the world as composed of objects, for choosing between courses of action, and for interacting in simple ways with these objects, we realize that we have come a long way in understanding the function of the brain. But when we realize that we have paid little attention to emotion and motivation or to that full richness of perception we call creativity, we see that we still have a long, long way to go. The purpose of this last chapter, then, is to suggest that—despite the vast range of human thought and behavior we have not yet touched upon from our cybernetic approach—our approach can evolve to apply to this range.

In Section 8.1 we discuss language and mental development to show that even in such well-trodden areas of study of human thought and behavior, our approach seems capable of providing fresh insights. Then in Section 8.2 we try to put the problem of understanding the brain into perspective, returning to the rather general themes laid out in Chapter 1, and then closing the book with a speculative discussion of some possible social implications of our studies.

8.1 LANGUAGE AND MENTAL DEVELOPMENT

Each of the topics "language" and "mental development" is so vast that no multivolume work could do full justice to them. Our purpose in this single section of a single book, then, must be a modest one. It is simply to show that a number of the principles that have guided our work can provide insights in thinking about language and mental development, and thus encourage us in the belief that our studies can indeed be integrated into a comprehensive program of what might be called cybernetic psychology. We emphasize again, though, that we are here viewing cybernetics as encompassing a broad program of artificial intelligence and brain theory, rather than an attempt to reduce all functioning to the interaction of a number of feedback circuits.

We shall confine ourselves to putting forward three proposals: that the notion of an internal model will help us understand language, and that comparative studies will aid this understanding; that the spatial frame of action that was central to our frog model will also provide the substrate for an understanding of human mental development; and that the ideas of Section 5.4 on hierarchies of motor control may be built upon, in a manner consistent with our discussion in Sections 6.1 and 6.2, to provide an integrated view of mental development and learning.

PROPOSED.   *That the notion of an internal model will help us understand language, and that comparative studies will aid this understanding.*

In Section 6.2, we presented the notion of an output feature cluster (OFC) as the "building block" for potential interaction of the organism with its environment, suggesting that a virtue of a long-term model (LTM) was that it enabled the organism to use different cues from different modalities on different occasions to activate a given OFC. In short, a given situation or object can be re-cognized (known again) in many different ways. But given this ability, which humans would seem to share at least with all mammals, the ability to use signs seems almost immediate. Many organisms, knowing an animal by its appearance, may come to know it by its cry; and in those cases where the brain is so structured as to enable the organism to make this association on the basis of experience, then the cry might as well be an arbitrary grunt or howl. Thus the ability to recognize signs would seem to be on a par with the ability to perceive the world in terms of objects (yielding "noun" recognition) and inter-actions with them (yielding "verb" recognition).

What distinguishes humans, it would seem, is then not so much the ability to recognize signs as it is the ability to assign them to new simplexes and combine them to generate complex sentences. (Studies of the speech of brain-damaged humans help us probe the mechanisms involved. Here we shall instead discuss some comparative and developmental studies of language, and refer the reader to Geschwind [1970] and Luria's book [1966] for studying language in relation to cerebral organization.) Let us speculate, in this vein, on how humans might have "invented" language, and then discuss some experiments which help us understand the functional capabilities the feat would have required. Initially, humans might have used conventional cries to draw attention to a single object, or to encourage the listener to undertake some particular action. It would then be natural to suggest an action with respect to a particular object and so *concatenation*—the chaining together of signals—could then evolve. Concatenating the typical warning cry of the mother to her child with the signal for some forbidden action might then be the basis for *negation,* and the first step toward logic. Here then is the beginning of language as a means for communicating perceptions, and trying to share properties of internal models of the world. Where many linguists have taken *syntax* (the grammatical rules of the language) as primary to the study of language, we would see it as secondary in the evolution of language. If we did not understand the passive construction and registered only the elementary meanings (semantics) of "apple", "eat", and "boy", our model of the world would lead us to understand their concatenation as meaning what in English we convey by "the apple was eaten by the boy" rather than "the apple ate the boy". However, as we put more and more "semantic units" together, our model of the world can no longer let us infer a unique relationship between. And thus we may hypothesize that syntax evolved as subtle modifiers became required to distinguish the possible meanings of long concatenations of signs.

Linguists have often commented upon the diversity of sentences in a language: we seem not to have mastered a finite set of sentences, but rather to have learned how to *generate* a potentially unbounded variety of sentences. This book is almost entirely composed of sentences which had never been uttered before they were written for this book or the papers which preceded it. But this generative property would seem to accord well with its initial function as a means of communicating aspects of internal models, for each new context must then call forth, once the vocabulary achieves a basic level of richness and flexibility, a new sentence to express it.

It is interesting to read such studies as those of Ursula Bellugi on the linguistic development of the child from this viewpoint. She shows that the child discovers regularities in language, and then uses these to *resynthesize* a sentence. For example, a child of 2 may interpret "the cat was chased by the dog" as "the cat chased the dog." I would interpret this as showing that a child does not parrot the sentence but rather understands it (builds an internal model of what she thinks it says) and then expresses the model in a sentence with a structure she already knows.

To get a feel for the sentences the child produces, we may study how the child develops the use of negation:

1. At first she puts no or not in front of a sentence to be negated. After a time she utters such sentences as
   I no do it.
   He no want it.
   Mummy no cut it.
2. The negative element is placed inside the sentence, not as a direct imitation of adult sentences but rather as a reconstruction according to the child's own rule. When asked to repeat a sentence such as "I don't like it", a child of this stage (around 35 months in one case) pauses a while before saying "I no like it".
3. Later (3 months later for the child just mentioned) the negative becomes associated with the auxiliary system.
   He don't want it.
   I can't have it.
   I don't want some.

Such grammatical refinements (fine tuning) as changing "I don't want some" to "I don't want any" do not come till later. It should also be noted that including a negative can "take up room", and so may yield "economized forms" as when "Catherine have shoe on" is negated to yield "Catherine no shoe". Thus, besides acquiring new rules, the child increases "capacity". A child may have more to say than she can express. Between stages 2 and 3 (the stages may be 2 or 3 months apart) the child seems to use "It's" as a variant of the pronoun, not as a combination of two elements, as in "It's goes". That is, the child may segment its sentences differently from the way adults do.

Why does the child change her grammar toward that of the adult when she can already make herself understood? Cutting down the number of rules accounts for some changes, but not for "fine tuning" like "who" versus "whom". Perhaps after the child has learned how to express an idea so that she can be understood, she is then free to learn the "fine tuning" of increased grammaticality which will increase her circle of listeners by imitation. In any case, we repeat the observation made earlier that the child does not parrot sentences but reconstructs them according to her own rules. This reinforces our objections in Section 6.4 to the seductive simplicity of a "Kodachrome" model of human memory, which regards memory of an event as some sort of faithful encoding awaiting retrieval at some later time. I would suggest that it will prove more fruitful to regard the fabrication of a unique and absolute representation of each experience as neither economical in neuronal terms nor flexible in dealing with novel stimuli, and that the crucial task in learning may be seen as the discovery of which features or rules make different events usefully similar.

Let me close this brief discussion of language with two observations on comparative studies. Bronoski and Bellugi [1970] analyzed the attempts of Gardner and Gardner [1969] to teach chimps sign language. Earlier attempts to teach chimps to speak had failed, but the Gardners had realized that this might reflect an inadequate control of the vocal musculature in the chimpanzee rather than a lack of linguistic ability per se. In fact, using sign language the chimpanzee was able to reach what Brown and Bellugi [1964] characterized as Class 2 in the linguistic development of children. This shows that although these particular aspects of language that pertain to speech are not shared by the chimpanzee, such basic linguistic abilities as the use of concatenation are. Complementing such studies, Marler [1970] asks "Birdsong and Speech Development: Could There Be Parallels?", for while birds do not have concatenation or language they can learn complex sound patterns. Marler shows ways in which the analysis of the relative degrees of genetic fixedness and learned "dialect" in various types of bird-song may provide valuable cues in probing the evolution of, and brain mechanisms for, our own speech abilities.

PROPOSED. *That the spatial frame of action that was central to our frog model will also provide the substrate for an understanding of human mental development.*

Given our emphasis on the "where" of action-oriented perception, the origin of the child's conception of space would seem to be of great interest to us. Let us briefly mention some careful experiments showing that the human baby is born with a spatial field in which reaching by hand is coordinated automatically with locations in the visual orienting field.

Bower, Broughton, and Moore [1970a, b] and Trevarthen [personal communication] found that even in the first week of life, a baby could reach for a seen object (although inaccurately) and could focus her gaze upon its hand when no object is present. Further, the baby does not have to alternately fixate hand and object to guide the hand to the object, for the baby can swipe as accurately if lateral blinders prevent her from seeing the initial position of the hand until a ballistic movement is initiated. Thus, since we are prepared to believe that the visuomotor coordinating mechanisms of the frog (which we attempted to model in Section 7.2) are genetically specified, it is encouraging to our reliance on comparative studies that we should now have evidence that a similar mechanism is apparently genetically specified in humans. (Trevarthen notes that eye-hand coordination is, however, initially slow and relatively imprecise; but that there is a rapid and regulated development which apparently involves the better integration of controlling mechanisms by feedback from practice.)

To add to this evidence for an inbuilt spatial frame, we should mention other evidence which accords well with our suggestion that we have evolved to perceive objects rather than sense intensity of stimulation or size of retinal stimulation as isolated variables. Bower et al. [1970a] show that infants only 1 to 3 weeks old will already show more of an avoiding response to an approaching object than to a puff of air alone, or to a movie projection of the approaching object. Earlier Bower had shown that a 2-month-old infant will respond to two views of a given cube at different distances as being more alike than the two views of a small cube nearby and a large cube far away which yield the same retinal image. In robotics and traditional psychology we often seek the minimal set of cues sufficient to identify an object; the preceding data suggest, but do not prove, that the brain makes judgments on many variables rather than on one variable at a time, and this may accord well with some variant of the hologram metaphor of Section 6.4.

In another experiment, Bower found that 2-month-old infants were distressed if a different object emerged from one they had just seen disappear behind a screen, suggesting that some aspects of object constancy appear early. This would seem to me to fit in well with what we judged in Section 6.2 to be the import of Shepard's data: that we perceive an object by setting up an internal model which can be easily modified to adjust to the movements of the object. If basic transformations of simple objects are as basic as we might expect them to be, the baby's surprise would not be surprising. Presumably, then, one aspect of mental development is the ability to model objects of increasing complexity, and "hold on to" these models for increasing lengths of time. Some of the data related to the next proposition suggest, unsurprisingly, that this is indeed so.

PROPOSED. *That our ideas on hierarchies of motor control may be built upon to provide an integrated (though incomplete) view of mental development and learning.*

Regarding the OFC as the "building block" for potential interaction with the environment, we would take the growth of long-term memory (LTM) to involve not only the learning of more and more cues to gain wider access to a given OFC (cited in our comments on language), but to also involve the formation of new OFC's. In line with the discussion of hierarchies of motor control in Section 5.4, we would expect this process to involve the "splicing" of existing structures, and the "fine tuning" of the result into new entities. This is exemplified by the role we assigned to identification procedures (Section 3.4) in learning a motor skill such as driving: by verbal instruction, a human can summon the basic "action routines" or "OFC's" which are to be combined, but much rehearsal and practice is then required to yield well-coordinated behavior. From this viewpoint it may not be helpful to make too sharp a distinction between learning ("updating" LTM) and mental development (cumulative effects of "updating" LTM); perhaps we may use mental development to refer to those effects of long-term memory which yield whole new *styles* of interaction with the environment.

To relate our approach to experimental work in mental development, we should introduce the concept of *schema*. Piaget speaks of *sensorimotor schemata* in a sense akin to that in which we use OFC's if we include with the OFC the specification of the varieties of sensory stimulation which will yield access to it. [Perhaps the main difference comes in our emphasis—relating the slide-box metaphor of Section 4.1 to the transformation schemes of Sections 6.2 and 6.3—on the ability of OFC's to be integrated and transformed within the representation of a spatial framework. Given our discussion of "nested analysis" in Section 4.3, we should also add that in many situations it is misleading to speak of the varieties of sensory stimulation which will yield access to an OFC, since often the *context* (pattern of already activated OFC's) will play a greater role in activation than sensory input, as in the role posited to the reference beam during dreaming, in the hologram metaphor of Figure 9 in Chapter 6. As a simple example of context dependence within the artificial intelligence approach, note how strongly the robot's interpretation, in Section 4.4, of the command "Push the large cube to the door" depended upon its current model of its environment.] Kagan [1970] is not so much interested in the motor aspects, and so views a schema as an "equivalence class" of sensory patterns which may be defined by observing differences in the way in which the subject pays attention to different stimuli.

Where Bower and Trevarthen, as reported above, studied hand-eye coordination, Kagan [1970] emphasized experiments in which the child's "level of attention" was measured by seeing how long the child's gaze would rest upon an object or pattern. His report of the newborn child's visual behavior is also consistent with the claim that the human newborn has "inbuilt" visuomotor mechanisms akin to those we attempted to model in Sections 6.4 and 7.2: Too bright light will cause the child to close her eyes, but if her eyes are open she will search not only for a light source, but for a patterned light source, with her gaze holding and crossing contour edges. The time which a child will spend gazing at a figure seems to depend upon the total length of contour in the figure. At each age there is a critical "complexity level" which gains maximum attention in that with either more or less complexity, the child's attention drops off. With increasing age, the maximum point on the attention curve shifts to higher and higher complexity levels. Kagan comments that "the preferential orientation to change is clearly adaptive, for the locus of change is likely to contain the most information about the presence of his mother or of danger", which reminds us of our theoretical analysis of visual preprocessing in Section 2.4.

During the second month, simple complexity measures seem less relevant than schemata (in Kagan's sense) in describing the foci of the child's attention. The child seems to elaborate her range of schemata by paying most attention to sensory patterns which differ moderately from known schemata. This situation, described as *the discrepancy principle* [Kagan, 1970], is caricatured in Figure 1, where we see that the child pays little attention either to stimuli which are very familiar, or to stimuli which are completely unfamiliar.

We may use this point to suggest that the world of the infant is *not*—as William James would have had it—a "buzzing, blooming confusion". To gain a feel for this, consider the following display:

Я СТРОИТ

To the average non-Cyrillist this is not a buzzing, blooming confusion, although it is certainly rather meaningless. She might commit it to memory as "R back to front, blank, CTRO, N back to front, T." However, to anyone who knows Russian, it can be succinctly encoded in terms of three syllables, "Ya stroy-eet." In fact, and this is the adult analog of the discrepancy principle, our usual reaction to seeing such an array is simply to notice that it is not meaningful to us and then ignore it. (Compare our

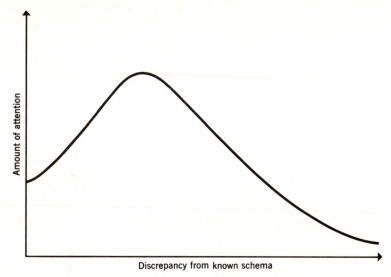

FIGURE 1 A graphical representation of the discrepancy principle, showing how attention reaches a peak for slight discrepancies from a known schema and then decreases as the discrepancy becomes even greater.

reaction to new schools in art.) In the same way, I would suggest that the naive child simply ignores most of her environment. As time goes by and she accumulates certain basic patterns, then she will notice more complex patterns to the extent that they can be built up in a fairly simple fashion either as composites or by tuning of what she already recognizes. The rest remains meaningless, but not buzzing, blooming, or confusing. It is only that which is on the verge of being encoded, but cannot quite be grasped, that causes confusion. As time goes by, the more complex patterns themselves become units on which she can build, and so her perceptions can encompass more and more aspects of her environment without any increase in instantaneous activity since they build on past structures. (The discussion of language development suggests that there is an increase in STM "capacity", which aids in expanding the range of the child's perception, too.)

An example of such a cumulative effect can be seen in the child's changing attention to pictures of human faces. At 1 week, and in fact even at 8 weeks, a face and a meaningless pattern of equal contour length receive equal attention. Children are tested with both photographs and outline drawings of faces and, as shown in Figure 2 for the drawings, these may be regular or irregular. Note, too, the motor skills involved in "visual exploration" including tiny eyeball oscillations which may qualify as (largely unconscious) "skills" for finding contours and equivalence relations. The changing patterns of attention of the child would seem to fit well with the discrepancy principle. During the first weeks of life the fact that photographs of either regular or irregular faces elicit equivalent epochs of attention would suggest that the child has no schema for the face and so both types of face are equally discrepant from any established schema. The fact that, between 2 and 4 months, the photograph of a strange face becomes optimally discrepant from the schema, more a focus of attention than familiar faces or irregular faces, would suggest that schemata for familiar faces have

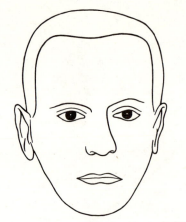

FIGURE 2   Before and after: a face and its rearrangement.

by then been built up. During the second half of the first year, it would seem that a general face schema becomes very well established, for photographs of regular or irregular faces, though discriminable, come to be looked at for short and equivalent periods of time.

What is perhaps most important about the foregoing discussion, based on Kagan [1970], is that it reminds us that perceptual changes can arise out of an active searching of the environment which involves no more activity than that used to shift visual attention. As we have already emphasized, our action-oriented approach to perception must be complemented by a study of its role in model-building for future action, so that achieving familiarity with differing patterns of sensory stimulation may occur during visual exploration of the environment as much as during acquisition in motor skills. It should be clear that our three proposals cover but a few aspects of language and mental development; and it should further be clear that these are indeed proposals for research rather than accepted dogmas. But if the proposals seem worthwhile, and their relationship with the rest of the book seems to be a natural one, then the aim of this section will have been achieved.

8.2   POSSIBLE SOCIAL IMPLICATIONS

One of my good friends, much concerned with putting our science in the context of ourselves as human beings, posed the following questions to me in relation to the material presented in the rest of this book:

> What *kind* of understanding of brain and behavior can be forecast?
> What will a mechanistic theory mean for our concept of ourselves?
> How can we ensure happy and beneficial uses of our knowledge?
> What imaginative and positive possibilities does it open up?
> What responses or changes can we expect in our social and political environment if we stimulate it with the possibility of the control which an exact knowledge of the brain might make possible?

It would have been easy to reply "My book is about experiments and theories and attempts to objectively assess the relationship between them", and politely decline to consider them here, objecting that answering these questions does not fit within this framework, and, in any case, would take me outside my special knowledge. But, having debated these issues with friends and students, having tried to awaken audiences, both large and small, to the ways in which cybernetics can change ourselves and our society, and having tried to convince students that they should attempt to relate their scientific studies to their social concerns, I feel bound to make some answer here. But in doing so, let me make it clear that the ratio of personal opinion to incontrovertible fact is even higher here than elsewhere in the book, and that it is certainly possible to disagree violently with some of the pronouncements of this section without in any way diminishing your agreement with the brain theory of Part III. Though I hope that some of my comments are valuable in themselves, the reason I have answered my friend's questions here is not to provide you with the right answers, but rather to convince you that these questions are worth answering, and that science should not be separated from life.

What kind of understanding of brain and behavior can be forecast? What imaginative and positive possibilities does it open up?

We have certain words for describing overall properties of our mental activity, such as "consciousness" and "intelligence" which, as we saw in Section 4.1, must be taken to refer not to single entities, but rather as multiple properties, each based on a cooperative phenomenon, that is, a product of interaction between a highly structured array of millions upon millions of neurons. When we consider that physics is as yet unable to explicitly solve highly simplified equations that describe a three-dimensional magnet, we see that even if the ordinary laws of the physical scientist were adequate to account for all aspects of what we consider to be intelligent or conscious behavior, we would still have a long way to go before we could explain such phenomena as intelligence and consciousness from those physical laws. In fact, we may find that as we study more complicated systems by the methods of physical science, so will more "correction terms" be required in the physical laws. We found we needed to modify Newtonian mechanics to get relativity when we entered the domain of the very fast; and we needed to modify them to get the laws of quantum mechanics when we entered the domain of the very small. Thus we must not be unprepared to have to find yet new laws of physics when we enter the domain of the very complex. But the fact remains that these would still be the laws of matter, of energy, of physics, and not mystical laws postulating properties of some entity which does not evolve from the highly cooperative phenomena of physical entities.

The human brain is so complex that exact prediction of its behavior is essentially impossible, but that approximate prediction at different levels of description may well be possible. It is too much to understand the detailed interaction of 10 billion neurons, but we may understand how the neurons in one layer of a brain structure may act together to yield a certain type of activity (and thus predict how changes in cellular activity induced by drugs will change the type of activity in that layer) ; we may understand how the layers of a structure may yield the overall function of a subsystem (and so find better ways of building visual prostheses to provide preprocessed light signals to the visual cortex of a blind human) ; we may understand how subsystems with different gross modes of activity may interact when combined in different ways (and so provide the basis for a truly rational neurosurgery) ; we may understand how different types of relationship with other people and the rest of the environment can change the growth of a human's mind (and so make education a joyous part of life instead of a tedious ritual conducted in the secrecy of the classroom) ; and, continuing up the hierarchy from neurophysiology and psychology to sociology and political science, if we can understand how small groups of people may help and encourage one another, perhaps we can build upon this to form a peaceful and creative world.

It should be noted that, as we progressed up this "shopping list" of imaginative and positive possibilities, the time-scale of achievement came to seem longer and longer. Understanding the effect of drugs on small parts of the brain and building visual prostheses are now within our reach; a rational neurosurgery which can remove a tumor or cure epilepsy with minimal disruption to the personality still seems elusive but not impossible; while the tasks of education and world peace are so mired in prejudice and old wive's tales, and so lacking in a common framework for rational discussion, that hopes for any cumulative progress at times seem dark indeed. But perhaps the very fact that we can descry such a progression is some cause for encouragement. If we just use a car to get to work, we need know nothing about engines, but if we want the best performance from it we must know all the fine details of the ignition system, the carburetor, and so on. Perhaps if we resolutely approach our study of brain theory and artificial intelligence in terms of its relationship to "getting the best performance" from ourselves as human beings, then we may be on the way to making some contribution to our global problems.

It would be pretentious to suggest that we only need more cybernetics to bring world peace and an end to pollution (!!)—a check-out clerk at the supermarket who smiles at you instead of begrudging every working minute may make a greater contribution to human happiness than a misanthropic cybernetician. What I am suggesting, though, is that humanity faces immense problems, and science and technology will have to form part of their solution. Some scientific contributions to the solution of these problems will come from scientists who are not thinking about those problems, but it does not seem unreasonable to expect that a scientist concerned with relating his study of the brain to better education may contribute more than a scientist whose only concern is for making bigger and bigger thermonuclear bombs. However, although it does not seem unreasonable, it may be wrong, which is why I repeat that this section should be treated as a basis for debate rather than a set of pat answers. The educator, despite his good intentions, may be deluded into overrating his theory and end up by crippling the minds of thousands of children, while the thermonuclear scientist may (let us fervently hope!) come to a time when nuclear warfare is a thing of the past, and find that he has provided the basic insight for a new and pollution-free source of energy. Our problem, whether we seek to understand the brain or to improve our world, is that we have little true appreciation of the complexity of the systems we study or the patience and length of time required to gain some true understanding.

What will a mechanistic theory mean for our concept of ourselves?

I have stressed that a mechanistic theory does not entail reducing humans to machines of a dull sort, but rather extends our understanding of what mechanism can be. Given that there are many humans who lavish immense care and attention to keep their cars in perfect condition, but ignore their children (or beat them when they can't ignore them), one might even suggest that if people were to view each other "only" as intricate mechanisms they would be far kinder to each other! In any case, one need love another no less for appreciating something of the bodily and neural mechanisms which underlie their charm. For much of our everyday relationships with people, the language we have evolved over the millenia will express what we want to say; but if we would find new techniques for meditation, or a drug to dispel depression, then we must probe within for the law of human functioning. In short, a mechanistic theory—if appreciated for its full subtlety—need not destroy a humanist conception of ourselves (though it is probably incompatible with an overly literal Biblical conception) but may enrich it by helping us get a better measure of our true complexity and diversity.

Physical explainability is compatible with our cherished belief in human uniqueness. When we consider the large amount of information that is contained in the genetic code of each person, which is different almost always except in the case of twins, and when we add to this the huge variety of experiences which each person encounters (and here twins do differ), then we see that it is inevitable that, as systems with a brain which can store so much of this individual experience, we must end up as unique individuals. We must beware, when we use the metaphor "humans are machines", of the fallacy that we have reduced men to machines that we currently know. When Darwinian theory of evolution made it possible to say that "humans are animals", there was violent reaction because many people were quite convinced that they were not just animals. The point is, of course, that evolution did not reduce us to the level of the other animals. Rather, it broadened our concept of animal to indicate that there was an essential continuity in all living things on earth, and that man was not set apart from that continuity. While, through comparative anatomy and physiology, we can gain much insight from this continuity, at the same time we can realize and study those things which set man apart from the other animals—just as, I presume, a cat with a human amount of consciousness could set cats apart and study that which is essentially feline. In saying that man is a machine, we must not ape those Darwinists who insisted that man was but a monkey, and ignored the differences. Rather, we must accept the challenge to grow our ideas of mechanism, so that we may eventually understand just what extra powers relative to present-day machines a mechanism must have if it is to share more and more of our human attributes.

In pondering the apparent freedom and spontaneity of our thought, we must realize that this stems from the complexity of our internal models of our worlds, and from the fact that most of the "mechanistic underpinning" is unconscious. We make a very bad mistake when we equate the computing that our brain does with the thoughts of which we are conscious. It is very hard to understand by introspection the actual process of retrieving information from memory, for it often seems as if consciousness posed a question, and the rest of the brain supplied the answer—just as at an information desk we may ask a question and an elaborate machinery, of which we are unaware, produces the answer.

It is known that if there is any kind of definite cause and effect relationship between the lifelong sequences of electric pulses leaving and entering the brain, it can be implemented by a suitable switching network. However, we must treat this statement with care, because it does not mention the size of the network involved; the challenge to she who would explain the workings of the brain is not to show that some hypothetical machine could carry out certain tasks, but rather to show how a machine which can fit into a human skull can do the task. And this is not always easy to see.

Again, in trying to understand the mechanism of the brain, we must think how far computers have come in a few decades and compare this with the fact that hundreds of millions of years of evolution were required to get the central nervous system to its present complexity. However, this comparison of decades with millions of years is somewhat misleading, because in the case of computers there has been conscious design by an active intelligence, whereas in the case of evolution, we ascribe the "design" to undirected factors interacting with one another, without the intervention of an external intelligence. In any case, we must be aware of the immense gap between current computer programs and general human intelligence. Also we should note that most current programs only simulate those aspects of problem-solving close to the verbal level. Thus they do not really explain how we think, but rather indicate an orderly level underlying the random seeming output. Of course, it is one of the challenges of this type of research to see whether, in fact, we can ascribe such intermediate levels to actual functioning within the brain. Let me assert again the dependence of human intelligence upon a highly structured brain, which has sufficient mechanisms and sufficient storage capacity to be able to mediate and accommodate a great deal of learning during a lifetime. Just as a computer has to have certain basic routines wired in before it is possible for us to program in higher-level languages, so must there be a basic substrate of genetically determined brain structure, memory mechanisms and thus behavior in the newborn baby if she is to learn to develop into an intelligent adult.

How can we ensure happy and beneficial uses of our knowledge? What responses or changes can we expect in our social and political environment if we stimulate it with the possibility of the control which an exact knowledge of the brain might make possible?

I cannot pretend to know the answers to these important questions, but I can at least make some comments which may help provide a framework within which answers may evolve. To answer the first question, we need both a greater self-awareness than we now possess (what constitutes a happy and beneficial use?) and a faith that science can be an ingredient in achieving happiness. I shall indicate some steps toward self-awareness, and indicate why I do not share the disillusionment in science and technology which has become so fashionable of late. The second question invites us to pretend to know more than we do, for we have already seen that an exact knowledge of the brain is far off. It is not clear that an exact knowledge of the brain would have made Attila the Hun more of a scourge, and advances in the neurosciences would have had little to add to the horror of Hitler's genocide of the Jews, or the agony of being napalmed in Vietnam. In some sense, then, the answer to the second question must merge with that of the first. We have to determine what we, as humans, really want (and this no doubt will change from time to time, since we are creatures of fashion), and we have to find a system of government (more or less of it, as the case may be) that will help us achieve our goals. It is only as part of this process that we can determine whether the neurosciences are to be used to help us use the full capability of our brains or are to be used to reduce the use of those brains to a restricted set of functions decreed by some limited ideology or regime.

To close this discussion, let me briefly describe why I believe that we *can* build a technology which will adapt to the individual rather than a technology that demands the individual to adapt to it, and indicate within this some of the processes involved in increasing our self-awareness. For many people nowadays, the computer has become the symbol both of technology and of conformity—as that thing that forces us to identify ourselves as a string of numbers, causing people to cry out in protest, "I am human! Do not spindle, fold or multilate *me*!" However, this antagonistic view of technology would seem to be based on the same limited view of mechanism which we have already sought to dispel in reconciling a mechanistic viewpoint with a true humanism. For example, few people realize that computers can, paradoxically, mass produce individuality, enabling technology to have that flexibility which allows individuality to flourish. There seems to be a strange reversal at work here. If one is prepared to return to a primitive life-style, one's idiosyncracies may flourish. But having discovered the comforts of electricity and plumbing, and having come to rely on a modicum of modern medical care, it is too easy to become just a consumer, awash in a sea of standardized products. To regain our individuality will of course require individual commitments and experiments in music and literature, personal relations, and our "inner lives", but what may be less obvious is that the process may be helped by using the computer to allow assembly lines to tailor-make products without losing the economies of mass production, and to enable bureaucrats to look up from their paperwork to talk to the people behind the statistics. However, rather than cataloging the novel uses to which computers may eventually be put, I would rather argue that a true science of human action must be predicated on a complex view of the human brain that, once assimilated, can only foster the evolution of a convergence of technology and the humanities that all too few people can visualize today.

As we have repeatedly stressed, both brain and society form systems with billions of variables, for which the sort of science in which one believes that one has captured reality by writing down two or three equations is inadequate. We have sketched ways in which science must grow if it is to more adequately encompass such complex systems. But it is clear that, given the incomplete state of our formal theories, we must complement them with our "everyday" knowledge as members of society. In short, our rational analysis of society must strike a balance between precise description of certain subsystems and, quite frankly, intuition and feeling about other problems. This position is not anti-intellectual; rather it calls for a scrupulous honesty which can recognize when formal approaches have and have not surpassed the implicit understanding given by having a brain and body evolved for life in a complex world. The current split that seems to be growing between the "technocracy" on the one hand and the "counterculture of the youth and the hippies" on the other hand (as spelled out by Roszak in *The Making of a Counterculture*) is, I think, one that can be mended as we come to better understand the strengths and limitations of science vis-à-vis discussing systems as complex as society. In other words, as we study more and more complex systems, we must understand that design engineering is as much a product of creativity of feeling and empathy crucially tempered by technical knowledge as it is the straightforward exercise of limited technical expertise.

Such problems of large numbers as urban population introduce new problems of scale which we cannot solve by goodwill alone unaided by technology. In a society with as many people as ours, then, we have to find some way of simultaneously increasing our understanding of what we can be as individuals in a society, but also seeing how we can develop a technology better suited to our needs. But such demands raise paradoxes. We now know that it is possible to avoid dying from all manner of diseases by proper medical care, and it would not be easy for us to go back to seeing our loved ones die at an early age, wracked by some hideous ailment, though we may not welcome the undue prolongation of a pained existence for the aged. While blessing technology for removing much of the evil of early death, we at the same time curse it for providing us with the problem of overpopulation.

Kurt Vonnegut, Jr., in his book *The Sirens of Titan*, tells us a legend that should give us some thought as to how we choose our goals. Tralfalmadore is a planet which is populated (or "machinated"?) only by machines. Of course, the machines, being very intelligent, wonder about where they came from, and though none knows for sure for their origin is shrouded in antiquity, there is a legend that once upon a time Tralfalmadore was populated by living beings, not machines, who were always seeking to understand their purpose in life. As their knowledge increased, they were able to see that most of their activity didn't qualify as being toward a higher purpose, and so they built machines that could take over these clearly unimportant functions. As time went by, more and more of what had originally occupied their time was being turned over to the machines, until eventually the machines were so sophisticated that the beings were able to assign them the task of finding out the beings' higher purpose. The machines, being more objective and more efficient, soon were able to report back that the beings didn't have a higher purpose! Hating nothing more than purposeless creatures, the beings set about slaughtering each other. It turned out the machines could do that better, too. . . .

So, there always comes a stage at which, no matter how good our objective science is, a rational approach to life demands that we say, "I'm going to postulate certain things, and structure my life in a way that fits in with those postulates". Perhaps the postulate we should make here is that "Individual humans are worthy". Unfortunately, when we leave the safe confines of mathematics, deducing from postulates is not at all easy. If individual humans are worthy, perhaps one might argue that we should have as many as possible, and that each woman should thus spend her whole life in pregnancy to increase the number of worthy individuals who can consecrate themselves. I would rather believe that this postulate means that we have an obligation to make the world, and the society which is the interface between the world and the individual, a place in which each individual can in some sense express herself fully; that we must stop overpopulation while there is still wilderness left where we can appreciate the grandeur and the silence. I don't know how to push through the implications of our "axiom", but I think it is well for those of us who are used to thinking in terms of well-set scientific criteria which can be developed objectively to realize that when we get into the domain of social affairs there really are no ultimate "givens".

On a naive level we might think that the good society is one in which everybody is happy—the politics of ecstasy. However, brain experiments (for a recent review see Olds [1969]) have shown that "ecstasy" is all too easy to achieve. One experiment involved placing an electrode in what has been called the "pleasure center" of a rat's brain and teaching it that if it presses a lever at one end of a box it will get "a charge", but that it then has to go to the other end of the box to press another lever to get the next charge, and so on. Stimulation of the "pleasure center" appears to be so desirable that if an electrified grid is placed between the two levers, which delivers a shock so intense that a starving rat will not cross it to get to food, a rat will nonetheless keep running back and forth across it, enduring great pain as long as it can ensure stimulation of its pleasure center at each end. Such an experiment raises horrible visions of a society in which everything is wrong save that the citizens all have their little electrodes rosy. Why do we feel uneasy about such a society, if indeed everyone has achieved ecstasy?

Perhaps the resolution is in the observation: "The brain has billions of neurons. Think of all you can do with that. If you're just going to keep charging some small pleasure center and go oo, oo all the time, you've thrown away your birthright." This suggests that one quality of a "good" society is that in it people can really make use of the truly fantastic power of their brains.

Some people will solve the problem of their own relationship to modern society by settling some of the remaining open land, opening a commune, tilling the soil relatively free from the strains of modern society. But the number of such people is terribly small as a percentage of the population (especially if the commune is to be genuinely self-supporting), and we must face the tension between how we realize our own selves and how we contribute to society-wide solutions. In finding these solutions, we have, on the one hand, to feel with our senses, our whole being, to know what it is that we really want out of a society, but on the other hand we must understand very well the problems of scale which call for technological solutions which do not just give us bigger gadgets but really help us achieve our humanly felt needs.

As the epitome of this we can take a great cathedral. Whether we are religious or not, in a cathedral our senses soar, as we feel the rise of the building, and bathe in the beauty of light playing through stained glass. And yet, if the builders of that cathedral hadn't been brilliant engineers, it would have fallen down three hundred years ago.

As we reshape our own society, we must use our knowledge to achieve this aesthetics, this joy.

References and Further Reading

Before giving a detailed bibliography, we devote a paragraph to each chapter of the book, suggesting material which may interest the reader who wishes to read further the themes of that chapter. No attempt has been made at completeness, and readers wishing to pursue the matter even further should go to a good college or university library and browse through books on the shelves adjacent to books cited here, and look at other issues of journals containing cited articles. To follow up a book or article of exceptional interest, the reader should refer to *Science Citation Index*, a quarterly that lists, under the title of a paper, all those papers which have been published in the previous three months and in which it is cited. The list of references also contains numerous papers not cited in the text which will provide useful leads for further reading.

CHAPTER 1

Four major shaping influences in cybernetics and theoretical neuropsychology have been Wiener [1948], Hebb [1949], Ashby [1960], and the papers collected in McCulloch [1965]. A general reading list of other books in these areas might include (in alphabetical order) Altman [1966], Arbib [1964], Burns [1968], Craik [1943], Deutsch [1960], Evans and Robertson [1968], Fair [1963], Herrick [1929], Hinde [1970], Luria [1956], Magoun [1963], Miller, Galanter, and Pribram [1960], Neisser [1967], Pribram [1971], von Neumann [1958], Wooldridge [1963], and Young [1964].

For multiauthor overview of neurophysiology the reader may wish to consult Field, Magoun, and Hall [1959–1960], Mountcastle [1968], Quarton, Melnechuk, and Schmitt [1967], and Schmitt [1970]. Herrick [1926], though somewhat out-dated, gives a still highly pertinent view of the evolution of the brain, which may be supplemented by the section on "Evolution of Brain and Behavior" in Schmitt [1970]. The problem of reliability of brain function is treated in Chapter 3 of Arbib [1964], following Winograd and Cowan [1963]. Further discussion of the philosophy of science may be found in Ackermann [1970], Hanson [1968, 1971], Kuhn [1970], and in *The Myth of the Metaphor* (Turbayne [1970]).

CHAPTER 2

In addition to the papers cited in the chapter itself, a number of books which may help the reader in weighing the frame of reference initiated in this chapter are Arnheim [1969], Gibson [1966], Gregory [1966, 1969b], Hebb [1949], Ingle, Schneider, Trevarthen, and Held [1967], Ingle and Schneider [1970], and Neisser [1967]. Perhaps the most accessible single reference for Section 2.2 is Katz [1966], though any good text of neurophysiology will provide a wealth of extra material. Good pictures of details of neural structure can be found in such sources as Bullock and Horridge [1965] and (for the cerebellum) Eccles, Ito, and Szentágothai [1967]. For models of such structures "in action" see Harmon and Lewis [1966] and Rall [1970]. See also Bullock [1959, 1962], Hodgkin [1964], Horridge [1968], Ramon-Moliner [1962], and Sholl [1956]. For vivid pictures of the brain see Netter [1962], and the diachrome inserts in Krieg [1957]. For other views of neuroanatomy see, for example, Altman [1966], Brodal [1969], Crosby, Humphrey, and Lauer [1962], Gardner [1963], Grossman [1967], Nauta [1963], Nauta and Karten [1970], Ochs [1965], and Ranson and Clark [1959]. Views on neural specificity may be found in Jacobson [1970], Sperry [1951], and Weiss [1941].

CHAPTER 3

Some of the ideas here were presented in Arbib [1964], and have found much deeper mathematical elaboration in Arbib [1969] and Kalman, Falb, and Arbib [1969]. Arbib and Zeiger [1969] give a general system theory of identification while Nilsson [1965] discusses machine learning. See also Arbib [1972]. Other approaches to system theory may be found in Wymore [1967] and Klir [1969]. See also Mesarovic [1968] and Rosen [1970]. Perhaps the best introduction to quantum mechanics may be found in Feynman [1965]. The feedback analysis of biological system (Wiener [1948]) has been elaborated by many authors; for textbook expositions, see Milhorn [1966] and Milsum [1966]. The view of Pitts and McCulloch's use of transformations follows Arbib [1971]. For Klein's ideas on geometry in relation to groups of transformations see Klein [1908].

CHAPTER 4

Many of the early papers in artificial intelligence have been collected by Feigenbaum and Feldman [1964]. Early attempts to relate this area to psychology are by Miller, Galanter, and Pribram [1960] and Reitman [1965]. Three texts have recently appeared: Banerji [1969], Nilsson [1971], and Slagle [1971]. Nilsson proved especially helpful in preparing our discussion of heuristic search. See also Ernst and Newell [1969] and Simon [1969]. For the notion of internal model presented within a cybernetic framework, see Craik [1943, 1966], Gregory [1969a], MacKay [1955, 1963], Minsky [1961, 1965], and Young [1964]. For some of the robot work see Nilsson and Raphael [1967] and Rosen [1968], as well as papers in the continuing "Machine Intelligence" series, Michie et al. [1967 on]. For the "action frame" see Trevarthen [1968]. Uhr [1966] is an excellent collection of papers on pattern recognition. For an AI approach to human problem solving, see Newell and Simon [1972].

CHAPTER 5

The general approach of this chapter was heavily influenced by Greene [1964, . . .]. General references for the chapter are Evarts et al. [1971] and Roberts [1967]. For further analyses of walking, see Bernstein [1967], Gray [1968], Hildebrand [1960, 1965, 1966], Paillard [1960], Tricker [1967], Weiss [1941], and Wilson [1966, 1967]. For neural substrates see also Bell and Dow [1967], Dow and Moruzzi [1958], Brooks [1969], Denny-Brown [1966], Eccles [1967], Eccles, Ito, and Szentagothai [1967], Phillips [1966], Pinneo [1966], and Werner [1970]. See also Arbib, Franklin, and Nilsson [1968], Boylls and Arbib [1962], Braitenberg and Onesto [1960], Marr [1969], Merton [1953], Mittelstaedt [1962], and Szentagothai [1968]. Suggestions for further reading on neuroanatomy have already been given in connection with Chapter 2.

CHAPTER 6

This chapter is based on Arbib and Didday [1971] and Arbib and Dev [1972]. Shepard's work was reported by Shepard and Metzler [1970], and a contrasting computer approach to representation may be seen in Colby and Gilbert [1964]. For a clear exposition of holography per se see Gabor et al. [1971]; and for an approach to neural "holography" see Westlake [1970], which has an excellent bibliography of other sources, and Pribram [1971].

CHAPTER 7

The bases for this chapter are Kilmer, McCulloch, and Blum [1968, 1969] and Didday [1970]. For Section 7.1 background, see Dell [1963], Glaser [1966], Jouvet [1967], and Magoun [1963]. In building upon the "frog model", one might try to relate eye movements to visual perception, as has been done, among many others, by Hebb [1949], Simon and Barenfeld [1969], and Noton and Stark [1971]. For a critique of the Noton-Stark theory, see Arbib [to appear] which also proposes a countertheory, leaning heavily on the data on subcortical mechanisms of vision in Ingle and Schneider [1970]; see especially Humphrey [1970]. Robinson [1968] gives a review of the neural control of eye movements.

CHAPTER 8

In addition to the cited papers, the reader may find the books by Cherry [1961], Chomsky [1957, 1965, 1968], Church [1961], and Lenneberg [1967] helpful in his study of language; those of Flavell [1963], Furth [1969], Harris [1957], Kimble [1968], and Piaget [1928, 1954] helpful in his study of mental development; those of Arnold [1968], Cofer and Appley [1964], Murray [1964], and Peters [1968] will aid in the restitution of the "emotional" component. For theoretical approaches see Simon [1967], Loehlin [1968], and Friedman [1967] on emotion and motivation; and Greene and Ruggles [1963], Papert [1963], Gyr, Cafagna, and Brown [1967], Hormann [1962, 1964], Johnson [1967], and Quillian, Wortman, and Baylor [1965] on mental development. For the questions of philosophical and social implications, see, among many others, Armstrong [1968], Boring [1946], Dennett [1969], Eccles

[1966], Herrick [1929], MacKay [1966], Martin and Norman [1970], Pylyshyn [1970], Roszak [1969], Smart [1963], and Smythies [1968].

REFERENCES

R. Ackermann [1970]. *The Philosophy of Science.* New York: Pegasus.

J. Altman [1966]. *Organic Foundations of Animal Behavior.* New York: Holt, Rinehart and Winston.

J. Apter [1945]. The Projection of the Retina on the Superior Colliculus of Cats. *J. Neurophysiol.,* **8**, 123–134.

J. Apter [1946]. Eye Movements Following Strychninization of the Superior Colliculus of Cats, *J. Neurophysiol.,* **9**, 73–85.

M. A. Arbib [1964]. *Brains, Machines and Mathematics.* New York: McGraw-Hill.

M. A. Arbib [1969]. *Theories of Abstract Automata.* Englewood Cliffs, N.J.: Prentice-Hall.

M. A. Arbib [1971]. How We Know Universals: Retrospect and Prospect. *Math. Biosciences* (Warren McCulloch Memorial Issue), **II**, 95–107.

M. A. Arbib [1972]. Automata Theory in the Context of Theoretical Neurophysiology. In R. Rosen, Ed., *Textbook of Theoretical Biology.* New York: Academic Press.

M. A. Arbib [to appear]. Eye Movements and Visual Perception.

M. A. Arbib and R. L. Dev [1972]. The Organization of Action-Oriented Memory for a Perceiving System II. The Hologram Metaphor. *J. Cybernet.,* forthcoming.

M. A. Arbib and R. L. Didday [1971]. The Organization of Action-Oriented Memory for a Perceiving System I. The Basic Model. *J. Cybernet.,* **1**, 3–18.

M. A. Arbib and H. P. Zeiger [1969]. On the Relevance of Abstract Algebra to Control Theory. *Automatica,* **5**, 589–606.

M. A. Arbib, G. F. Franklin, and N. Nilsson [1968]. Some Ideas on Information Processing in the Cerebellum. In E. Caianiello, Ed., *Proceedings of the Summer School on Mathematical Models of Neuronic Networks.* Berlin: Springer-Verlag, pp. 43–58.

D. M. Armstrong [1968]. *A Materialistic Theory of Mind.* London: Routledge and Kegan Paul.

R. Arnheim [1969]. *Visual Thinking.* Berkeley: University of California Press.

Magda E. Arnold, Ed. [1968]. *The Nature of Emotion: Selected Readings,* Harmondsworth: Penguin Books Ltd.

W. R. Ashby [1960]. *Design for a Brain.* New York: John Wiley and Sons.

F. Attneave [1954]. Informational Aspects of Visual Perception. *Psych. Rev.,* **61**, 183–193.

R. B. Banerji [1969]. *Theory of Problem Solving: An Approach to Artificial Intelligence.* New York: Elsevier.

H. B. Barlow [1959]. Sensory Mechanisms, The Reduction of Redundancy, and Intelligence. *Symp. on Mechanization of Thought Processes,* London: H. M. Stationery Office, pp. 535–539.

H. B. Barlow [1969]. Trigger Features, Adaptation and Economy of Impulses. In K. N. Leibovic, Ed., *Information Processing in the Nervous System.* New York: Springer-Verlag, pp. 209–230.

H. B. Barlow, C. Blakemore, and J. D. Pettigrew [1967]. The Neural Mechanism of Binocular Depth Discrimination. *J. Physiol.,* **193**, 327–342.

C. Bell and S. Dow [1967]. Cerebellar Circuitry. *Bulletin of the Neurosciences Research Program,* **5**, MIT.

N. Bernstein [1967]. *The Coordination and Regulation of Movements,* Oxford: Pergamon.

R. L. Beurle [1956]. Properties of a Mass of Cells Capable of Regenerating Pulses. *Phil. Trans. Roy. Soc.* (London), Ser. B, **240**, 231–277.

R. L. Beurle [1962]. Functional Organization in Random Networks. In H. Von Foerster and G. W. Zopf, Jr., Eds., *Principles of Self-Organization*. New York: Pergamon, p. 291.

E. G. Boring [1946]. Mind and Mechanism. *Am. J. Psychol.*, **54**, 173–192.

T. G. R. Bower, J. M. Broughton, and M. K. Moore [1970a]. The Coordination of Visual and Tactile Input in Infants. *Perception and Psychophysics*, **8**, 51–53.

T. G. R. Bower, J. M. Broughton, and M. K. Moore [1970b]. Demonstration of Intention in the Reaching Behaviour of Neonate Humans. *Nature,* **228**, 679–681.

C. C. Boylls and M. A. Arbib [1972]. The Cerebellum: A Case Study in Brain Theory. *Progr. Biophys.*

V. Braitenberg and N. Onesto [1960]. The Cerebellar Cortex as a Timing Organ. *Congress Inst. Medicina Cibernetica,* First Naples Atti., 239–255.

A. Brodal [1969]. *Neurological Anatomy,* 2nd ed., Oxford University Press.

J. Bronowski and U. Bellugi [1970]. Language, Name and Concept. *Science,* **168**, 669–673.

J. Brookhart [1967]. Tutorial on the Cerebellum. *NRP Conference on Information Processing in the Cerebellum,* Salishan, Ore.

V. B. Brooks [1969]. Information Processing in the Motosensory Cortex. In K. N. Leibovic, Ed., *Information Processing in the Nervous System,* New York: Springer-Verlag.

R. Brown and N. Bellugi [1964]. Three Processes in the Child's Acquisition of Syntax. In E. H. Lenneberg, Ed., *New Directions in the Study of Language.* Cambridge, Mass.: The MIT Press.

T. H. Bullock [1959]. Neuron Doctrine and Electrophysiology. *Science,* **129**, 997–1002.

T. H. Bullock [1962]. Transfer Functions at Synaptic Junctions. In R. W. Gerard and J. W. Duyff, Eds., *Information Processing in the Nervous System,* Vol. III, *Proc. XXII Internat. Congr. Physiol. Sci.,* Amsterdam: Excerpta Medica, pp. 98–108.

T. H. Bullock and G. A. Horridge [1965]. *Structure and Function in the Nervous System of Invertebrates,* Vol. I. San Francisco: W. H. Freeman.

B. De Lisle Burns [1968]. *The Uncertain Nervous System,* London: Edward Arnold.

Colin Cherry [1961]. *On Human Communication.* New York: John Wiley and Sons.

N. Chomsky [1957]. *Syntactic Structures.* The Hague: Mouton.

N. Chomsky [1965]. *Aspects of the Theory of Syntax.* Cambridge, Mass.: The MIT Press.

N. Chomsky [1968]. *Language and Mind.* New York: Harcourt Brace and World.

J. Church [1961]. *Language and the Discovery of Reality.* New York: Vintage Books.

C. N. Cofer and M. H. Appley [1964]. *Motivation: Theory and Research.* New York: John Wiley and Sons.

K. M. Colby and J. P. Gilbert [1964]. Programming a Computer Model of Neurosis. *J. Math. Psych.,* **1**, 405–417.

B. G. Cragg and H. N. V. Temperley [1954]. The Organization of Neurones: A Cooperative Analogy. *EEG Clin. Neurophysiol.* **6**, 85–92.

K. J. W. Craik [1943]. *The Nature of Explanation.* Cambridge: Cambridge University Press.

K. J. W. Craik [1966]. The Mechanism of Human Action. In S. L. Sherwood, Ed., *The Nature of Psychology: A Selection of Papers, Essays and Other Writings by Kenneth J. W. Craik.* Cambridge: Cambridge University Press, pp. 9–90.

E. C. Crosby, T. Humphrey, and E. W. Lauer [1962]. *Correlative Anatomy of the Nervous System.* New York: The Macmillan Company.

G. D. Dawson [1958]. The Central Control of Sensory Inflow. *Proc. Roy. Soc. Med.,* **51** (7), 531–535.

P. Dell [1963]. Reticular Homeostasis and Critical Reactivity. In G. Moruzzi, A. Fessard, and H. H. Jasper, Eds., *Brain Mechanisms; Progress in Brain Research,* **2**, pp. 82–103 (Discussion: pp. 103–114).

D. C. Dennett [1969]. *Content and Consciousness.* London: Routledge and Kegan Paul.

D. Denny-Brown [1966]. *The Cerebral Control of Movement: The Sherrington Lectures VIII,* Springfield, Ill.: Charles C Thomas.

M. Dertouzos [1967]. PHASEPLOT: An On-line Graphical Display Technique. *IEEE Trans. Electron. Computers,* **EC-16**, 203–209.

M. Dertouzos and H. L. Graham [1966]. A Parametric Display Technique for On-line Use. *AFIPS Conf. Proc.,* **29** (1966 Fall Joint Computer Conf.), 201–209.

J. A. Deutsch [1960]. *The Structural Basis of Behaviour.* Chicago: University of Chicago Press.

R. L. Didday [1970]. The Simulation and Modelling of Distributed Information Processing in the Frog Visual System, Ph.D. Thesis, Information Systems Laboratory, Stanford University, August 1970.

J. Doran and D. Michie [1966]. Experiments with the Graph Traverser Program. *Proc. Roy. Soc. A,* **294**, 235–259.

R. S. Dow and G. Moruzzi [1958]. *The Physiology and Pathology of the Cerebellum.* Minneapolis: University of Minnesota Press.

R. O. Duda and P. E. Hart [1970]. Experiments in Scene Analysis. *Proc. First Natl. Symp. on Industrial Robots,* Chicago, Ill. April 2–3, 1970.

C. P. Duncan [1949]. The Retroactive Effect of Electroshock on Learning. *J. Comp. Physiol. Psychol.,* **42**, 32–44.

J. C. Eccles, Ed. [1966]. *Brain and Conscious Experience.* New York: Springer-Verlag.

J. C. Eccles [1967]. Circuits in the Cerebellar Control of Movement. *Proc. Nat. Acad. Sci.,* **58**, 336–343.

J. C. Eccles, M. Ito, and J. Szentágothai [1967]. *The Cerebellum as a Neuronal Machine.* New York: Springer-Verlag.

G. W. Ernst and A. Newell [1969]. *GPS: A Case Study in Generality and Problem Solving.* New York: Academic Press.

C. R. Evans and A. D. J. Robertson, Eds. [1968]. *Cybernetics: Key Papers,* Baltimore, Md.: University Park Press.

E. V. Evarts, E. Bizzi, R. E. Burke, M. DeLong, and W. T. Thach, Jr. [1971]. Central Control of Movement. *Neurosci. Res. Prog. Bull.,* **9**, 1–170.

C. M. Fair [1963]. *The Physical Foundations of the Psyche.* Middletown, Conn.: Wesleyan University Press.

E. A. Feigenbaum and J. Feldman, Eds. [1964]. *Computers and Thought.* New York: McGraw-Hill.

R. P. Feynman, R. B. Leighton, and M. Sands [1965]. The Feynman Lectures on Physics, Vol. 3, *Quantum Mechanics.* Reading, Mass.: Addison-Wesley.

J. Field, H. W. Magoun, and V. E. Hall, Eds. [1959–1960]. *Handbook of Physiology,* Section 1, *Neurophysiology,* Washington, D.C.: American Physiological Society.

K. Fite [1969]. Single Unit Analysis of Binocular Neurons in the Frog Optic Tectum. *Exp. Neurol.,* **24**, 475–480.

J. H. Flavell [1963]. *The Developmental Psychology of Jean Piaget.* Princeton, N.J.: Van Nostrand.

L. Friedman [1967]. Instinctive Behavior and Its Computer Synthesis. *Behav. Sci.,* **12**, 85.

H. G. Furth [1969]. *Piaget and Knowledge.* Englewood Cliffs, N.J.: Prentice-Hall.

D. Gabor, W. E. Kock, and G. W. Stroke [1971]. Holography. *Science,* **173**, 11–23.

A. R. Gardner and B. T. Gardner [1969]. Teaching Sign Language to a Chimpanzee. *Science,* **165**, 664–672.

E. Gardner [1963]. *Fundamentals of Neurology.* Philadelphia: W. B. Saunders.

N. Geschwind [1965]. Disconnexion Syndromes in Animal and Man, Part I. *Brain,* **88**, 237–295; Part II, *Brain,* **88**, 585–644.

N. Geschwind [1970]. The Organization of Language and the Brain. *Science,* **170**, 940–944.

J. J. Gibson [1966]. *The Senses Considered as Perceptual Systems.* London: George Allen & Unwin.

E. M. Glaser [1966]. *The Physiological Basis of Habituation,* Oxford: Oxford University Press.

Sir James Gray [1968]. *Animal Locomotion*. London: Weidenfeld and Nicholson.

P. H. Greene [1964]. New Problems in Adaptive Control. In J. T. Tou and R. H. Wilcox, Eds., *Computer and Information Sciences*. Washington: Spartan.

P. H. Greene [1967]. Models for Perception and Actions. *Proceedings of the First Annual Princeton Conference on Information Sciences & Systems*, Dept. of EE, Princeton University, 245–253. In relation to which, see numerous articles by Russian workers in *Biophysics*, the English translation of the Russian *Biofizika*, in the section entitled, "Biophysics of Complex Systems. Mathematical Models."

P. H. Greene [1968]. A. Essential Features of Purposive Movements; B. Cybernetic Problems of Sensorimotor Structure: Introductory Remarks and Survey of a Study; C. Seeking Mathematical Models of Skilled Actions; D. An Aspect of Robot Control and Nervous Control of Skilled Movements; Coordination of Two Effectors and Transfer of Adaptation, *Institute for Computer Research, Quarterly Progress Report No. 16*, Sections III A–D.

P. H. Greene [1970]. *The Theory of Tasks: Cybernetic Problems of Sensorimotor Structure*. Book in preparation (Preliminary material may be found in Greene [1967/1968]).

P. H. Greene and T. Ruggles [1963]. CHILD and SPOCK (Computer Having Intelligent Learning and Development; Simulated Procedure for Obtaining Common Knowledge). *IEEE Trans. on Military Electronics*, **MIL–7**, 156–159.

R. L. Gregory [1961]. The Brain as an Engineering Problem. In W. H. Thorpe and O. L. Zangwill, Eds., *Current Problems in Animal Behaviour*. Cambridge: Cambridge University Press.

R. L. Gregory [1966]. *Eye and Brain, the Psychology of Seeing*. New York: McGraw-Hill.

R. L. Gregory [1969a]. On How So Little Information Controls So Much Behaviour. In C. H. Waddington, Ed., *Towards a Theoretical Biology, 2 Sketches*. Edinburgh: Edinburgh University Press.

R. L. Gregory [1969b]. *The Intelligent Eye*. New York: McGraw-Hill.

S. P. Grossman [1967]. *A Textbook of Physiological Psychology*. New York: John Wiley and Sons.

E. M. Gurowitz [1969]. *The Molecular Basis of Memory*. Englewood Cliffs, N.J.: Prentice-Hall.

A. Guzman [1967]. *Some Aspects of Pattern Recognition by Computer*. MAC-TR-37 (Thesis) MIT.

A. Guzman [1968]. Decomposition of a Visual Scene Into Three-dimensional Bodies. *Proc. Fall Joint Comp. Conf.*, 291–304.

J. W. Gyr, A. C. Cafagna, and J. S. Brown [1967]. Quasi-Formal Models of Inductive Behavior and Their Relation to Piaget's Theory of Cognitive Stages. *Psychol. Rev.*

J. W. Gyr, J. S. Brown, R. Willey, and A. Zivian [1966]. Computer Simulation and Psychological Theories of Perception. *Psychol. Bull.*, **65**, 174–192.

N. R. Hanson [1968]. *Patterns of Discovery*. Cambridge: Cambridge University Press.

N. R. Hanson [1971]. *Observation and Explanation*, New York: Harper Torch Books.

L. D. Harmon and E. R. Lewis [1966]. Neural Modeling. *Physiol. Rev.*, **46**, 513–591.

D. B. Harris, Ed. [1957]. *The Concept of Development*. Minneapolis: University of Minnesota Press.

P. Hart, N. Nilsson, and B. Raphael [1968]. A Formal Basis for the Heuristic Determination of Minimum Cost Paths. *IEEE Trans. Syst. Sci. Cybernetics*, **SSC–4**, 100–107.

H. K. Hartline [1938]. The Response of Single Optic Nerve Fibers of the Vertebrate Eye to Illumination of the Retina. *Am. J. Physiol.* **121**, 400–415.

D. O. Hebb [1949]. *The Organization of Behavior*. New York: John Wiley and Sons.

R. Held [1965]. Plasticity in Sensory-motor Systems. *Sci. Am.*, **213**, 84–94.

R. Held and A. Hein [1963]. Movement-Produced Stimulation in the Development of Visually Guided Behavior. *J. Comp. Physiol. Psychol.*, **56**, 872–876.

C. J. Herrick [1926]. *Brains of Rats and Men*. Chicago: University of Chicago Press.

C. J. Herrick [1929]. *The Thinking Machine*. Chicago: University of Chicago Press.

M. Hildebrand [1960]. How Animals Run. *Sci. Am.,* 148–157.

M. Hildebrand [1965]. Symmetrical Gaits of Horses. *Science,* **150**, 701–708.

M. Hildebrand [1966]. Analysis of the Symmetrical Gaits of Tetrapods. *Fol. Biotheoretica,* **IV**, 9–22.

R. A. Hinde [1970]. *Animal Behaviour: A Synthesis of Ethology and Comparative Psychology,* 2nd ed. New York: McGraw-Hill.

A. L. Hodgkin [1964]. *The Conduction of the Nervous Impulse.* Springfield, Ill.: Charles C Thomas.

A. M. Hormann [1962, 1964]. Programs for Machine Learning, Parts I and II. *Inform. Control,* **5**, 347–367; **7**, 55–77.

G. Adrian Horridge [1968]. *Interneurons—Their Origin, Action, Specificity, Growth, and Plasticity.* London and San Francisco: W. H. Freeman.

D. H. Hubel and T. N. Wiesel [1962]. Receptive Fields, Binocular Interaction and Functional Architecture in the Cat's Visual Cortex. *J. Physiol.,* **160**, 106–154.

D. H. Hubel and T. N. Wiesel [1965]. Receptive Fields and Functional Architecture in Two Non-Striate Areas (18 and 19) of the Cat. *J. Neurophysiol.* **28**, 229–289.

D. H. Hubel and T. N. Wiesel [1968]. Receptive Fields and Functional Architecture of Monkey Striate Cortex, *J. Physiol.* **195**, 215–243.

D. A. Huffman [1971]. Impossible Objects as Nonsense Sentences. In B. Meltzer and D. Michie, Eds., *Machine Intelligence.* Edinburgh: Edinburgh University Press, Vol. 6, pp. 295–323.

N. K. Humphrey [1970]. What the Frog's Eye Tells the Monkey's Brain. *Brain Behav. Evol.,* **3**, 324–337.

D. Ingle [1968]. Visual Releasers of Prey-Catching Behavior in Frogs and Toads. *Brain Behav. Evol.* **1**, 500–518.

D. Ingle and G. E. Schneider, Eds. [1970]. Subcortical Visual Systems. Published as *Brain Behaviour and Evolution,* **3**, Nos. 1–4.

D. Ingle, G. E. Schneider, C. B. Trevarthen, and R. Held [1967]. Locating and Identifying: Two Modes of Visual Processing (A Symposium). *Psychol. Forsch.,* **31**, Nos. 1 and 4.

M. Jacobson [1970]. *Developmental Neurobiology.* New York: Holt, Rinehart and Winston.

E. Roy John [1967]. *Mechanisms of Memory.* New York: Academic Press.

A. R. Johnson [1967]. A Structural Preconscious Piaget: Heed Without Habit. *Proc. National Electronics Conf.,* **XXIII**, 29–32.

M. Jouvet [1967, Feb.]. The States of Sleep. *Sci. Am.,* **216** (2), 62–72.

J. Kagan [1970]. Attention and Psychological Change in the Young Child. *Science,* **170**, 826–832.

R. E. Kalman, P. L. Falb, and M. A. Arbib [1969]. *Topics in Mathematical System Theory.* New York: McGraw-Hill.

E. R. Kandel, W. T. Frazier, and R. E. Coggeshall [1967]. Opposite Synaptic Actions Mediated by Different Branches of an Identifiable Interneuron in Aplysia. *Science,* **155**, 346–349.

B. Katz [1966]. *Nerve, Muscle and Synapse.* New York: McGraw-Hill.

M. J. Keating and R. M. Gaze [1970]. Rigidity and Plasticity in the Amphibian Visual System. *Brain Behav. Evol.* **3**, 102–120.

W. L. Kilmer and T. McLardy [1970]. Hippocampal Circuitry. *Am. Psychol.,* **25**, 563–566.

W. L. Kilmer, W. S. McCulloch, and J. Blum [1968]. Some Mechanisms for a Theory of the Reticular Formation. In M. Mesarovic, Ed., *Systems Theory and Biology.* New York: Springer-Verlag, pp. 286–375.

W. L. Kilmer, W. S. McCulloch, and J. Blum [1969]. A Model of the Vertebrate Central Command System. *Int. J. Man-Machine Studies,* **1**, 279–309.

D. P. Kimble, Ed. [1968]. *Experience and Capacity.* New York: New York Academy of Science.

F. Klein [1908]. *Elementary Mathematics from an Advanced Standpoint: Geometry.* (English translation is published in paperback by Dover Publications, Inc.)

G. J. Klir [1969]. *An Approach to General Systems Theory.* New York: Van Nostrand Reinhold.

J. Konorski [1967]. *Integrative Activity of the Brain.* Chicago: University of Chicago Press.

W. J. S. Krieg [1957]. *Brain Mechanisms in Diachrome,* 2nd ed. Brain Books, Box 9, Evanston, Ill.

S. Kuffler [1953]. Discharge Patterns and Functional Organization of Mammalian Retina, *J. Neurophysiol.* **16**, 37–68.

T. S. Kuhn [1970]. *The Structure of Scientific Revolutions,* 2nd ed. Chicago: University of Chicago Press.

K. S. Lashley [1929]. *Brain Mechanisms in Intelligence.* Chicago: University of Chicago Press. (Reprinted 1963 with a new introduction by D. O. Hebb, Dover, New York.)

K. S. Lashley [1951]. The Problem of Serial Order in Behavior. In L. A. Jeffress, Ed., *Cerebral Mechanisms in Behavior: The Hixon Symposium.* New York: John Wiley and Sons, pp. 112–136 (Discussion: 136–146).

E. H. Lenneberg [1967]. *Biological Foundations of Language.* New York: John Wiley and Sons.

J. Y. Lettvin et al. [1961]. Two Remarks on the Visual System of the Frog. In W. Rosenblith, Ed., *Sensory Communication.* Cambridge, Mass.: The MIT Press, p. 757.

J. Y. Lettvin, H. Maturana, W. S. McCulloch, and W. H. Pitts [1959]. What the Frog's Eye Tells the Frog's Brain. *Proc. IRE,* **47**, 1940–1951.

R. B. Livingston [1963]. Goal-Seeking Controls Affecting Both Motor and Sensory Systems. *Int. J. Neurol.,* **4** (1), 39–59.

J. C. Loehlin [1968]. *Computer Models of Personality.* New York: Random House.

A. R. Luria [1966]. *Higher Cortical Functions in Man.* New York: Basic Books.

A. R. Luria [1968]. *The Mind of a Mnemonist.* New York: Basic Books.

D. M. MacKay [1955]. The Epistemological Problem for Automata. In C. E. Shannon and J. McCarthy, Eds., *Automata Studies.* Princeton, N.J.: Princeton University Press, pp. 235–251.

D. M. MacKay [1963]. Internal Representation of the External World. *AGARD Symposium on Natural and Artificial Logic Processors,* Athens, mimeographed, 14 pages.

D. M. MacKay [1966]. Cerebral Organization and the Conscious Control of Action. In J. C. Eccles, Ed., *Brain and Conscious Experience.* New York: Springer-Verlag, pp. 422–445.

H. W. Magoun [1963]. *The Waking Brain.* Springfield, Ill.: Charles C Thomas.

P. Marler [1970]. Birdsong and Speech Development: Can There be Parallels? *Am. Sci.* **58**, 669–673.

D. Marr [1969]. A Theory of Cerebellar Cortex. *J. Physiol.,* **202**, 437–470.

J. Martin and A. R. D. Norman [1970]. *The Computerized Society.* Englewood Cliffs, N.J.: Prentice-Hall.

Warren S. McCulloch [1965]. *Embodiments of Mind.* Cambridge, Mass.: The MIT Press.

P. A. Merton [1953]. Speculations on the Servo-Control of Movement. In *The Spinal Cord,* A CIBA Foundation Symposium, J. and A. Churchill, Ltd., London, pp. 247–255 (Discussion: 255–260).

M. Mesarovic, Ed. [1968]. *Systems Theory and Biology.* New York: Springer-Verlag.

D. Michie et al. [1967 on]. *Machine Intelligence,* Vols. 1, 2, 3, . . . , 6, . . . Edinburgh: Edinburgh University Press.

Howard T. Milhorn, Jr. [1966]. *The Application of Control Theory to Physiological Systems.* Philadelphia, London: W. B. Saunders.

G. A. Miller, E. Galanter, and K. H. Pribram [1960]. *Plans and the Structure of Behavior.* New York: Henry Holt and Co.

P. M. Milner [1970]. *Physiological Psychology.* New York: Holt, Rinehart and Winston.

J. H. Milsum [1966]. *Biological Control Systems Analysis.* New York: McGraw-Hill.

M. L. Minsky [1961]. Steps Toward Artificial Intelligence. *Proc. IRE,* **49**, 8–30.

M. L. Minsky [1965]. Matter, Mind and Models. In W. A. Kalenich, Ed., *Information Processing 1965, Proceedings of IFIP Congress 65,* Vol. 1. Washington, D.C.: Spartan Books, pp. 45–49.

M. Minsky, Ed. [1968]. *Semantic Information Processing.* Cambridge, Mass.: The MIT Press.

H. Mittelstaedt [1962]. Control Systems of Orientation in Insects. *Ann. Rev. Entomol,* **7**, 177–198.

V. B. Mountcastle, Ed. [1968]. *Medical Physiology,* 12th ed., Vol. II. St. Louis: The C. V. Mosby Co.

E. J. Murray [1964]. *Motivation and Emotion.* Englewood Cliffs, N.J.: Prentice-Hall.

R. Narasimhan [1963]. *Syntactic Descriptions of Pictures and Gestalt Phenomena of Visual Perception.* Report No. 142, Digital Computer Laboratory, University of Illinois, Urbana, Ill.

R. Narasimhan [1969]. *Picture Languages.* Technical Report No. 75, Computer Group, Tata Institute of Fundamental Research, Bombay.

W. J. H. Nauta [1963]. Central Nervous Organization and the Endocrine Nervous System. In A. V. Nalbandov, Ed., *Advances in Neuroendocrinology,* pp. 5–21.

W. J. H. Nauta and H. J. Karten [1970]. A General Profile of the Vertebrate Brain, with Sidelights on the Ancestry of Cerebral Cortex, in Schmitt [1970], pp. 7–26.

F. Navas and L. Stark [1968]. Sampling or Intermittency in Hand Control System Dynamics. *Biophys. J.,* **8**, 252–302.

U. Neisser [1967]. *Cognitive Psychology.* New York: Appleton-Century-Crofts.

F. H. Netter [1962]. Nervous System. Vol. I the Ciba Collection of Medical Illustration. Summit, N.J.: CIBA.

A. Newell, J. C. Shaw, and H. A. Simon [1959]. Report on a General Problem-Solving Program. *Pro. Int. Conf. Inf. Processing.* UNESCO House, Paris, pp. 256–264.

A. Newell, J. C. Shaw, and H. A. Simon [1960]. A Variety of Intelligent Learning in a General Problem Solver. In M. Yovitts and S. Cameron, Eds, *Self-Organizing Systems,* New York: Pergamon, pp. 153–189.

A. Newell and H. A. Simon [1972]. *Human Problem Solving.* Englewood Cliffs, N.J.: Prentice-Hall.

N. J. Nilsson [1965]. *Learning Machines.* New York: McGraw-Hill.

N. J. Nilsson [1971]. *Problem-Solving Methods in Artificial Intelligence.* New York: McGraw-Hill.

N. J. Nilsson and B. Raphael [1967]. Preliminary Design of an Intelligent Robot. *Comp. Inf. Sci.,* **II**, 235–259.

D. A. Norman [1969]. *Memory and Attention.* New York: John Wiley and Sons.

D. Noton [1970]. A Theory of Visual Pattern Perception. *IEEE Trans. Systems Sci. Cybernet.,* **SSC-6**, 349–357.

D. Noton and L. Stark [1971a]. Scanpaths in Eye Movements During Pattern Perception. *Science,* **171**, 308–311.

D. Noton and L. Stark [1971b]. Eye Movements and Visual Perception. *Sci. Am.,* **224** (2), 34–43.

S. Ochs [1965]. *Elements of Neurophysiology.* New York: John Wiley and Sons.

J. Olds [1969]. The Central Nervous System and the Reinforcement of Behaviour. *Am. Psychol.,* **24**, 114–132.

J. Paillard [1960]. The Patterning of Skilled Movements. *Handbook of Physiology, Section I: Neurophysiology,* **3**, 1679–1708.

S. Papert [1963]. Étude comparée de l'intelligence chez l'enfant et chez le robot. *La Filiation des Structures*. Études d'Épistémologie Genétique, XV, Paris: Presses Universitaires de France.

R. S. Peters [1968]. *The Concept of Motivation*. London: Routledge and Kegan Paul.

C. G. Phillips [1966]. Changing Concepts of the Precentral Motor Area. In J. C. Eccles, Ed., *Brain and Conscious Experience*. New York: Springer-Verlag, pp. 389–421.

J. Piaget [1928]. *Judgment and Reasoning in the Child*. London: Routledge and Kegan Paul.

J. Piaget [1954]. *The Construction of Reality in the Child*. New York: Basic Books.

L. R. Pinneo [1966]. Electrical Control of Behavior by Programmed Stimulation of the Brain. *Nature, 211,* 705–708.

W. H. Pitts and W. S. McCulloch [1947]. How We Know Universals: The Perception of Auditory and Visual Forms. *Bull. Math. Biophys., 9,* 127–147.

K. Pribram [1969]. The Neurophysiology of Remembering. *Sci. Am.,* January.

K. Pribram [1971]. *The Languages of the Brain*. Englewood Cliffs, N.J.: Prentice-Hall.

Z. W. Pylyshyn, Ed. [1970]. *Perspectives on the Computer Revolution*. Englewood Cliffs, N.J.: Prentice-Hall.

D. Quartermain, R. M. Paolino, and N. E. Miller [1965]. A Brief Temporal Gradient of Retrograde Amnesia Independent of Situational Change. *Science, 149,* 1116–1118.

G. C. Quarton, T. Melnechuk, and F. O. Schmitt, Eds. [1967]. *The Neurosciences: A Study Program,* New York: Rockefeller University Press.

M. R. Quillian, P. M. Wortman, and G. W. Baylor [1965]. *The Programmable Piaget: Behavior from the Standpoint of a Radical Computerist*. Dittoed Memorandum, Cambridge, Mass.

W. Rall [1970]. Dendritic Neuron Theory and Dendrodendritic Synapses in a Simple Cortical System, in Schmitt [1970], pp. 552–565.

E. Ramon-Moliner [1962]. An Attempt at Classifying Nerve Cells on the Basis of Their Dendritic Patterns. *J. Comp. Neur., 119,* 211–227.

R. E. Ransmeier and R. W. Gerard [1954]. Effects of Temperature, Convulsion and Metabolic Factors on Rodent Memory and EEG. *Am. J. Physiol., 179,* 663–664.

S. W. Ranson and S. L. Clark [1959]. *The Anatomy of the Nervous System: Its Development and Function,* 10th ed. Philadelphia: W. B. Saunders.

Walter Reitman [1965]. *Cognition and Thought*. New York: John Wiley and Sons.

L. G. Roberts [1963]. *Machine Perception of 3-Dimensional Solids*. Lincoln Laboratory, MIT, Tech. Rept. No. 315.

T. D. M. Roberts [1967]. *Neurophysiology of Postural Mechanisms*. London: Butterworths.

D. A. Robinson [1968]. The Oculomotor Control System: A Review. *Proc. IEEE, 56* (6), 1032–1049.

A. S. Romer [1970]. *The Vertebrate Body,* 4th ed. Philadelphia: W. B. Saunders.

C. A. Rosen [1968]. Machines that Act Intelligently. *Sci. J.,* 109–114.

R. Rosen [1970]. *Dynamical System Theory in Biology*. New York: Wiley-Interscience.

T. Roszak [1969]. *The Making of a Counterculture*. Garden City, N.Y.: Doubleday.

A. L. Samuel [1959]. Some Studies in Machine Learning Using the Game of Checkers. *IBM J. Res. and Dev., 3,* 210–229.

A. Samuel [1967]. Some Studies in Machine Learning Using the Game of Checkers II, Recent Progress. *IBM J. Res. and Dev., 11,* 601–617.

M. E. Scheibel and A. B. Scheibel [1968]. The Brain Stem Core—An Integrative Matrix. In M. Mesarovic, Ed., *Systems Theory and Biology*. New York: Springer-Verlag, pp. 261–285.

M. E. Scheibel and A. B. Scheibel [1969]. Terminal Patterns in Cat Spinal Cord III. Primary Afferent Collaterals. *Brain Res., 13,* 417–433.

M. E. Scheibel and A. B. Scheibel [1970]. Elementary Processes in Selected Thalamic and Cortical Subsystems—The Structural Substrates, in Schmitt [1970], pp. 443–457.

F. O. Schmitt, Editor-in-Chief [1970]. *The Neurosciences Second Study Program.* New York: The Rockefeller University Press.

G. E. Schneider [1969]. Two Visual Systems, *Science, 163*, 895–902.

R. Shepard and J. Metzler [1970]. Mental Rotations of Three-Dimensional Objects, *Science.*

D. A. Sholl [1956]. *The Organization of the Cerebral Cortex.* Oxford University Press.

H. A. Simon [1967]. Motivational and Emotional Controls of Cognition. *Psych. Rev., 74,* 29–39.

H. A. Simon [1969]. *The Sciences of the Artificial.* Cambridge, Mass.: The MIT Press.

H. A. Simon and M. Barenfeld [1969]. Information-Processing Analysis of Perceptual Processes in Problem-Solving. *Psych. Rev., 76,* 473–483.

J. Slagle [1971]. *Artificial Intelligence: The Heuristic Programming Approach.* New York: McGraw-Hill.

J. J. C. Smart [1963]. *Philosophy and Scientific Realism.* London: Routledge and Kegan Paul.

J. R. Smythies, Ed. [1965]. *Brain and Mind.* London: Routledge and Kegan Paul.

Ye. N. Sokolov [1963]. *Perception and the Conditioned Reflex.* London: Pergamon Press.

R. W. Sperry [1951]. Mechanisms of Neural Maturation. In S. S. Stevens, Ed., *Handbook of Experimental Psychology.* New York: John Wiley and Sons, pp. 236–280.

R. W. Sperry [1966]. Brain Bisection and Consciousness. In J. C. Eccles, Ed., *Brain and Conscious Experience.* New York: Springer-Verlag, pp. 298–313.

J. Szentagothai [1968]. Structuro-functional Considerations of the Cerebellar Neuron Network. *Proc. IEEE, 56* (6), 960–968.

G. A. Talland [1968]. *Disorders of Memory and Learning.* Baltimore, Md.: Penguin.

H. L. Teuber [1960]. Perception. *Handbook of Physiology: Section I, Neurophysiology,* **III,** 1595–1668.

O. K. Tichomirov and E. D. Poznyanskaya [1966]. An Investigation of Visual Search as a Means of Analyzing Heuristics. *Soviet Psychol., 5,* 2–15.

S. S. Tomkins and S. Messick, Eds. [1963]. *Computer Simulation of Personality.* New York: John Wiley and Sons.

C. B. Trevarthen [1968]. Two Mechanisms of Vision in Primates. *Psychol. Forsch., 31,* 299–337.

R. A. R. Tricker and B. J. K. Tricker [1967]. *The Science of Movement,* New York: American Elsevier.

C. M. Turbayne [1970]. *The Myth of the Metaphor,* rev. ed., Columbia, S.C.: University of South Carolina Press.

A. M. Turing [1950]. Computing Machinery and Intelligence. *Mind,* **59,** 433–460.

L. Uhr, Ed. [1966]. *Pattern Recognition.* New York: John Wiley and Sons.

L. Uhr and C. Vossler [1961]. A Pattern Recognition Program that Generates, Evaluates and Adjusts Its Own Operators. *Proc. Western Joint Computer Conference,* pp. 555–569.

E. von Holst and H. Mittelstaedt, Das Reafferenzprinzip. *Naturwiss., 37,* 464–476.

J. von Neumann [1958]. *The Computer and the Brain.* New Haven, Conn.: Yale University Press.

P. Weiss [1941]. Self-Differentiation of the Basic Patterns of Coordination. *Comparative Psychology Monographs,* Serial No. 88, **17,** No. 4.

G. Werner [1970]. The Topology of the Body Representation in the Somatic Afferent Pathway, in Schmitt [1970], pp. 605–617.

P. R. Westlake [1970]. The Possibilities of Neural Holographic Processes within the Brain. *Kybernetik, 7,* 129–153.

I. C. Whitfield [1967]. *The Auditory Pathway.* London: Edward Arnold.

N. Wiener [1948]. *Cybernetics.* Cambridge, Mass.: The Technology Press.

N. Wiener [1961]. *Cybernetics,* 2nd ed. Cambridge, Mass.: The MIT Press.

D. M. Wilson [1966]. Insect Walking. *Ann. Rev. Entomol.,* **11,** 103–121.

D. M. Wilson [1967]. Stepping Patterns in Tarantula Spiders. *J. Exp. Biol. Gr. Br.,* **47,** 133–157.

T. Winograd [1971]. *Procedures as a Representation for Data in a Computer Program for Understanding Natural Languages.* Report MAC TR-84, Cambridge, Mass.: Project MAC, MIT.

S. Winograd and J. D. Cowan [1963]. *Reliable Computation in the Presence of Noise.* Cambridge, Mass.: The MIT Press.

P. H. Winston [1970]. *Learning Structural Descriptions from Examples.* Report MAC TR-76, Cambridge, Mass.: Project MAC, MIT.

D. E. Wooldridge [1963]. *The Machinery of the Brain.* New York: McGraw-Hill.

A. W. Wymore [1967]. *A Mathematical Theory of Systems Engineering.* New York: John Wiley and Sons.

J. Z. Young [1964]. *A Model of the Brain.* Oxford: Oxford University Press.

Author Index

237

Subject Index